Treating Gambling Problems

Wiley Series on Treating Addiction

Series editors, Robert Holman Coombs and William A. Howatt

TREATING DRUG PROBLEMS
Authur W. Blume

TREATING ALCOHOL PROBLEMS
Frederick Rotgers
and
Beth Arburn Davis

TREATING GAMBLING PROBLEMS
William G. McCown
and
William A. Howatt

Treating Gambling Problems

William G. McCown

William A. Howatt

John Wiley & Sons, Inc.

In Memory of Bob Coombs, who unfortunately left us before he saw the final product of this book. This is the third book in the Wiley Addiction series, and we are proud to be able to keep this series going in his memory.

CONTENTS

Chapter 2: Recognizing Gambling Disorders: Signs and Symptoms

Chapter 4: Developing an Effective Treatment Plan

Chapter 5: Recovery Theories, Programs, and Tools

Chapter 6: Continuing Care: When and How Should Clients Be Discharged

Chapter 7: Posttreatment Recovery Management: Models and Protocols of Relapse Prevention

Chapter 8: New Beginnings: Moving Beyond the Addiction

ACKNOWLEDGMENTS

Foremost, I want to acknowledge the contribution of my clients, from whom I have learned so much.

I would like to personally thank Dr. Bill Howatt and also Lisa Gebo, the series editor from John Wiley and Sons, who have been incredibly patient and supportive.

I would also like to thank Dr. Howatt's assistant, Carolyn Hill, for her expertise in project management, editing, and organization. I understand she was a driving force in getting this book across the goal line.

Linda Chamberlain has remained a "like mind" for 15 years, but always a much better clinician.

Reece Middleton, Janet Miller, and all of my friends at Louisiana Association of Compulsive Gambling have been helpful in passing along wisdom.

The clients and staff at "Middle Pines" and "Gulf Coast" Addiction Centers deserve special note for patience. Jim Z. set up and maintained the bulletin board and Internet services described in several chapters. Thanks also, Ross Keiser.

"John" in South Carolina and "Ted" in Arkansas provided helpful criticism and extensive input from perspectives different from mine. I appreciate their flexibility and hope that we all are richer.

Chris Johnson and Jay Bulot in the Department of Gerontology and Sociology at the University of Louisiana at Monroe have been friends of similar interest and furnished a great deal of advice and just plain enthusiasm. Joe McGahan has just begun to teach me about social psychology and I am appreciative! Thanks as always to Sean Austin and Bob Abouee.

To Greg Stolcis and Gordie Flett—guys, you made me hang in there.

Finally, to Louisiana: *"Lache pas la patate."*

SERIES PREFACE

Most books on addiction are written for only 10 percent of those who deal with addicted people—typically, for experts who specialize in addiction. By contrast, we designed the Wiley Series on Treating Addictions primarily for the other 90 percent—the many health service providers and family members who, though not addictionologists, regularly deal with those who suffer from various addictive disorders.

All volumes in this series define addiction as "an attachment to, or dependence upon, any substance, thing, person or idea so single-minded and intense that virtually all other realities are ignored or given second place—and consequences, even lethal ones, are disregarded" (Mack, 2002).

Considering that over one's lifetime more than one fourth (27 percent) of the entire population will suffer from a substance abuse problem (Kessler et al., 1994), many family members and all human services providers will, sooner or later, be confronted with these problems. Unfortunately, few have received any training to prepare them for this challenging task.

Research is linking problem gambling behavior to a constellation of addictive disorders, such as alcohol and drugs, at rates higher than the general nonproblem-gambling population. Two leading researchers in North America on problem gambling (Korn and Shaffer, 2002 p. 171) reported that "Gambling is an emerging public health issue based on epidemiology, social costs, and quality of life concerns." The reality is that the prevalence of gambling problem behaviors has been creeping up over the last 25 years, and the net result is that gambling has become a multibillion-dollar profit center for governments. No one knows exactly how much revenue gamblers actually spend each year because much of the gambling that occurs is not regulated. What we do know is that gambling is a real social issue that is challenging governments and businesses to debate exactly what their social responsibilities are and what actions should be taken. While these debates roar on, people with problem gambling issues continue, and there is a need for more professionals to take action. The goal of this book is to provide professionals with a user-friendly resource that will move them from merely identifying problem gambling to facilitating a process for people to reclaim control of their lives.

We are pleased to provide the thoughts of Dr. McCown, a professional in the trenches working with clients, who has spent much time and research in discovering how professionals can help clients navigate through problem gambling. In addition to his impressive academic and professional background, we also would like to acknowledge his tireless commitment to communities and organizations in need of his expertise and skills through such casualties as Katrina and Tsunami.

We believe you will find the information in this book invaluable for a clearer understanding and sensitivity to the personal, social, and cultural dynamics of people living with gambling problems, and what one can do to assist them through the healing.

William A. Howatt, PhD, EdD
Series Editor

PREFACE

This book was conceived by the late Dr. Robert Coombs and his associate, Dr. Bill Howatt, as a practical guide for the treatment of disordered gambling. Bob realized that many clients with problem and pathological gambling who receive treatment are unlikely to be treated by specialists, such as Certified Addictions Counselors. For better or worse, most clients are now treated by counselors or therapists in general mental health practices or by other helping professionals. Bob intended this book for professionals, whose primary population is not gambling, but who see the value and need to increase competencies in treating this population. As gambling problems become more common, this description will include many more clinicians. In addition, this book will serve as an excellent reference for medical doctors, nurses, teachers, and other professionals who may cross this population and who are looking for more insight as to options for treatment.

When Bob first mentioned the concept of this book, I told him that it was a great idea, but I protested that he could easily find a more qualified author. First, I was not a Certified Gambling Counselor. I had been forced to learn things the hard way, as a broadly trained psychologist, who gradually gained a background in gambling, based on my background in addictions and perception of current need.

"Aha—So far, your qualifications are perfect."

Next, I objected that there were scores of more *serious* clinicians and scholars than me. Certainly, he could find a more "reputable name" for this book. He reiterated that this was not his goal. Instead, his hope was for a pragmatic, "hands-on" volume, to make the treatment of gamblers *less formidable* for the typical nonspecialist clinician.

Bob had a way of being insistent about these things.

I reminded Bob that my administrative and therapeutic mistakes, programmatic errors, misdirection of resources, misunderstandings of clinical situations, and occasional franks misdiagnoses, could fill a small file.

"Great! What an opportunity to help others avoid your errors!"

Bob was a bit of an optimist.

Dr. Howatt, the other Bill in this project, in his own persistent way similar to Bob, would not let me out of this book. I was pretty much 90 percent done, then the pressures of life hit. In the throws of supporting a state crisis in Louisiana, a national crisis providing Arabic translation, and a book crisis trying to get a book complete with no time and constant outside demands, the final caveat was that I was expecting my first child. Dr. Howatt kindly agreed to help me finish this book and for that I am grateful.

As explained in the preface, this book follows the chapter guidelines and outline suggested by Bob and Dr. Howatt. Chapter 1 is an overview of problem and pathological gambling, including definitions and a distinction between the two terms. Counselors are often benefited by understanding group and individual risk factors. Although there are risk factors associated with developing a gambling disorder, anyone with a sufficient reinforcement history can develop a wagering problem. Recently, data have shown that gambling treatment works, something we could not claim perhaps five years ago.

Chapter 2 discusses the signs and symptoms of problem and pathological gambling. The paradox is that, although gambling is extraordinarily destructive, it is often hard to detect. Disordered gambling does not furnish definitive laboratory tests or even consistent reports from the neighbors about raucous behavior. However, there are numerous clues to the presence of gambling disorders that a careful clinician may find. Structured interview questionnaires and screening instruments may be helpful in detecting the presence of problem or pathological gambling.

Chapter 3 concerns the pragmatics of using and protecting scarce treatment resources. The chapter opens with a practical problem that isolated clinicians face: How can I find colleagues who can help me treat gamblers? For the isolated clinician, this is a topic that is rarely addressed in the literature and was one that Bob Coombs often pointed out was critical for client *and* counselor well being. The chapter next covers a number of down-to-earth topics such as selecting the right professional for treatment, the "do's and don'ts" of referrals, some concrete strategies for getting a person to a professional, advice about dealing with crisis situations, and risk-management strategies.

Chapter 4 involves some of the "nuts and bolts" of conducting an intake and developing an effective treatment plan for people with gambling problems. The chapter stresses that in order for a treatment plan to be truly effective, it must begin at intake. The chapter emphasizes that the intake interview should be motivational, and its purpose is to gather information. It also discusses problems with confidentiality and compliance with the Heath Insurance Portability and Accountability Act (HIPAA). Admittedly, no one knows much about HIPAA as it involves treating clients with gambling disorders, but this discussion is a start, and I hope it generates awareness and dialogue.

Chapter 5 concerns treatment strategies for problem and pathological gamblers. This is not a "how to" chapter, such as you might find in a detailed manual-driven intervention. There are now several outstanding sources for these in the literature, which are discussed in this chapter. Instead, we summarize various popular types of treatment and discuss where to access more comprehensive resources.

Chapter 6 highlights continuing care for people with a gambling problem. It highlights the stages of recovery and how various treatments may be appropriate for each stage. Successful discharge planning is able to use family and community resources and to organize resources where they are not available. Ethical concerns involving discharge are discussed in this chapter.

Chapter 7 emphasizes posttreatment recovery management. Since many instances of gambling disorders are considered potentially chronic, they will need to be managed throughout long periods, perhaps life. Clients will need to develop proactive strategies for preventing and dealing with "triggers" for relapses. This includes developing relapse prevention plans appropriate for different stages of treatment. Other resources include those in the community and family, as well as pastoral counseling.

Finally, Chapter 8 discusses what the client's life can be like after gambling recovery. This includes the possibility that he or she can live a richer, fuller life than otherwise imagined. Each recovered gambler's life is different and the positive direction cannot be measured in advance. However, almost invariably, when people change, they report that their lives have a real and deeper meaning. This chapter is brief because there is not one single path to a posttreatment lifestyle. Some clients find that they are able to use the emptiness of their time spent gambling in a constructive and positive manner. Others simply prefer to forget that period and move on.

All of the clinical vignettes are true stories. Identifying information has been removed through a two-part process to preserve anonymity.

The volume deliberately excludes a few popular topics. Notably, these include prevention, although some of the suggested resources are very helpful concerning this topic. It also excludes treatment of adolescent and elderly gamblers. Adolescent treatment usually requires additional training, and it is unlikely that a clinician can develop minimal competence without more extensive supervision. Furthermore, it is still unlikely that adult generalist mental health counselors and practitioners will be referred adolescent gambling cases. Regarding elderly, their treatment needs are usually so diverse and complex that they also demand specially trained practitioners.

Bill McCown, PhD

ABOUT THE AUTHORS

William A. Howatt, PhD., EdD., has more than 18 years experience as an addiction counselor. He is an internationally acclaimed alcohol and drug addictions specialist, gambling addictions specialist, registered professional counselor, registered social worker who has also completed post doctoral work in addiction studies at UCLA School of Medicine. He is a faculty member of Nova Scotia Community College where he teaches in the addiction counselor program for the School of Health and Human Services. He is author of numerous books including The Addiction Counselor's Desk Reference and is coeditor of the Treating Addictions Series (both published by Wiley).

William G. McCown, PhD., is a clinical psychologist with over 20 years of addiction-treatment experience. He combines appreciation of traditional approaches to treatment with a commitment to evidence-based methods. An international consultant, he pioneered one of the first Internet-based treatments for disordered gambling. He is presently Associate Professor at the University of Louisiana at Monroe, where he carries on an active research program.

CHAPTER I

Conceptual Foundations of Gambling Disorders

TRUTH OR FICTION

QUIZ

After reading this chapter, you should be able to answer the following questions:

1. Gambling is a *new addiction* that first appeared in the twentieth century. True or False?

2. Gambling is primarily a compulsion, like perfectionism or excessive hand washing. True or False?

3. Problem gambling and pathological gambling are two separate and distinct disorders. True or False?

4. Most people with gambling problems lose control every single time they gamble. True or False?

5. Clinical difficulties involving gambling seem to be increasing. True or False?

6. True pathological gamblers develop problems regardless of wagering opportunities. True or False?

7. The treatment of pathological gambling is identical to that of other addictions. True or False?

Answers on p. 31.

Introduction to Gambling

Gambling is the attempt to win something on the outcome of a game or event that depends on chance or luck. The purpose of this chapter is to educate professionals and clinicians about *pathological* and *problem* gambling. Gambling is not inherently pathological, immoral, or associated with any psychological problems. An overwhelming majority of people who choose to wager do so in moderation and without evident problems. There is no evidence that this majority is at any risk of developing the problems described in this chapter and throughout this book.

However, in North America, approximately between 2 and 6 percent of the population has, or has had, gambling-related problems. Estimates vary according to the research methodology used. For example, researchers find different estimates depending on what time frame and frequency gambling is assessed (e.g., within the last month, within the last year, within a lifetime). Findings also are influenced by where they are obtained. For example, proximity to a gambling venue possibly contributes to the risk for developing a problem. However, this may be changing with the onset of additional wagering options, including those available on the Internet and growth in casinos across North America.

Although the behaviors involved in disordered gambling do not involve a specific substance of abuse, they facilitate a syndrome that is similar to the *classical* chemical, or other, addictions. Similarities include compulsion, loss of control, and continued use despite negative consequences. These are the "Three Cs of addiction" (Blume, 2005), and they are detailed in a later section. For people with a gambling dysfunction, the dependence, craving, and disruption to their lives are often as severe as in any addiction. What is confusing to family and others is that gambling does not involve a specific substance; consequently, the addiction to gambling seems (to them) less legitimate and understandable.

Not everyone with a gambling disorder demonstrates the stereotype of progressively severe impairments. In the world of gambling, what walks like a duck and quacks like a duck—may not be a duck at all. It is relevant to understand that, just because a person appears to meet the criteria of being a pathological or problem gambler, it does not always prove to be true. Some show patterns of periodic difficulties that may or may not be related to external events, such as life stressors; others "mature out," gradually curtailing destructive gambling over months or years. The reasons for these varied patterns are not well understood. Still, others show more abrupt spontaneous remission that occurs when disordered gambling problems disappear without informal or formal treatment. The frequency of spontaneous remission is unknown, as are its definitive mechanisms.

Certain cultural, economic, racial, and ethnic groups may be at higher risk for developing gambling problems. The specific pathways for developing a gambling disorder are not necessarily the same in diverse groups or in any two people. Rather, gambling disorders may represent a common outcome or destination from a variety of different pathways.

The need for this book comes from the fact that many general therapists, counselors, and other mental health professionals now are encountering, or will soon encounter, someone with a gambling problem. Yet, gambling and gambling problems are not new. On the contrary, people have been gambling since recorded history, presumably even earlier. Betting on horses began almost as soon as these animals were domesticated. Ancient Chinese and Egyptian texts indicate that gambling was common, though excessive gambling was a concern. The Biblical book of Judges (Chapter 14) highlights the role that gambling played at ancient feasts and weddings, when Sampson apparently tried to provoke warfare by wagering on who could solve a riddle (The Holy Bible). Many historical accounts discuss various forms of wagering that existed in Europe during the Dark Ages and during the Renaissance. During the sixteenth and seventeenth centuries, some of the seminal advances in the mathematics of probability and statistics were based on attempts to understand and capitalize on the odds afforded to gamblers.

In North America, the popularity of gambling has followed various periods of expansion that some observers have labeled *waves*. Undoubtedly, historians disagree about these exact time frames, and it is our belief that gambling expansion never completely ceased, even during its least popular periods. Some accounts suggest that the first wave began with colonization, where colonists gambled heavily, with the possible exception of the Puritans. Later, Scotch-Irish immigrants probably wagered even more frequently, primarily to fight the tedium of frontier life. The first race track was established on Long Island more than one hundred years before the Declaration of Independence. Playing the lottery became a voluntary tax and form of civic pride, as well as a universal form of amusement. All of the 13 original colonies had some form of lottery.

Many classic card games followed the Mississippi River up from New Orleans, blending French and Creole influences into the New World. These included poker, which had firmly developed a variety of different rules by the 1840s. The mystique of this game contributed to the American folklore of the prewar antebellum South and period of Western expansion. The *gentleman's game* of craps also originated in Europe and became popular in New Orleans, partly because it resisted *fixing*. Fixing displayed an ugly side to the romanticized notions of riverboat and frontier gambling. Violent sharks, thugs, and cons often attempted to rig whatever games were available. The solution for these players was often quick, vigilante justice.

Slaves may have turned to gambling as one of the few amusements that they could afford and conceal. Unfortunately, little is known about the folk gambling culture that developed during these conditions of oppression. Following the American Civil War, gambling popularity increased until the United States public became disgusted with recurrent lottery and race track corruption, beginning a period of rapid legal restrictions. This abruptly ended the first wave of North American gambling.

Some argue that the next wave of gambling in the United States, perhaps from the 1890s to the early part of the 1900s, was tied in part to advances in gambling technology. At the race track, the set starting gate and, particularly the tote board (or parimutuel machine), reduced the appearance of corruption. Tote boards feature odds that are constantly being updated. The public is basically betting against itself, with players trying to outsmart each other as they might in the stock exchange. No longer were odds set by various bookmakers, who were corrupt and might fix a race. Instead, all the money bet at a track was pooled together and divided according to odds set by the crowd's ever-changing choices. In the United

States, this type of wagering smacked of the populism that a growing democracy liked. This led to the perception of fairness, though with many notorious exceptions and attempts to defraud the public, which continue on through today.

The mechanical slot machine, called the *fruit machine* in Britain, or one-armed bandit in some circles, was another innovation spawned from a renewed interest in legalized gambling. Invented in 1895 by Charles Fey, a locksmith and machinist in San Francisco, these amusement devices proved immensely popular and became a backbone of legal casinos in Nevada and later New Jersey and elsewhere. Nevada legalized most forms of gambling in 1931. The potential profitability of slot machines for the player increased when the mechanical reel was replaced with increasingly sophisticated electric and electronic variations. This eventually resorted in enormous revenue for slot machine owners, since so many more patrons played them, often for hours at a time.

The third wave began after the 1930s in the United States with the return of bingo and parimutuel betting, and on into the 1960s with the renewed popularization of state lotteries. Atlantic City saw gambling as a cure for a moribund economy and opened casinos in the late 1970s. This trend was followed with riverboat gambling, ostensibly for its romantic, quixotic appeal and attempt to restore rustbelt city economies. Native American casinos, often falling under less stringent regulation, became immensely popular and circumvented state law. Only two states, Utah and Hawaii, presently do not have some legalized form of gambling; however, this is now overshadowed by the ability to access Internet and cable or satellite television wagering.

In Canada, all gambling was made illegal by the Canadian Criminal Code of 1892. Still, there are many very colorful accounts of frontier gamblers that rival those on the Mississippi. Canadian gambling never really went away. It just moved *down the block* or out to the frontier. In 1969, the federal government began reducing its involvement with gambling, turning over regulation to provinces and territories, which accepted the expansion at varying paces. In 1985, provinces were allowed to oversee video slot machines and video lottery terminals. These have become immensely popular, very lucrative, and there is concern regarding their potential for causing excessive gambling problems.

Some form of legally sanctioned gambling is now available in all ten provinces, with casino gambling now available in many provinces as well.

IMAGINE THAT!

The odds of being struck by lightning are 1 in 240,000. With slot machines, the odds of winning the top prize at maximum coin play ranges from 1 in 4,096 up to 1 in 33,554,000.

Source: British Columbia Partnership for Responsible Gambling (2004).

IMAGINE THAT!

The profits from government gaming operations are almost $13 billion nationally, but the costs of gambling addictions are not known. Some of these could be quantified, including medical care, policing, courts, prisons, social assistance, and business losses. However, no simple dollar figure can measure the devastation to the lives of those affected by pathological gambling.

Source: Canada Safety Council (2006).

In legal circles, the words *gamble* and *gambling* sometimes are used for the activities that run afoul of applicable criminal laws, and the more innocent sounding *gaming* is employed for activity specifically legalized by state or federal regulations. The most rapidly expanding form of gambling or gaming is available in some areas on the Internet. A new law in the United States, HR4411, prohibits gambling over phone lines; the debate is whether or not this means the Internet as well. In the United States, there is a movement of prohibition on Internet gambling, while for the rest of the world, it is extremely profitable for the site owners who peddle the sites. However, this unregulated Internet market still does not come close to the volume of money gambled through illegal person-to-person sports wagering at bars and through *bookies, agents, contacts,* or people with other such monikers. By some accounts, this illegal industry may amount to twice the size of the entire legal gaming market.

Definitions of Problem and Pathological Gambling

The terms *problem* and *pathological* gambling often are used interchangeably. This is not quite accurate, as counselors soon discover in their encounters with the variety of gambling disorders that exist. The formal diagnosis of a gambling disorder is *Pathological Gambling* and it is defined by the current edition of the *Diagnostic and Statistical Manual–Fourth Edition, Text Revised* (DSM-IV-TR; American Psychiatric Association, 2000). To receive this diagnosis, a person must meet five of the ten criteria listed in Table 1.1.

The *DSM-IV-TR* classifies this disorder as an "Impulse-Control Disorder Not Elsewhere Classified" (APA, 2000, p. 613). Similar disorders, according to the *DSM-IV-TR*, include kleptomania and trichotolomania (hair pulling). Gambling is not listed as an "addictive disorder." The *DSM-IV-TR* does not classify any disorders as "addictive" or "nonaddictive" per se, but it does classify chemical dependencies based on their degrees of severity. To date, there is just one level of severity for pathological gambling in the *DSM-IV-TR*.

Definitional Distinctions

Many clinicians use the term *problem gamblers* to describe people who meet some (e.g., three of the criteria), but not the minimum five criteria that obtains the *DSM-IV-TR* diagnosis for pathological gambling. This also has become popular with researchers and will be discussed later regarding classification schemas. To avoid repetition, we may use more generic phrases, such as *impaired gambler* or *aberrant gambler* to refer to people with gambling disorders of any type, unless we need to designate between specific levels of severity. Recently, the prolific gambling researcher Nancy Petry (2005a) has suggested the term *disordered gambler* for people who meet *some* or *all* of the criteria for a *DSM-IV-TR* diagnosis. Often, this will be a useful term.

Table 1.1: Criteria for Pathological Gambling

---

1. Is preoccupied with gambling (e.g., reliving past gambling experiences, handicapping or planning the next venture, or thinking of ways to get money with which to gamble)

2. Needs to gamble with increasing amounts of money to achieve the desired excitement

3. Has repeated, unsuccessful efforts to control, cut back, or stop gambling

4. Is restless or irritable when attempting to cut down or stop gambling

5. Gambles to escape problems or relieve a dysphoric mood (e.g., helplessness, guilt, anxiety, depression)

6. After gambling loss, often returns to "get even" (i.e., "chasing" one's losses)

7. Lies to family members, therapist, or others to conceal the extent of gambling involvement

8. Has committed illegal acts such as forgery, fraud, theft, or embezzlement to finance gambling

9. Has jeopardized or lost a significant relationship, job, educational or career opportunity because of gambling

10. Relies on others to provide money to relieve a desperate financial situation caused by gambling

---

Source: Reproduced by permission, American Psychiatric Association, 2000.

The terms *compulsive gambling* and *compulsive gambler* are older and were made popular by early researchers and the self-help group known as Gamblers Anonymous (GA). In general, these terms will be avoided because they are easily confused with unrelated psychiatric conditions, such as *Obsessive Compulsive Disorder* or *Obsessive Compulsive Personality Disorder.*

There are clinicians, often those involved in self-help groups, who emphasize the subjective nature of diagnosing gambling problems. They state that the *DSM-IV-TR* reiterates that subjective complaints are important in ascertaining whether a person has a gambling problem. It is not the specific number of criteria that a person does or does not have that make a diagnosis; it is whether or not the person *believes* a gambling problem exists. This is not a misconception about aberrant gambling, but rather a different way to view the problem that offers strengths and weaknesses. It originates from the *Disease Model* of addiction, which is well-ingrained in North American addiction treatment, especially in the United States.

Chapter 2 discusses other diagnostic lists, such as the 20 Questions of Gamblers Anonymous (GA). Although unscientifically derived, meeting criteria from these screening tools frequently assists people in rethinking their current gambling behaviors and in accepting a treatment plan. By formal criteria, these people are classified in most cases as "sub clinical," yet it can hardly be said they are living free of gambling problems. Petry (2005a) has noted that, with the present definition provided by the *DSM-IV-TR*, these people would have to get worse before receiving a diagnosis making them eligible to receive treatment. As professional care providers, this does not make sense as it is ascribing that a client must deteriorate before we are allowed to intervene. This goes against everything we understand about how to treat mental health problems. Many clinicians agree that it is a misunderstanding of the nature of addiction to deny people treatment because they miss one or two of the required *DSM-IV-TR* criteria. From our perspective, there are obvious benefits and economic savings to early intervention and prevention versus waiting for problems to worsen before intervening.

Some researchers and practitioners state that gambling cannot be a *true* addiction because it does not involve any specific substances that are ingested, such as alcohol, nicotine, or heroin. Many others, including most treatment providers in the field of pathological gambling, believe that this difference is semantic and trivial (Grant & Potenza, 2005). We believe gambling is a real, addictive disorder that can paralyze a person as much as any drug can. The use of mnemonic of the Three Cs of Addiction—Feelings of *Compulsion, Loss of Control,* and *Continued Use, Despite Consequences*—is an effective strategy for assessing the frequency, duration, and intensity of addictive behaviors such as gambling, drugs, alcohol, work, sex, Internet, and so forth.

An Introduction to the Three Cs of Problem and Pathological Gambling

The first "C," *Compulsion,* involves an intense desire to irrationally gamble once a cue is present or a specific thought regarding gambling is triggered. A compulsion is an uncontrollable behavior sparked by an irrational idea, called an *obsession.* While these urges are not identical to the compulsions seen in anxiety disorders (such as *DSM-IV-TR* Obsessive Compulsive Disorder), they share similar overwhelming internal feelings that seem coercive and inescapable. They are seemingly *beyond reasonableness.* Anniversaries, various moods, physical events, people, places, practically anything can serve as powerful cues for eliciting an incapacitating need to gamble in people with a gambling-related disorder.

Sylvia, a lawyer for a large firm, who played video poker for several hours a night, phrased this well when she said, "Imagine resisting the hardest thing, like laughing when you are tickled, or worse, maybe sneezing when you need to. My compulsion to gamble was worse than that. It was a behavior that I just couldn't resist."

Some clinicians and researchers believe that the pivotal point in the development of any addiction is *Loss of Control,* the second of the three Cs. For the gambler, this involves an inability to *reliably* control or moderate wagering frequency or amount. *It is important to realize that this loss of control is not necessarily evident every time a disordered gambler places a bet.* However, once wagering has begun, the pathological gambler cannot be certain of the ability to show restraint. On some occasions, a pathological gambler may be able to wager in a limited fashion, adhering to a preset monetary limit. Based on the gambler's history, the probability of following this restraint is questionable and may not be very high. As the wife of a pathological gambler stated, "He doesn't spend the car payment every time he goes gambling. But he does it enough that I am scared to death."

Some argue that loss of control involves yet another C, *chasing.* As it is referred to in literature, chasing actually has two distinct purposes or meanings for the gambler. First, it is the process of betting more money for financial recouping. This is usually a variety of what is known as the Martingale system, developed in the eighteenth century. Many gamblers develop pathological patterns when they begin increasing their wagers to make up for previous gambling losses (Petry, 2005a). The Martingale guarantees failure. The mathematics show that making up for previous losses only is possible in the long run if the gambler has an unlimited bankroll and the bookmaker or casino has no limit on the size of bets it accepts. What inevitably happens is that the gambler goes tragically *bust* or broke, like Ben, a 19-year old college student in New York who owed over $130,000 to bookies from chasing his losses. This occurred after only 6 months of gambling, trying to recoup his initial losses.

The other use of the term is the attempt to *out wager* the habituation and tedium that accompany the grind of chronic gambling. Often, a financially solvent disordered gambler finds that it takes a greater amount to experience the excitement of an earlier time. Gambling is no longer fun. He or she *chases* that first big success by gambling progressively larger amounts. This also leads to quick financial devastation.

Periods of successful chasing are invariably followed by financial irresponsibility. For example, a windfall from an unlikely payout may be immediately wagered again, despite the fact that the gambler has many creditors. No one, it seems, can chase successfully and then walk away. Don, a securities professional, noted, "My trading was so crazy that I was losing money all over the place. Then, I'd score something through just plain luck. Rather than quit and pay my mortgage, I was overcome with the thought that this was going to be my day. I'd lose everything that I had earned, and then some. I went through thousands of dollars like this."

The final C in this mnemonic is a pattern of continued gambling despite *Consequences.* For the disordered gambler, gambling continues despite financial and legal problems, shame, scorn from social systems, and many other tangible costs. While the pathological gambler may or may not be in *denial,* the gambler is aware that there are consequences to the behavior. This is what makes the behavior so hard to understand. The gambler may fluctuate between promising to change *tomorrow* and being unable to limit wagering once it has begun or when responding to cues. The individual is usually on a downward spiral of depression, stress, family alienation, and financial and personal ruin. In this mental state, this individual is at risk of serious felonious behavior and/or suicide. Sometimes the progression downward is slow; at other times, and for reasons that are not clear, it may occur rapidly. For Ben, discussed previously, he continued to borrow from his mother's credit cards in the belief that one day he would make enough money to cancel out his year of losses. He did not and was imprisoned.

For some who reach this stage, there is a reluctant awareness that gambling, in the long run, is certainly a losing proposition. They no longer can fool themselves into believing that luck will bail them out. By now they realize that gambling is a game of chance first, and skill second—if at all. Even with this realization, they still continue to irrationally wager. Sometimes pathological gamblers will admit that even severe losing is better than not wagering at all.

As mentioned, it is this final C that is so difficult for the outsider to understand, but at the same time lets others realize that the gambler is not simply acting immorally or selfishly. Aberrant gamblers act recklessly and foolishly. They behave in self-defeating ways that simply seem *crazy*. They may lose their job, lie to loved ones, rob, steal, and occasionally even kill in order to continue wagering. It is no wonder that *loss of control* seems to be a reasonable description for people in the end stages of extreme, pathological wagering.

Myths versus Facts about Problem and Pathological Gambling

The following are some of the most pervasive myths that surround pathological gambling. No clinician or family member can hope to understand pathological gambling until these myths are recognized as untruths or part truths. Our colleagues wish these came from our imaginations or distant memories; but, unfortunately, they came from *recent, angry* telephone calls, letters, emails, or classroom discussions. See if you can find the patterns of extremes represented in the viewpoints that are expressed.

1. Myth: "Gambling is a relatively new problem that is due to contemporary problems of lax morals, social evil, or modern greediness."
   Fact: History records many colorful accounts of people risking something of value for the hope of gain.

2. Myth: "Gambling is evil—it is invariably harmful and turns everyone who undertakes it into someone less honorable or at least someone who does not live up to his or her potential."

Fact: Based on the number of people who pursue gambling without ever developing noticeable problems, this is simply not true. Over 80 percent of North Americans over age 18 have wagered; almost 60 percent of North Americans have done so in the past year (Taylor, Funk, & Craighill, 2006). For an overwhelming majority, gambling is a pleasant, social activity, often with costs that are no greater than those of other amusements, such as ball games, movies, concerts, or hobbies.

3. Myth: "Pathological gambling is a victimless activity. All this talk about 'treatment and intervention' is just a fancy way to invent more problems for you wealthy professionals to solve."
Fact: Criminal activity, disruption of the family and other social units, and the cost to society from unsecured debt and squandered life opportunities are all caused by pathological gambling. Many victims of problem gambling often are silent. They may be family members, including children, who can comment little about the ways in which gambling affects their lives. By one account, each pathological gambler negatively impacts six to eight people. While these numbers probably cannot be accurately calculated, it is clear that disordered gambling is more than just a personal, victimless matter.

4. Myth: "Gambling is someone else's problem, not mine.... Gambling does not affect 'nice people,' religious people.... It is basically a problem that weak people acquire through selfish behavior. Face it—it is basically a fancy word for a moral problem."
Fact: Problem and pathological gambling can affect anyone who wagers as well as the individual's family, friends, and members of social institutions who do not wager.

5. Myth: "Gambling is a choice, or a result of a lack of willpower. People with true moral character or deep spiritual values do not develop problems from gambling and, if they do, can change their behavior through their effort and willpower."
Fact: As previously stated, while the initial decision to engage in gambling or other risky activities may involve moral elements, once a pattern of problematic gambling is established it is outside of the individual's volitional control. Treatment providers believe that no one solves the problem through willpower. If resolution and fortitude could solve the problem, then no one would request treatment. Counselors or therapists could simply provide feedback, give advice, and watch the positive results. How easy life would be! However, most researchers and clinicians believe that, by the time a pattern of pathological wagering is established, talk of morality, character, and values is usually of little help to the gambler and his or her family.

6. Myth: "Once people develop pathological gambling, they are basically without hope, as Freud and other psychoanalysts seemed to imply. Basically, it is best just to cut your losses with such people, not even wasting any resources on treatment."

Fact: Treatment for gambling can work. Millions have recovered from gambling disorders and millions more will, if they understand that treatment and recovery are possible. Data from controlled studies now demonstrate that very substantial change is possible. One purpose of this book is to assist the mental health professional, health care professional, clergy person, or other important provider in understanding what works in gambling treatment. Another purpose is to remind professionals and family that change is not necessarily speedy or easy.

7. Myth: "So, my kid has a gambling problem. I'll just do what my dad did for me. I'll make him go outside and get the biggest stick he can find and if that stick isn't big enough, I'll make him get a bigger one. Then, I'll beat it out of him."
Fact: Sorry, that approach does not work at all—ever.

8. Myth: "Addictions are not preventable. Since they are diseases, you have to let them develop and *then* you treat them. This means that if a person shows signs of having a gambling problem, the person has no choice but to 'bottom out,' just like an alcoholic without insight."
Fact: The course of many diseases, even chronic ones, may be arrested. For example, the direction and damage of hypertension can take an entirely different course if treated aggressively. The belief that a disease has to reach extremely damaging proportions before it can be treated shows a misunderstanding of the concept of *disease* and thus confuses the notion of treatment with that of insight, which was once purportedly necessary for recovery from addiction. Surprisingly, this view remains common in gambling recovery, perhaps as much as it was 20 years ago in the alcohol or other drug fields.

The bottom line: No one believes you have to have a stroke in order to treat your high blood pressure. You do not have to start losing teeth to learn to brush and floss. At one time, perhaps people needed to experience addiction to make efforts to avoid it, but most practitioners no longer believe that initial insight is necessary for the successful treatment of addiction.

> **IMAGINE THAT!**
> "There are two kinds of gamblers: The losers and the pathological liars."
>
> *Source: Graffiti on a hallway, Iowa Casino.*

Transient versus Chronic Problems

Another prevalent myth is that everyone who develops gambling problems develops them in the same ways. In a sense, this myth is a response to the gambler prototypes from the mid-twentieth century, much as our stereotype of drug dependence is based on heroin users during the 1940s and 1950s. Many of us pigeonhole pathological gamblers as down-and-out horse players or perhaps *degenerate* card players hiding in smoky rooms or back alleys. We may envision an older, white male, having spent many years arriving at his unfortunate station in life.

For some, the progression from an occasional gambler to a dysfunctional one may follow this stereotypical path. For others, the progression is speedy, more direct, and frankly, catastrophic. Some paths may meander, encircling like an errant planet that ultimately gets caught in the orbit of its target. There is now emerging evidence that gambling problems that occur in a subgroup of women seem to follow this more rapid developmental course (Petry, 2005a).

In some situations, disordered gambling will reach a plateau of frequency and intensity. In still other situations, no easily discernable patterns are present. Heavy, problematic, and even blatantly pathological gambling may stabilize or decrease. It may fluctuate wildly between extremes. Other cases seem to recur through time, following a pattern that is strikingly similar to depression or bipolar disorder, which will be discussed further in the next section.

There is also evidence that some people experience nonrecurrent (single or very few) episodes of moderate or even extreme pathological gambling. For example, a 31-year-old business person attending a convention at a gambling resort wagered her checking account funds and "maxed out" her credit cards in 2 days. This was her first and only severe gambling experience. Five years later, she has not made any other bets and looks back on this episode with extraordinary regret and utter embarrassment. "I can't believe it was me who was that stupid," she recalls. However, little is known regarding people who engage in this process of an occasional gambling *fling* or one-time pathological wagering that they do not repeat.

Patterns may incorporate any of these features for reasons that are not understood. We can guess that particular pathways relate to wagering opportunities, a lack of social supports, an absence of social sanctions, erroneous cognitive beliefs regarding wagering, and possibly some personality factors. There is also growing evidence that genetic factors may be involved, particularly those that affect neurotransmitters including the noradrenergic, serotonergic, and dopaminergic systems.

POINTS TO REMEMBER

Gambling is a real, addictive disorder that can paralyze a person as much as any drug or alcohol substance can.

- Pathways for developing problem or pathological gambling are diverse.

- The Three Cs of addiction are Compulsion, Loss of Control, and Continued Use Despite Consequences and are an effective mnemonic device for assessing the frequency, duration, and intensity of addictive behavior, including disordered gambling.

- Treatment providers believe that no one solves a gambling problem through willpower.

Spontaneous Remission and Maturing Out

Another myth regarding pathological gambling is that once a person develops a gambling problem, the person will invariably have it for life in its full intensity. But, in fact, among those who develop a gambling problem, as many as 40 to 60 percent will demonstrate substantial clinical remission without professional or formal intervention. This number is approximately the same as with other addictions and the mechanisms involved are not known. People who follow this pattern are said to be *maturing out*. They will not meet the current criteria of pathological gambling, but do show evidence of having met the criteria in the past (Petry, 2005a).

No large studies have refuted this finding, which has been replicated with various groups, using different methodologies. This result should not be surprising, as many chronic disorders in mental health and also in medicine show patterns of spontaneous remission. Examples are anxiety, depression, and bipolar disorder in psychiatry. In internal medicine, they include lupus, hypertension, seizure disorders, and even allergies. These disorders may disappear, though often they recur with environmental triggers, sometimes increasing in severity.

It is not known whether pathological gambling that spontaneously remits is likely to return at a later time. This is illustrated in Figure 1.1, in which different groups of hypothetical people who mature out of addiction are *followed* for a number of years. Based on knowledge regarding alcohol and other drugs (AODs), it is likely that many cases of spontaneous remission will show a varied course and may return.

The concept of spontaneous remission rubs many counselors the wrong way. They may have experience with disordered gamblers who *plan* on maturing out, often when their bankrolls run dry. The counselor may have recalled being told, "I'll quit when I'm broke, but not before I'm old." Furthermore, spontaneous remission has been used by insurance companies and various legal authorities as an excuse for denying needed gambling treatment. These and other concerns leave some clinicians uneasy regarding discussions of spontaneous remission. Regardless, it does occur quite frequently and future research may use the experiences of people who show spontaneous remission as starting points for new treatment methods.

It is impossible for the clinician to know who will experience spontaneous recovery or a maturational healing, although the factors from research concerning other addictions include awareness that the addiction is problematic and the existence of positive spousal support. The relationship between negative life events and spontaneous remission is not clear. In one of the few studies, gamblers were more likely to quit when they viewed gambling as interfering with their views about themselves. The impetus was not necessarily one event, but the emotional reaction to a number of events. A reduction in negative life events and an increase in positive events seemed to facilitate self change or its maintenance.

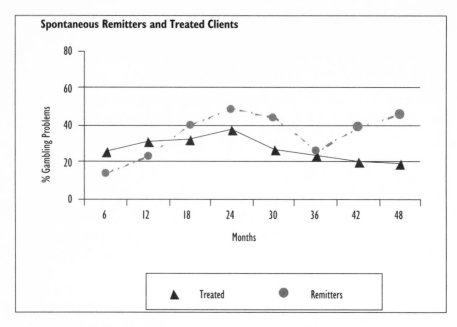

Figure 1.1: Percent of treated and spontaneously remitted clients with self-described gambling problems following initial gambling cessation.

From what we know about schizophrenia and affective disorders, such as bipolar disorder and depression, addictions that spontaneously remit indeed may be more likely to periodically return. There is evidence that many disorders show what is called *periodicity*, meaning they may be triggered by initial, extreme life stress, and then resolve in time often without treatment. However, once they are triggered, subsequent gambling occurrences are likely, and they are triggered by lower levels of stress or fewer environmental cues than before. As well, relapses tend to occur more frequently, more severely, and with less environmental precipitants. This is illustrated in Figure 1.2.

Because there are no clues or cues for whether a person will mature out or have a gambling problem for life, trained clinicians never count on spontaneous remission or maturing out as strategies for treatment. It is important for clinicians to understand that this can happen, but it should not shorten a well-thought-out treatment plan.

Clinical versus Nonclinical Populations: Why Some Gamblers Do Not Mature Out

To state it simply, and to repeat a phrase that will become frustratingly common throughout this text, *we simply do not know* the answer. Attempts to determine why some gamblers spontaneously mature out or quit problematic gambling are hampered by a lack of studies in the scientific literature.

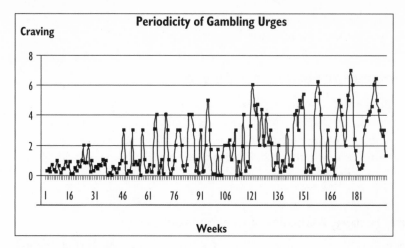

Figure 1.2: Periodicity of gambling urges in a client who spontaneously remitted from disordered gambling.

Despite the fragmented literature, some factors seem relevant. Understanding the real odds of winning and losing may discourage pathological gamblers from continuing this behavior (Benhsain, Taillefer, & Ladouceur, 2004). Many gamblers report that the realization that they were "suckers" was so offensive that they abandoned gambling altogether. As one pathological gambler stated, "When it occurred to me that you never beat the House, I was so disgusted that I had to quit. I am not that bad of a loser that I would be someone else's sucker."

Based on what we know about alcoholism and drug addiction, we may surmise that opportunities for gambling and cultural acceptance both play an undeniable role in whether a person matures out of problem wagering. Just as alcohol availability increases the likelihood of alcohol dependence, the availability of a gambling venue increases the likelihood that a borderline problem will become more encompassing. People who live near a casino are more than twice as likely as others to develop gambling problems. As mentioned, this may be becoming less relevant since virtually every Internet-connected computer in North America and Europe has access to legalized or semi-legalized wagering. Gambling opportunities are literally only clicks away. Cable and satellite television also offer gaming or horse racing channels dedicated to providing hundreds of wagering opportunities in a short time span.

We also can hypothesize that an early age of onset is associated with more serious problems. If research in other addictions is an indication, the earlier people start and the greater their opportunity to participate, the more likely they are to develop a gambling problem. Furthermore, they will probably have a worse prognosis. This is made even worse if their social conditions in life, such as absence of education, life skills, and opportunities, make them particularly vulnerable (Tims, Leukefeld, & Platt, 2001). This is of special concern because evidence suggests that poorer and younger people are gambling at a higher rate than in previous generations. More research is needed in this area.

Risk Factors for Gambling Disorders

We know little about the risk factors for developing severe pathological gambling (Ladouceur & Shaffer, 2005) due to the sparse attention paid to general gambling problems compared to other addictions. However, we may speculate, with reasonable certainty, that research from other addiction areas and laboratory studies may be applicable to people with gambling problems of various ranges.

Exposure, History, Attitudes, and Expectancies

Wagering is rewarded on a variable ratio of reward. This aspect of conditioning probably accounts for part of the explanation of why pathological gambling is addictive (Weatherly, Sauter, & King, 2004). Anecdotal accounts and some researchers suggest that people who *score big* or experience a windfall profit early in their gambling histories may be at particularly high risk. One casino manager said recently that he believes half of the people who experience a "very large financial gain" will "give it back to us" within a year. While some researchers dispute this, a general consensus is that a big win may act to bias a person's cognitions and emotions toward the belief that gambling is a predictable process that affords the player the opportunity to score consistently huge payoffs.

Recently, clinicians have seen other risk factors for acquisition of problem gambling, such as a person's total hours of Internet exposure and participation in risky financial transactions. New venues for wagering are developing almost yearly and often cannot be anticipated. For example, some high school students have gone beyond wagering on college sports and now bet on the outcome of local high school matches. Professionals involved with high schools must be vigilant to assess youths at risk of developing gambling problems.

Irrational expectations regarding pay-offs are risk factors for at least a subset of gamblers (Benhsain et al., 2004; Walker, 1992). Presumably they include a strong belief in luck, in the possibility of beating games of chance, or that games of chance show detectable patterns. People with gambling problems, especially with pathological gambling, expect to win in the long run, sometimes even in the short run. Often, these expectations seem to resist normal extinction mechanisms and become pathological, defying usual behavioral and cognitive theories that apply to others. Promising treatments that have strong empirical support focus on changing these irrational expectations (Toneatto & Millar, 2004).

Some people are more apt to develop a gambling problem when they consider gambling an illicit or forbidden activity. This may explain why sometimes the most intense gambling occurs among people with the deepest sentiments against it, such as deeply religious people who are in a state of rebellion against social or religious figures. Furthermore, the excitement associated with the lack of inhibition is increased in people who consider gambling *bad* or *evil*. When excessive wagering is seen as simply unhealthy, perhaps a bit like eating potato chips, it may lose some of the luster associated with its apparent tawdriness and then may become less tempting.

Personality Variables

The classic work of Custer and Milt (1985) identified two major types of gamblers—Action gamblers and Relief gamblers. These are useful models, though *models do not typically encompass every condition* and serve more as useful guides or maps. A clinician who tries to pigeonhole someone into a model may not understand fully the function of models.

Action gamblers, the majority of whom until recently were male, appear to be motivated by the positive reinforcing qualities of gambling-related arousal. While gambling, they usually experience intense excitement, a euphoric *rush* while winning, self importance, and feelings of omnipotence and power. Furthermore, they may often demonstrate, or appear to demonstrate, a reckless disregard for their losses. It is believed that the action gambler usually needs to bet more and more frequently in order to maintain the rewarding experiences.

Relief gamblers wager primarily for distraction, rather than for thrills or to enhance their egos. In other words, they are thought to be seeking negative reinforcement or a reduction in anxiety, depressive rumination, and other dysphoric states. However, gambling (like alcohol, commonly abused drugs, and other life distracters) is an exceedingly unreliable and costly mood-altering method. Its frequent failures result in increased use. When abused, it results in more anxiety and depression, causing a vicious circle.

Blaszczynski's Types

More than 60 years of research suggests that many personality factors may be a risk for some forms of disordered gambling. The prolific gambling researcher Alex Blaszczynski and his associates (Steel & Blaszczynski, 1996) have argued that there are four *personality types* at risk for developing the most severe pathological gambling problems.

The first type is essentially *no discernable type,* meaning those who have no substantial personality factor that contributes to their pathology. They are *normal* people who become exposed to excessive gambling perhaps through a large win or lifestyle factors. They may live near a casino or may be involved in the

---

IMAGINE THAT!

"My church makes a lot of money off of those Las Vegas nights. The idea is to make it as glitzy and really almost as sinful as possible, without sinning, if you know what I mean. I don't know that we will be doing it again, though. The last time we had one of those 'Casino Nights' one of the card dealers got into a fight with one of the players about cheating. It got that violent over *imaginary money*."

Source: Southern Church Pastor, now minus two church members.

gaming industry. Regardless of having no apparent predisposition, they develop severe gambling problems that cause personality-related behaviors.

A second type is composed of people who have serious preexisting *neurotic* spectrum disorders or other psychiatric conditions. An example might be a person who has anxiety or depression and gambles as a result of these conditions. This group likely corresponds to the relief gambler described earlier. In the language of many personality theorists, these people probably have a high degree of trait neuroticism, a personality characteristic that is related to emotionality and negative affect. An example is a person who gambles in response to the loneliness following the separation from a spouse.

A third type may have specific *biological vulnerabilities* to gambling and perhaps to other addictions as well. These people are highly impulsive and appear to have a strong biological component and difficulty regulating their moods. Perhaps they gamble as a form of mood regulation. A current theory is that they have abnormalities involving the neurotransmitter dopamine, causing reward deficits that will be discussed in later chapters. A radio commentator recently described these gamblers as "addicted to the action" because the action "makes them calm" and indeed they seem to be. They tend to enjoy taking chances and learn more slowly from their mistakes than others.

A fourth type is composed of people with *antisocial personality traits* that do not condition to signals of punishment in the way that the rest of us do. There is certainly some overlap between groups three and four. Groups two, three, and four are not mutually exclusive. It is possible for someone to have temperamental or intrapsychic variables or predispositions that propel the person to excessive gambling. That same person, quite independently, might have problems with various neurotransmitters or neurohormonal regulatory or reward systems. This might make people more addiction prone to a variety of stimuli and substances, not just gambling.

Specific Contradictory Personality Variables

A number of often contradictory personality factors are considered related to pathological gambling (Aasved, 2002). Some of the disparity in the literature may be due to the fact that subtypes of gamblers were included in the studies. Table 1.2 shows some personality variables that have been cited in research or clinical literature that are associated with gambling problems. Many of these traits are controversial and have not been replicated in other studies. Still, clients often find them useful in self-evaluating risk and self discovery.

It is clear that many types of personalities gamble excessively. Many personality extremes can be stretched into the hypothetical *gambling personality*. Not surprisingly, there is no single type of personality highly correlated with gambling problems, although personality may be a cofactor in the development of the disorder.

Table 1.2: Personality Characteristics Purportedly Causally Related to Gambling

Assertiveness	Conformity
Boredom proneness	Easily entertained personalities
Disagreeableness	Agreeableness
Need for interpersonal intimacy: High	Need for interpersonal intimacy: Low
Extraversion	Introversion
Female-ness	Male-ness
Gullibility	Paranoia
Magical Thinking	Concreteness
Generosity	Selfishness
Narcissism	Desire for Anonymity
Aggressiveness	Passivity
Need for achievement: High	Need for achievement: Low
Type A personality traits	Type B personality traits
Assertive personality traits	Avoidant and compliant traits
Need for rejection	Need for acceptance
Neuroticism	Excessive Stability
Sensation seeking	Passivity
Rebelliousness	Conformity
Need for acceptance: High	Self-punishment
Need for power: High	Need for power: Low
Manic subclinical traits	Depressive subclinical traits

Opposite and exclusive personality traits may relate to different types of gambling and when a person is likely to gamble during the life cycle. For example, extraverts may be at risk during specific periods and enjoy games in which they can be seen winning or losing. Introverts, on the other hand, may be less likely to enjoy flashier aspects of casinos but may develop gambling problems from other wagering opportunities.

Research now shows that major personality traits, as broadly measured, are relatively stable throughout much of life. Some of these broad personality variables are related to addictive disorders, such as high impulsivity. Others may make people more likely to become addicted following specific situations, such as high levels of trait neuroticism, which may interact with uncontrollable life stress.

Most clinicians are aware of the importance of personality in acquiring and maintaining addictive behaviors; however, they do not find it useful to directly treat an *addictive personality*. It is unlikely that one single addictive personality exists, despite what the media and popular accounts proclaim. Researchers and clinicians now understand that it is far more efficient to change extreme addictive behavior than it is to change personality traits. On the other hand, when their clients talk about having addictive personalities, clinicians help the clients use these insights to foster behavioral changes.

Comorbid Psychiatric Disorders

There are several well-recognized comorbid, or co-occurring, psychiatric disorders that are important risk factors for pathological gambling. These also are called comorbidities (Winters & Kushner, 2003). Based on the summary of existing literature, disordered gamblers are more likely than the general population to have the co-occurring or comorbid disorders listed in Table 1.3.

These disorders, and the diagnostic confusion that they generate, are discussed more fully in Chapter 2. Additional chapters will highlight the problems of comorbidity in treatment management and compliance.

Biology and Genetic Factors

Most researchers, and practically everyone who has recovered from a serious gambling problem, believe that the brains of gamblers work differently than those of others—but how? Some researchers believe that the underlying pathology of aberrant gambling is related to a reduced sensitivity of the brain's *reward system* (Reuter et al., 2005). This may be acquired through life experiences, may be based on genetic factors, or may be a combination of the two. Early experience might alter the ability of the reward system to function adequately and predispose a person to developing a gambling problem. There is increasing evidence from other addictions that, once specific brain mechanisms are overstimulated, it is unlikely that they will return to their balanced state prior to addiction (Kelley & Berridge, 2002).

Mounting evidence suggests that pathological gamblers show deficits in a specific portion of the brain associated with *deficits in impulse control*, especially under conditions of excitement. Essentially, they fail to show an adequate ability to inhibit or stop responses, even under conditions of losses. These people do not avoid punishment as well as the rest of us. It is easy to see how they might be more likely to continue gambling, despite serious financial setbacks.

Table 1.3: Co-occurring Disorders with Problem and Pathological Gambling

Alexithymia (inability to describe emotions)

Antisocial Personality Disorder

Anxiety Disorders

Attention-Deficit Disorder

Avoidant Personality Disorder

Bipolar Disorder

Borderline Personality Disorder

Dependent Personality

Depression

Dyslexia and Other Learning Disabilities

Impulse Control Disorders Other than Gambling

Narcissistic Personality Disorder

Other Addictive Disorders

Paranoid Personality Disorder

Schizoid Personality Disorder

Schizotypal Personality Disorder

Various Communication Disorders

Source: From Winters and Kushner (2003), Petry (2005), and other sources.

Several neurotransmitters have been implicated in disordered gambling. These include serotonin, norepinephrine, dopamine, and beta endorphins (Aasved, 2004). Fiorillo (2004) reviews the somewhat controversial nature of dopamine. Dopamine appears to be a major neurotransmitter involved with pleasure. It also appears to be released under conditions of uncertainty, a relatively novel finding that has been verified on a cellular level. Fiorillo notes, "If dopamine is increased by reward uncertainty and it is reinforcing, then it seems likely that it would contribute to the reinforcing and potentially addictive contribute of gambling, which is defined by reward uncertainty" (p. 123).

There is now data suggesting substantial genetic influence in pathological gambling (Potenza, Xian, Shah, Scherrer, & Eisen, 2005). Care needs to be taken in interpreting the findings of these studies, which were conducted on middle-aged men. However, they are congruent with the notion that differences in reward sensitivity may underline gambling addiction. Certainly, the picture is much more complex than anyone presently imagines. The next few years should produce important breakthroughs.

Coexisting Addictive Disorders

The *DSM-IV-TR* has proven to be a reliable tool in defining addictive disorders up to a certain point. For example, in drug addictions, the *DSM-IV-TR* can provide criteria to classify between abuse and dependency. It also provides the criteria needed to obtain a pathological gambling diagnosis. But nowhere is there a definition for sex, work, alcohol, buying, or food addiction (which is different then eating disorders). Statistically, a person with any addictive disorder, such as alcohol, has a higher chance of becoming addicted to gambling or another addictive disorder. As this field grows, there will be more research linking prevalence of gambling to drug addictions.

Epidemiology of At-Risk Populations

Despite common stereotypes, disordered gamblers can be male or female, teen, young adult, middle-aged, and older people. Aberrant gamblers are found among the poor and the wealthy. Every race and religion is included; every ethnicity or nationality is at risk.

Historically, the poor and people who are socially or economically disenfranchised have been more likely to develop gambling problems. This trend remains, and gambling among the most disenfranchised appears to be growing at an alarming pace. Statistically, Black and Asian people are more likely to become disordered gamblers, even controlling for economic factors (Welte, Barnes, Wieczorek, & Tidwell, 2004). The reasons for these patterns are not clear, but may relate to a cultural tolerance of gambling due to a history of economic deprivation, or because these groups had few other leisure options, such as oppressed people in the slavery period.

Because pathological gambling once took years to develop, gambling was believed to be a problem primarily for middle-aged people. However, gambling is increasing fastest among the young and the elderly, and there is evidence that pathological gambling is increasing fast in these groups as well.

During the last 10 years, elderly people have been recognized as being at particularly high risk for gambling problems. Many are addicted to such harmless pastimes as church-related bingo. Occasional gaming-industry marketing approaches target elderly patrons all too successfully. Because elderly people have limited leisure opportunities, they are at higher risk for financial devastation.

Studies suggest rates of disordered gambling may be from 7 to 12 percent for high school students. Many students are gambling much earlier and more frequently than their peers from a generation ago. Research finds above 80 percent of high school students admit to some history of gambling and about 14 percent

---

TESTING YOUR KNOWLEDGE

1. Rates of gambling in the North American population appear to be between _____ and _____.

2. Rates for younger people tend to be _____ than those of older people.

3. The *DSM-IV-TR* classifies gambling as a Disorder of _____.

4. Gamblers Anonymous prefers to use the term _____.

5. The term _____ is often used for cases of gambling disorders that are not as severe as those that have the full pathological symptoms.

Answers on page 31.

---

state that they have gambled on school property. High-stakes poker is now a highly popular cable television show for high school-aged people; and participation in games such as Texas Hold 'em has become a national craze. For some students in late high school and early college, gambling with peers is the only organized source of socialization.

In the college years, students may be at particularly high risk for exposure to new and particularly dangerous wagering opportunities. Outfitted with a credit card, which is often necessary for college transition, these students often are tempted to participate in sports wagering or other Internet gambling. Advertisements for these wagering opportunities are commonly encountered where students visit. To uninformed individuals, who do not realize that their gambling odds may be incredibly poor, the attraction can be overwhelming.

Student athletes and people that work closely with them may be particularly vulnerable for developing wagering problems. As more people wager on college sports, there may be pressure for these athletes to fix games or small parts of games. This can be done very subtly. For example, some bookmakers accept wagers on how many strikes must be thrown before the first base on balls is recorded in a specific game. It is exactly this type of athletic performance that is easy to unobtrusively manipulate, and officials are appropriately wary. Still, occasional accounts that appear in the media suggest that the problem is not necessarily under control.

Today, with rapid play video terminals and Internet wagering, many younger people are showing an affect that has been labeled *telescoping*. This occurs when a person advances rapidly through stages of gambling that once developed more slowly. As previously mentioned, some authors believe that women also are more likely to experience these telescoping tendencies.

Gender Differences

In the past, men were more likely to develop gambling problems; however, now many authors argue that genders have achieved parity. History shows that women are more likely to be relief gamblers, while men are more likely to be action gamblers. It is not clear whether these trends will continue.

Clinical cases and self-help literature suggest that many female problem and pathological gamblers may have a number of psychological and social burdens that male gamblers do not. These are listed in Table 1.4.

It is likely that gender differences and their relationship between the two types of problem and pathological gambling styles will disappear in the next generation or two. There is already some evidence that women are rapidly becoming more action gamblers; and as many as one half of men who seek help for gambling appear to be relief gamblers. Since the development of a specific type of gambling disorder may relate to the opportunities that a person can access, it may be that women have more access to relief-oriented games.

Table 1.4: Purported Characteristics of Female Problem and Pathological Gamblers

- Gambling becomes a problem later in life, frequently after women reach age 30.

- Gambling problems are more likely to occur when women reach the "empty nest phase" when their children leave.

- Gambling problems are presumed to occur more often following a divorce.

- Women are presumed to gamble at games that are entirely luck based, compared to those that involve a minimal degree of skill.

- In the past, women tended to be very quiet about gambling, compared to men, who tended to boast.

- Women often show more irregular wagering patterns—weeks of intensity, followed by months or years of quietude, with a return to intensity.

- Women were often observed to be more in a "fugue state" while gambling, appearing numb to their surroundings.

- Self-help literature states women with gambling problems tend to avoid confrontation.

- It is believed that gambling is harder on children if the mother has the problem.

- Some authors believe that women may reach a point of desperation sooner, following a much more rapid declining path after their initial wagering experiences.

- Self-help groups often claim that women have a difficult time in early recovery because of overwhelming shame and guilt.

- Some self-help proponents believe that women are more likely to relapse.

Gambling, the Family, and Multicultural Considerations

Presently, it is not clear how families affect problem or pathological gambling or related behaviors. Practitioners often note that dysfunctional families tolerate or actually encourage problem gambling by another member. Many family therapists see these *Identified Patients* (IPs) as scapegoats or metaphors for problems of other members in the family system. While this perspective has not generated the clinical enthusiasm that it has in other areas of addiction, it is often useful, especially where families seem to assist or enable relapses (Federman, Drebing, & Krebs, 2000). Clinical impression suggests that, where there is a gambling-related disorder, many families show a tendency toward a specific type of dysfunctioning. They are simultaneously crisis prone and treatment resistant. They are in need of intervention, but seem to work hard to avoid making interventions successful.

As is the case with alcohol, some clinicians note that families that model gambling moderation (rather than total abstinence) are likely to produce children without gambling problems. From a sociological perspective, social gambling can be taught in the family context the way social drinking can be reinforced by a family's values. But there is no guarantee that these social gamblers will not evolve into problem gamblers regardless of the reinforcement and support.

The meaning attached to gambling and abusive gambling may differ in diverse cultures. In some Asian cultures, gambling is commonly accepted and may even be necessary for daily business dealings. Gambling abuses may or may not be tolerated, however, and subcultures run the gamut of being permissive to extraordinarily restrictive. Practitioners need to be careful to avoid stereotypes based on limited experiences of people in Western settings.

Most fundamentalist Islamic countries detest gambling, though this moral condemnation does not seem to have slowed the progression of pathological gambling in many people of this background. Sub-Saharan African and European descendents do not seem to show any particular pattern. Gambling rates seem to vary by country and historic period. Other groups, such as the dwellers of southern Louisiana, have had a colorful past that has often involved abuse of gambling and excessive alcohol.

The role of religion needs to be considered carefully by professionals. Historically, the more *Protestant* a person, family, or origin group is, the greater the tendency to regard gambling as morally aberrant. However, in many cases, this morality can cause a person to engage in periodic binges that may increase the severity of gambling problems. Binge gambling, like binge drinking, seems especially high among people with conservative backgrounds, who are temporarily in a location where they feel that they will not be detected.

Usually, a trained counselor who is sensitive is able to ask about a person's religious beliefs and how these beliefs might have influenced the individual's gambling patterns. Religious values may be an untapped source of strength that assists in motivating a client to change. Regardless, this is a sensitive topic to explore and must be dealt with gently when opportunities arise for exploration and discussion.

What the Future Holds for the Treatment of This Disorder

The field of gambling treatment has become more outcome oriented. At the same time, when professionals are beginning to gain recognition as being autonomous, techniques are being systematized and subjected to empirical critiquing. The days when a specific treatment approach is used simply because popular clinicians advocate them will be gone. Similarly, clinicians who require clients to undergo a specific treatment simply because it worked for the specific clinicians or their peers will be seen as atavistic—relics of the past.

The treatment of gambling disorders will also move more toward a truly *biopsychosocial model.* The clinical and scientific community has often given lip service to the concept that gambling addiction is multicausal and is related to constructs from biology, psychology, and social interaction. What this means in practice, however, is that researchers and clinicians emphasize the variables that are most in their range, experience, and professional licensing to change. This is an example of the old adage of "If you have a hammer, the world is a nail." For example, psychiatrists *naturally* gravitate to biological orientations toward gambling, such as models that emphasize serotonergic or dopaminergic imbalances. Psychologists tend to emphasize learning and the cognitive aspects of the acquisition of gambling behavior. Social workers and family therapists tend to emphasize the interaction of family units, especially couples.

In other addictions, sadly, there is a further tendency to further fragment fields by the subspecialty of the practitioner. For example, nurses working in sexual addiction may read separate journals and have separate theories than family therapists working in sexual addiction. This is most prominent where addiction research is most advanced—alcohol. This trend may be beginning in gambling treatment, but practitioners and researchers can stop it cold.

Perhaps in 10 years, this fragmented, segmented approach to gambling research and treatment will be avoided. It is possible that gambling research and treatment may escape the splintering by profession that other addictions have experienced. Only time will tell, but there is reason to be hopeful.

Where the Field Is Going

The treatment for gambling disorders is now where alcohol was 30 or 40 years ago. There are many more questions than answers. Seven years ago, when we wrote a book for clinicians who wanted to learn about pathological gambling, there was clearly an insufficient number of studies. It was questionable whether pathological gambling was a disorder that the average clinician would ever encounter. The demand for treatment was primarily inpatient, unlike today, where comparatively few people are treated in this intensive of a modality.

In the past 10 years, academics in the field have learned more, and researchers want the therapeutic community to pay attention to what they have found. We now have some idea of what works, at least some of the time. Clinicians want better treatment based on data, not charisma or authority. To paraphrase the late Robert Coombs, "Addictionology is at last becoming a profession" (personal communication, April 15, 2004).

In many cases, briefer treatments appear to be very effective. A major concern over the next 10 years will be in determining for whom brief treatments are an appropriate intervention. Emphasis may be on interfacing formal aspects of brief treatment with Gamblers Anonymous.

Undoubtedly, there will be greater work on the subtypologies of pathological gamblers. Research has largely been retrospective and suffers from the deficits inherent in that design. Furthermore, there will be more research linking theories of abnormal behavior to these subtypes, and biological differences will undoubtedly loom boldly in these findings.

The field will pay attention to the growing number of Internet gamblers. In 2003, worldwide Internet gambling made revenues of $5.7 billion, and it is expected to reach approximately $16.9 billion by 2009 (Groover, 2005). Kearney (2005) reports that, between 2002 and 2003, there was an increase of 42 percent in the revenues obtained through Internet gambling; Internet gambling is not expensive to obtain, transportation is not involved, and there are basically no usage charges. The rise of Internet gambling brings an increase in youths gambling, gambling problems, and criminal activity. Individuals who previously could not gamble due to age, disabilities, and societal positions, now can gamble anonymously on the Internet. Furthermore, Internet gambling increases the opportunity for some types of fraud, such as credit card fraud. Participation in Internet gambling also could increase an individual's engagement in other forms of gambling.

Furthermore, as more *average citizens* become involved in the stock market, this form of investing will likely result in expanded opportunities for pathological gambling. The tendency of young people to gamble at apparently higher frequencies will need more attention, and researchers need to determine whether prevention of gambling in this age group can help prevent the development of other disorders. Research also will be aimed at determining what works for which type of high-risk group, such as the elderly, certain ethnic groups, and women.

Perhaps with gambling disorders, we have finally learned from our treatment errors in other addictions. First, we have learned that prevention is more important than expensive, after-the-fact treatment. As discussed in many sources (e.g., Coombs & Howatt, 2005), mental health prevention can be divided into three levels for comparison. Primary prevention is directed toward preventing the initial occurrence of a gambling disorder, by limiting either gambling opportunities or other methods that limit development of exposure to risk factors. Secondary prevention seeks to arrest or retard existing gambling problems and their effects before they become unmanageable. Tertiary prevention seeks to reduce the occurrences of gambling relapses in people who are committed to treatment. Greater emphasis will be placed on primary and secondary prevention and in understanding the transitioning between low-risk and high-risk gambling.

Bornstein and Miller (2006) report video games as being more harmful than any other form of media because of their interactive involvement. Video games have been associated with substance abuse, poor school performance, low activity, and gambling. We are concerned about the possible breeding ground for future gamblers to which the video game industry may be contributing. Today this industry is collectively bigger than the movie industry, which has been around much longer. We have no clinical evidence, just years of clinical experience that suggests gambling problems will continue to increase because of the Internet infrastructure and video game training arenas providing young people adventure and escape from the real world. Both are prime drivers for adult gambling addictions. We encourage and promote the idea that video games, the Internet, and other sources of electronic entertainment be monitored by parents closely.

Emphasis also will be less on traditional gambling treatment modeled after substance abuse treatment, and more on that which is modeled after relapse prevention (Toneatto & Millar, 2004). People for whom gambling abstinence is not an appropriate goal, or for those who choose not to pursue abstinence, methods of harm reduction will become more common. Harm reduction is a policy or program directed toward decreasing the adverse health, social, and economic consequences of gambling without requiring abstinence (although abstinence can be one of the strategies). Whether it is possible to use harm-reduction techniques to divert people who are on a trajectory toward high-risk gambling activities is not known and is beyond the scope of this book.

Ultimately, the greater goal will be beyond gambling cessation to one of health promotion—the process of enabling people to increase control over and to improve their health.

Summing Up

There are similarities and distinctions between gambling and other addictive disorders. Those with anger and a lack of empathy toward people with addictions often become blatantly antagonistic toward people specifically with gambling disorders. Through progress in treatment, most of us have some understanding of how drug or alcohol addiction can cause devastation, and there are now fewer

POINTS TO REMEMBER

Despite common stereotypes, disordered gamblers can be male, female, teen, middle-aged, elderly, rich or poor, and any ethnicity or nationality; although, historically, the poor and socially or economically disenfranchised have been more susceptible to developing gambling problems.

- Some reports suggest that younger adults are having more problems with gambling than older adults.
- Video games have been associated with substance abuse, poor school performance, low activity, and gambling.
- The meaning attached to gambling and abusive gambling differs across cultures, families, and religions.
- Treatment for gambling disorders is effective for the majority of people with problems.

stigmas associated with alcohol and drug addictions. In contrast, gambling-related disorders are more likely to be viewed as a personal Achilles' heel or a great wrongdoing. If others do see problem or pathological gambling as a legitimate addiction, they are likely to see it as beyond treatment, "utterly beyond the worst of hopeless" as a probation officer recently said. One possible reason is that there are fewer public examples of recovered pathological gamblers who are leading successful lives, in contrast to recovered alcohol or drug-addicted people. A number of common myths have impeded understanding and treatment of problem and pathological gambling. These include the idea that excessive gambling is a moral failure or personal weakness.

Furthermore, gambling problems may be acute or chronic and vary in severity. Many personality variables, psychiatric conditions, and cultural factors, perhaps genetics as well, influence the development of disordered gambling. Perhaps even sheer accident—dare we say chance?—also plays a role.

There is definitive evidence that treatment for gambling disorders is effective. During the next few years, more scientifically based treatment will combine with successful mechanisms of prevention to boost the effectiveness of interventions.

Key Terms

Mature out. Gradually curtailing destructive behavior over months or years.

Spontaneous remission. Disordered gambling problems disappear without informal or formal treatment.

Pathological gambler. The formal diagnosis of a gambling disorder as defined by the current edition of the *Diagnostic and Statistical Manual–Fourth Edition, Text Revised* (*DSM-IV-TR*). To receive this diagnosis, a person must meet five of the ten criteria as indicated in Table 1.1.

Problem gambler. People who meet some (e.g., three of the criteria), but not the minimum five criteria that obtains the *DSM-IV-TR* diagnosis for pathological gambling.

Disordered gambler. A general term used to describe anyone with a gambling disorder.

Compulsion. An uncontrollable behavior sparked by an irrational idea, called an *obsession,* having overwhelming internal feelings that seem coercive and inescapable.

Chasing. First, it is the process of betting more money for financial recouping. Another use of the term is the attempt to *out wager* the habituation and tedium that accompany the grind of chronic gambling

Action gambler. A person that appears to be motivated by the positive reinforcing qualities of gambling-related arousal.

Relief gambler. A person who wagers primarily for distraction, rather than for thrills or to enhance his or her ego.

Comorbid. Co-occurring.

Recommended Reading

For an excellent summary and breakdown of the three Waves, see Roger Dunstan (1997) at http://www.library.ca.gov/CRB/97/03/Chapt2.html.

One of the best resources available for summarizing findings regarding risks of developing problem and pathological gambling is available at the web page of the Ontario Problem Gambling Research Centre (OPGRC): http://www.gamblingresearch.org/contentdetail.sz?cid=2007. This is presented as a model that is constantly being updated, in response to new findings regarding biological, psychological and social influences in development of aberrant wagering. It is particularly useful to researchers, as it links present findings to questions of immediate interest.

Bob Wildman's e-review contains over 8,000 citations directly relevant to gambling. It is a very readable and entertaining narrative that highlights everything from the history of gambling to contemporary theories. It is free and Dr. Wildman writes like a gifted science writer. You can access it at the web page of the OPGRC at http://www.gamblingresearch.org/ewildman.sz.

While it is not quite the "Latest Addiction on the Internet" as they claim, Addictionsearch.com (http://www.addictionsearch.com) is a great resource for summaries of many recent findings for a variety of pharmacological and non-pharmacological addictions; counselors or therapists may find yourselves spending hours following the links listed there. Warning Sign posted: the information is so good it may be "Addicting to the Interested."

The Addiction Counselor's Desk Reference by Coombs and Howatt (2005) is a volume written by the editors of this series. This book, which is also available as an electronic e-book, is an immensely practical guide book for all kinds of information you might want to know about addiction in your daily practice. Moreover, and for our purposes, it has an outstanding set of tools for intakes, treatment planning, and client action plans. This book is *highly recommended* as a time saver and as a rich source of practical ideas and summaries of pertinent theoretical information. Get it today!

This Must Be Hell: A Look at Pathological Gambling by Humphrey (2000) includes brief accounts of the lives of pathological gamblers—*very* useful for clinicians, gamblers, and their families.

Born to Lose: Memoirs of a Compulsive Gambler by Lee (2005) is a very honest, straightforward account of how a very bright man with a great deal of talent developed an immense gambling addiction. This is a great book for people who might have a gambling problem, their families, and for therapists as well.

Pathological Gambling: Etiology, Comorbidity, and Treatment by Petry (2005b) is the most current, comprehensive scholarly review of pathological gambling by a noted researcher, who has a talent for asking questions that practitioners need answered. This is also a user-friendly treatment guide filled with resources for the clinician. Clinicians can adopt the cognitive behavioral program that she recommends with very little revisions. The book includes 35 pages of handouts for her scripted interventions. If you treat one gambler, at any time in your professional career, you must have this book.

TESTING YOUR KNOWLEDGE

ANSWERS

1. 2 percent and 6 percent   2. Higher   3. Impulse control   4. Compulsive gambling   5. Problem gambling

TRUTH OR FICTION

QUIZ ANSWERS

1. False   2. False   3. False   4. False   5. True   6. False   7. False

CHAPTER 2

Recognizing Gambling Disorders: Signs and Symptoms

TRUTH OR FICTION

QUIZ

After reading this chapter, you should be able to answer the following questions:

1. The phenomenon of *denial* is unique to addictions and part of the progress of the disease. True or False?

2. Emotional signs and symptoms associated with gambling disorders vary according to whether a person is in an acute crisis. True or False?

3. Traditional psychological testing is usually helpful for screening and diagnosis of a gambling-related problem. True or False?

4. There is agreement that all screening instruments are equally effective for every type of clinical group. True or False?

5. The family and employer typically are not very good sources of information, since they are usually in denial about gambling. True or False?

6. Training in gambling, or special certification, is always necessary to successfully treat the problem or pathological gambler. True or False?

7. It is potentially unethical for professionals to treat a person with a gambling problem unless they feel confident in their abilities to do so successfully. True or False?

Answers on p. 65.

Developmental Stages in the Progression of Problem and Pathological Gambling Behaviors

Many counselors, psychiatrists, social workers, psychologists, therapists, medical personnel, and other professionals lack sufficient training and experience to accurately detect the likelihood that a person has a gambling problem. This may be true despite the professional's outstanding abilities and training in other areas. This chapter highlights the developmental stages in the progression of disordered gambling and how to recognize gambling disorders in clients when evidence is unclear. It also highlights sources of information that can be used to form an appropriate differential diagnosis.

Involvement in gambling usually happens on a continuum. Insight into the developmental phases of disordered gambling may help in an overall understanding of recognizing its signs and symptoms.

The Gambling Continuum

It is often helpful to picture four developmental phases in the progression to pathological gambling. These are based on a model that was popularized by psychiatrist Robert Custer and his associates (e.g., Custer and Milt, 1985). Although these phases are based on clinical experience rather than research, they are popular with clinicians; and clients often find this representation particularly helpful in describing their experiences.

Phase I: The *Winning Phase* is characterized by positive socialization into the gambling experience. A person sees gambling as a pleasant, often immensely enjoyable part of life and may also ascribe special attributes to gambling, such as a way to relieve chronic stress or boredom.

During this phase, gamblers are likely to remember their winning episodes and believe that they may have special talent. This is because there are few, if any, negative consequences for the infrequent wagering episodes or relatively small sums that are wagered. This phase may last indefinitely for social gamblers, or years for progressive gamblers. In some situations, perhaps with slot gamblers, this phase may be very brief, as it may rapidly lead to the next phase.

Also during this phase, problem gamblers in the making often develop irrational fantasies about winning or about their special abilities for beating the odds (e.g., he sees himself as an itinerant card player, going from town to town, raking in money; she pictures herself quietly stalking the casinos, staying just long enough to make "a big score"). Some argue that these fantasies of the big win play an important part in the development and maintenance of pathological gambling (Weatherly, Sauter, & King, 2004).

Phase II: The next phase involves *Losing*, where gambling episodes become more regular, habitual, and more integrated into the individual's life. Losses increase and are rationalized. Wagering sizes increase, in part to compensate for these losses. Moreover, gambling becomes a major leisure activity, often replacing other activities. Family and work obligations may suffer, the gambler may lie to a spouse, employer, or perhaps call in sick in order to gamble.

Kilman, a 27-year-old mechanic, was in the Losing phase. His comments were typical of people who rationalize their behaviors: "I know I spend a lot of money at the boats [the casino]. But it's the same cost as, say, some other hobby. If I was into NASCAR or boating, I'd be spending more. If I had a house I owned, I'd be spending more."

Gamblers at this stage may seem preoccupied with gambling and, although they report enjoying it, there is often a sense of necessity and dread, as if gambling is an obligatory task rather than an enjoyable activity. This anxiety often is triggered by substantial financial losses, which are potentially devastating. Often there is increased anxiety and worry from job pressures. Credit cards may be maxed out and lines of credit are exhausted. Money borrowed from social networks soon depletes any possibility of supportive contacts with friends. At this time, people may try to cut back or manage finances through creative methods. They may juggle ridiculously from credit card to credit card, or refinance their houses at exorbitant rates.

Typically during this phase, people show periods of remorse following their exceptional losses. This is similar to the behavior of a substance abuser who promises to quit tomorrow. However, once tomorrow arrives, these vows of quitting do not maintain themselves. The person begins to gamble, often with more intensity.

Chasing, which we have described earlier, may also become common and this behavior-feeling state deserves special note.

Phase III: The *Desperation* phase is characterized by increased psychiatric symptoms including frank anxiety, insomnia, depression, avoidance, and even phobic behavior. In some cases, the gambler may go without food or sleep for prolonged periods while gambling. Often, behavior seen during this phase is difficult to distinguish from bipolar disorder. Mood swings are common and temper outbursts, some quite serious, become routine. The individual may become socially avoidant or agoraphobic for no discernable reason.

The gambler's social life and supports continue to decline. Options for obtaining vital cash are usually completely exhausted. The possibility of illegal behavior is increased as people begin to look for quick money. During this phase, a person's social and psychological identity as a gambler is solidified.

Phase IV: In the final phase, the *Hopelessness* phase, the gambler finds there is nothing left. It is very possible this person is homeless and may be living on the streets. Malnutrition is not uncommon. Suicidal attempts are also common and even successful many more times than others may realize. Suicidal ideation is almost universal and is a constant theme in the daily thoughts of the gambler. Preoccupation is with lost wagering opportunities or "the one that got away." Life is beyond desperate. Without help, the gambler falls into a feeling of desperate, often life-threatening hopelessness.

From the previous description of the developmental phases leading to pathological gambling, The National Research Council (1999) has developed a useful classification tool to classify people along this continuum. This four-points classification tool will be referred to throughout this book.

Level 0 gambling is a designation for people who have never gambled. Sometimes researchers will differentiate between Lifetime and Past Year Level 0 gamblers, as with the other levels described in the following paragraphs.

Level 1 gambling is the category that involves the largest number of people, about 80 percent of us, ranging from individuals who wager almost never, to those who gamble frequently for recreational purposes but show no evidence of problems. This broad category includes people who play occasional church bingo, as well as those who spend regular vacations at casino resorts, spending very large, but planned-for, sums. The amount wagered or lost is irrelevant, if there is no evidence of problem behavior.

An example is Marge and Chuck, a hypothetical retired couple, who visit a casino once a year "for a big blow out." They spend thousands of dollars that they *can afford* to lose, since they have planned well and have sufficient assets. The pattern, which they have repeated for 20 years, does not affect them or anyone else negatively, and they do not meet the diagnostic criteria for pathological gambling.

Level 2 gamblers have developed some moderate, real, and often persistent difficulties in life that are directly due to wagering. While experiencing distress, their lives are not yet unmanageable *at this point*. However, they are usually thought of as being at risk for developing more severe pathology. Other terms used in the literature for this classification of people are problem gamblers, habitual, episodic, abusive gamblers, problem social gamblers, excessive social gamblers, and threshold pathological gamblers. The most common term *problem gambler* will be employed in this book to indicate Level 2 gamblers.

Petry (2005a) notes that, despite the fact that Level 2 gambling is common, we know very little regarding people in this phase of the continuum. Petry specifically notes that, because Level 2 gamblers are not included in the *DSM-IV-TR,* counselors and clinicians are not able to bill for services for these people, discouraging effective treatment. Since this *Level* actually represents a statistical cluster of people in an underlying continuum, there is going to be some overlapping and misclassification.

Furthermore, we know little about the developmental histories of Level 2 gamblers. For example, how many go on to become more severe gamblers, or how many level off at this severity?

Level 3 gambling involves people who meet the full *DSM-IV-TR* criteria of pathological gambling. There is clear evidence of intense, gambling-related problems, including craving, preoccupation, and even withdrawal symptoms if gambling opportunities are unavailable.

Recognizing Gambling Disorders

Remember, no model is completely accurate; it does not encompass reality, it only represents it. Often, gambling problems masquerade as other types of psychopathology. Sometimes the presentation of the client does not fit our stereotype of what a person with a gambling disorder looks like. We may fail to screen for these disorders and, as a result, clients show no progress. An example is presented in the following case study.

John

John, 56, a very successful lawyer, had been treated by at least a dozen therapists for vague and poorly understood mental health symptoms. The treatments he received were diverse. None had any effect on his principal complaint of anxiety, agitation, periods of depersonalization (during which nothing seemed real), and occasional periods of deep and numbing depression.

One day, while at work, John was so upset over a falling stock that he swore violently and very obscenely. "Look at that idiotic corporation! The psychotic board of directors couldn't run a church bake sale...Their quarterly earnings mean I'm down $25,000 in my retirement fund and it isn't 9:30!"

A coworker heard him and was taken aback because this was not in line with John's usually pleasant demeanor and affable personality.

The coworker proceeded to ask John a few questions about his "investment strategies." It became obvious to the coworker that John might be more interested in the frenzy of wild stock speculation than serious financial plans and strategies. The coworker had a husband with a background in mental health. She suggested that John contact one of the few gambling counselors in the region. John stated that he would do so and surprisingly complied, with no resistance.

When the counselor saw John a few days later, John was ecstatic over another unlikely "investment," but this one had paid off. John said to the counselor that with "this investment coming through" John had broken even for the week. "I really should quit investing my retirement. I've gotten to the point where the thrill of winning makes me do—uh—stupid things."

The counselor asked John a series of standard questions. Then she asked John if John had ever considered that his "investing" was actually a form of pathological gambling? John stated that he had suspected this for a long time, perhaps years. Then why, the counselor wondered, didn't he mention it to any of the many therapists that he'd seen?

"Well," John said completely honestly, "as best as I can remember, they just did not ask. I guess I just didn't seem like that type of person to them."

POINTS TO REMEMBER

- Gambling problems are often thought to exist and develop on a continuum.
- In most cases, development of severe gambling problems takes a prolonged period, although there is a trend toward more rapid progression.
- *Level 2* gamblers are best thought of as problem gamblers who do not meet all of the criteria for a *DSM–IV-TR* diagnosis of pathological gambling.
- Some, though not all, Level 2 gamblers will proceed to a more severe *Level 3*, a term for people who meet the *DSM–IV-TR* criteria of pathological gambling.
- People with Level 2 and Level 3 problem gambling show progressively more problems, with Level 3 people meeting the full criteria, according to official diagnoses.

This case is an example in which stereotypic clinical presentations often blind the clinician to the signs and symptoms of pathological gambling.

The Signs and Symptoms of Pathological Gambling

Signs of gambling problems are the behavioral signals that a clinician or counselor observes in order to make an appropriate diagnosis and obtain necessary information to establish a diagnostic formulation. Signs might include such factors as associations with specific peers, leisure activities, financial behavior, and sports interests.

Symptoms, for our discussion, are the unique thoughts, feelings, and psychiatric-related behaviors associated with the specific syndrome of pathological gambling. Examples include the grandiosity that comes from winning a series of long-shot bets, the anxiety that accompanies losing, and the suicidal thoughts that accompany desperation from chronic losses. It is generally not helpful for the working clinician to search for the meaning of symptoms or to see symptoms as having an interpretive or deeper value.

Unlike alcoholism or marijuana use, there are no consistent, definitive physiologically related clinical signs or symptoms associated with gambling. Consequently, a diagnosis of problem or pathological gambling usually depends on information furnished from the client or from others.

An overview for making sense of signs and symptoms is to realize that these sources of self and others are different vantage points of the problems of the same person. The sources do not necessarily have to furnish the same information. Many factors may limit the usefulness of information from one particular source. However, when multiple sources tend to agree, this can strengthen the conclusions we draw.

The source that is often the most *and* least helpful is information given directly from the client. Not surprisingly, clients may be unreliable oral historians or may minimize the extent of their wagering problems. Therefore, the clinician may be forced to rely on a secondary or indirect source, such as the client's objective history or personal circumstances, or from others who know the client. These include family members, coworkers, employers, and others.

When obtaining client information, it is helpful to the communication process to be familiar with the games and terms of gambling. Also, this will help in future client discussions around the true odds of gambling. For many of us, the world of gambling is just a blur of terms to which we cannot relate. To avoid getting lost in the lingo, become aware of how the different games of chance are played as well as the different terms used in gambling.

For example, *Tilt*—a term used by gamblers to refer to the process of losing control over gambling; *Bailout*—money given to a gambler that allows him or her to pay debts without suffering adverse consequences; and *Bad beat*—a term used by gamblers to describe a run of bad luck. In addition to asking the client what terms mean as they are spoken, build a glossary of terms used over a period of time.

It is very helpful to become familiar with the gambling lifestyle as well, not necessarily by experiencing it, but by reading about it. Arthur Blume's (2005) sister volume to this book, *Treatment of Drug Addiction*, highlights his preference for avoiding slang. But sometimes, with gamblers, there are no other terms than the vernacular; and it is valuable to understand these terms when clients refer to them.

Client Information

Data in this category fall under the classification of what personality psychologists call *S Data,* or self report. Identifying the signs and symptom of pathological gambling directly from clients is difficult, as it is in any other addiction. However, the clinician should not be judgmental and ascribe this to any predisposition gamblers may have to lie. For a number of reasons, clients may be less than objective in furnishing an accurate account of their past or present wagering histories. First, they may not be aware of the extent of their gambling problems. Furthermore, they may minimize the abnormality of their wagering because their peer groups provide abnormal feedback. They have little contact with *normal* reference groups and consequently minimize the significance of their own addictive behaviors because they lack appropriate objective knowledge. Similarly, this may be more likely when they have grown up within a family that has normalized excessive gambling.

Next, problem and pathological gamblers may minimize their gambling history because there is a human tendency to resist attempts by others to limit our pleasurable or rewarding experiences. This has nothing to do with the traditional concept of *denial* as made popular by the old-fashioned substance abuse theorists. Instead, this is human nature, as social psychologists have long contended. People want to continue to do what they enjoy doing and resent others telling them that they can't.

Also, because gambling experiences may occur under the conditions of emotional arousal, gamblers may recall them poorly in quieter circumstances. In psychology, this phenomenon is known as *state dependent learning* and is seen in a variety of phenomena, such as when people who learn specific material while they are drunk recall it better when they are drunk at a later time. Again, this is a potential reason for clients possibly furnishing an unreliable history.

Other reasons may include that the problem or pathological gambler may be distracted, may ramble, or may not focus on telling the information you need. It is often helpful to structure the content of the clinical interview around questions proposed by the National Council on Problem Gambling, shown in Table 2.1.

Table 2.1: 10 Questions about Gambling Behavior

1. Have you often gambled longer than you had planned?

2. Have you often gambled until your last dollar was gone?

3. Have thoughts of gambling caused you to lose sleep?

4. Have you used your income or savings to gamble while letting bills go unpaid?

5. Have you made repeated, unsuccessful attempts to stop gambling?

6. Have you broken the law or considered breaking the law to finance your gambling?

7. Have you borrowed money to finance your gambling?

8. Have you felt depressed or suicidal because of your gambling losses?

9. Have you been remorseful after gambling?

10. Have you gambled to get money to meet your financial obligations?

It is believed by proponents of this questionnaire that a positive answer to any one of these questions may indicate a gambling problem.

Source: Reprinted with permission, National Council on Problem Gambling.

Another set of questions that is usually more stringent for clients is the Gamblers Anonymous Twenty Questions, in Table 2.2.

Table 2.2: Gamblers Anonymous Twenty Questions

1. Did you ever lose time from work or school due to gambling?

2. Has gambling ever made your home life unhappy?

3. Did gambling affect your reputation?

4. Have you ever felt remorse after gambling?

5. Did you ever gamble to get money with which to pay debts or otherwise solve financial difficulties?

6. Did gambling cause a decrease in your ambition or efficiency?

7. After losing did you feel you must return as soon as possible and win back your losses?

8. After a win did you have a strong urge to return and win more?

9. Did you often gamble until your last dollar was gone?

10. Did you ever borrow to finance your gambling?

11. Have you ever sold anything to finance gambling?

12. Were you reluctant to use "gambling money" for normal expenditures?

13. Did gambling make you careless of the welfare of yourself or your family?

14. Did you ever gamble longer than you had planned?

15. Have you ever gambled to escape worry or trouble?

16. Have you ever committed, or considered committing, an illegal act to finance gambling?

17. Did gambling cause you to have difficulty in sleeping?

18. Do arguments, disappointments or frustrations create within you an urge to gamble?

19. Did you ever have an urge to celebrate any good fortune by a few hours of gambling?

20. Have you ever considered self destruction or suicide as a result of your gambling?

Most compulsive gamblers will answer yes to at least seven of these questions.

For general population screening, Sumitra and Miller (2005) urge that physicians screen using the following acronym: WAGER OFTEN. This is based on the *DSM-IV-TR* and may be useful in helping assist in the early detection of gambling. People who meet diagnostic criteria on routine physicals or other health screening may be appropriately referred for a level of care that is not necessarily as intensive as might be necessary later. Refer to Table 2.3.

Table 2.3: The WAGER Mnemonic

WAGER OFTEN: A mnemonic for diagnosing pathologic gambling disorder[a]
W ithdrawal. Feels restless or irritable when attempting to reduce or stop gambling (*DSM-IV-TR* criterion 4)
A ffects relationships. Has jeopardized or lost a significant relationship, job, or educational or career opportunity because of gambling (*DSM-IV-TR* criterion 9)
G oal is to get even by chasing losses. Gambles again to break even after losing money gambling (*DSM-IV-TR* criterion 6)
E scape. Gambles as a way to escape problems or relieve dysphoric mood, helplessness, guilt, anxiety, or depression (*DSM-IV-TR* criterion 5)
R escue. Relies on others to be rescued financially (*DSM-IV-TR* criterion 10)
O utside the law. Has committed illegal acts, such as forgery, fraud, theft, or embezzlement, to finance gambling (*DSM-IV-TR* criterion 8)
F ailure to control. Has made repeated unsuccessful efforts to reduce, control, or stop gambling (*DSM-IV-TR* criterion 3)
T olerance. Needs to gamble with increasing amounts of money or risks to achieve the desired excitement (*DSM-IV-TR* criterion 2)
E vades telling the truth. Lies to family members, healthcare providers, or others to conceal the extent of involvement with gambling (*DSM-IV-TR* criterion 7)
N eeds to think about next gambling venture. Is preoccupied with reliving past gambling experiences, handicapping or planning the next venture, or thinking of ways to get money with which to gamble (*DSM-IV-TR* criterion 1)

[a]*Cannot be better accounted for by a manic episode.*

Source: Diagnostic and Statistical Manual of Mental Disorders, fourth edition, text revision (DSM-IV-TR).

Coexisting Addictive Disorder Screening

One strategy for screening people with potential coexisting addictive disorders is Dr. William Howatt's (2006) *Addictive Disorders Screen-7* screening tool. This tool was designed to be used in assessing risk in the early stages of assessment. For example, after using one or more of the previous screening tools, a clinician could use this particular tool to assess for potential risks in other areas. Refer to Table 2.4.

Table 2.4: Addictive Disorders Screen–7 (ADS-7)

The Addictive Disorders Screen–7 (ADS-7) is an assessment tool to predict potential risk for seven addictive disorders: alcohol and drug dependency, compulsive buying, compulsive gambling, eating disorders, work addictions, and sex addictions. The ADS-7 has been designed to assess new clients' potential risk.

This risk measure has 49 questions, which are to be answered with regard to the individual's behavior over the past 6 months, including today. This measure has been designed to assess risk. It is not a diagnostic tool. The client's scores indicate potential risk in certain addictive disorders. The scoring grid will help establish potential risk levels.

The client reads each question carefully and selects the response that best fits his or her present situation. The scoring grid provides a measurement of frequency (number of times) for each question.

The ADS-7 will take approximately 20 minutes to complete.

Questions Over the last six months:	0 Never	1 Once	2 (Fewer than 3 times)	3 (Fewer than 6 times)	4 (More than 7 times)
1. Has family or peers expressed a concern about your drug use?					
2. Have you tried to stop gambling and been unsuccessful?					
3. Have you thought you have a problem with alcohol?					
4. Have you worried about food and calories?					
5. Have you not bought groceries or paid bills because of your buying habits?					
6. Have you lost interest in friends, hobbies, school, work, or other pursuits because of your drug use?					
7. Have partners, peers, or family members expressed a concern about your sexual behavior?					
8. Have you noticed a connection between your financial problems and gambling?					
9. Have you purged food or used laxatives or diuretics as a strategy for maintaining body weight?					
10. Have you noticed that during weekends you cannot relax unless you are working?					

	0	1	2	3	4
11. Have you missed work or family functions because of your sexual behaviors (e.g., people or cyber sex)?					
12. Have you driven any kind of motor powered vehicle under the influence of alcohol?					
13. Has family or friends suggested you have an eating disorder (anorexia or bulimia)?					
14. Have you started the day drinking to avoid feeling sick?					
15. Have you used sex (people or cyber sex) as a way to get away from the stress of the world?					
16. Have any relationships failed as a result of work?					
17. Have you felt depressed after a buying spree?					
18. Have you acted on an internal drive to eat large amounts of food at one sitting?					
19. Have you noticed that food seems to be a major source of pleasure for you?					
20. Have you lost time (e.g., blackouts) during a drinking episode?					
21. Have you lied about your sexual behaviors?					
22. Have you ever committed a crime to obtain drugs (e.g., stealing)?					
23. Have peers or family expressed a concern over the amount of time you work?					
24. Have you used sex as a way to escape from the world?					
25. Have you noticed you gamble to escape or as a means of excitement?					
26. Have you noticed it takes more alcohol to feel good?					
27. Have you lied about your eating habits?					
28. Have you lied about your buying habits?					
29. Have you chosen drugs over people or work?					

	0	1	2	3	4
30. Have you noticed that your sense of self-worth is directly related to your work?					
31. Have peers personally or professionally expressed concern about your drinking?					
32. Have you tried to control your sexual behavior (people or cyber sex) and failed?					
33. Have you tried to stop drinking?					
34. Have you lied about your gambling?					
35. Have you felt regret, guilt, or remorse over your drug use?					
36. Have you noticed gambling is causing stress at home, but you continue to gamble?					
37. Have you found yourself buying things knowing you cannot afford them?					
38. Have your buying habits created money problems for you?					
39. Have you experimented with different kinds of drugs to find a better high?					
40. Have you noticed that you feel most in control when you are working?					
41. Have you felt a deep sense of depression after sex (people or cyber sex)?					
42. Have you attempted to keep your buying secretive?					
43. Have you lied to family or peers to stay at work longer?					
44. Have you used a system to increase your chances of winning when you gamble?					
45. Have you lost money gambling and felt OK?					
46. Have you spent the majority of a day obtaining drugs?					
47. Have you made projects more complex and time consuming than they need to be?					
48. Have you attempted to control your eating habits and failed?					
49. Have you noticed buying helps you feel a sense of control?					

Chemical Dependency (Drug)	Chemical Dependency (Alcohol)	Compulsive Buying	Compulsive Gambling
1	3	5	2
6	12	17	8
22	14	28	25
29	20	37	34
35	26	38	36
39	31	42	44
46	33	49	45
Total: Risk Level:	Total: Risk Level:	Total: Risk Level:	Total: Risk Level:

Food Addictions	Workaholism	Sex Addictions	
4	10	7	
9	16	11	
13	23	15	
18	30	21	
19	40	24	
27	43	32	
48	47	41	
Total: Risk Level:	Total: Risk Level:	Total: Risk Level:	

Potential Risk Levels

0–2	Sub clinical concern	May not be a concern—however, it is still important to explore this area in more detail with the client.
2–8	Medium concern	Has the potential to be a serious concern. It is recommended that the client do a more in-depth assessment in this area.
9–28	Serious concern	This score indicates the client is at risk and there is a need for a more in-depth clinical assessment.

Why do we use these popular, but unscientific, screening tools, rather than more objective and scientifically designed clinical measures (discussed later in the chapter)? One reason is that they are already popular. Another reason may be because they are cheap, easy to use, and have proven to net positive outcomes in screening potential problem gamblers for getting on the road to recovery. Once risks are uncovered, it is important for the counselor to follow up with more statistically proven clinical measures to confirm findings. And finally, regardless if using a screening tool or clinical measure, ultimately clinical judgment and experience will be the most valuable tools a counselor can use to assist clients in defining their present issues.

Other Client Signs

Personality psychologists discuss *L Data*, or life-history data, as another source of information. This information is often inferred from what you can see or surmise about the client's life and history. It is sometimes most helpful when it conflicts with what the client or others have told you. For example, the client who says that she is comfortable visiting the casino every night, but who looks tired and defeated, is presenting conflicting S and L data.

Health signs and symptoms usually involve detection by a specialist practitioner, but there are many exceptions that more general care providers can note and pass on for referral. Gambling takes a physical and psychological toll. Clients may look in ill health, despite the fact that they claim to feel healthier and cheerful. For the medical practitioner, clients with gambling problems may present with a variety of stress-related physical, psychosomatic, and depression-related complaints. Often, a client may approach a family practitioner, internist, or other practitioner with somatic complaints typical of chronic stressors. The client may ask for a heavy dose of a benzodiazepine or of a stimulant. Clinicians should note sleep disturbances, headaches, vaguely defined physical ailments, low back pain, sleep problems, bursts of energy or tiredness, an unkempt appearance, heart palpitations without a cardiac cause, chronic hypertension, weight change, poor health care or hygiene, sudden moodiness, and gastrointestinal problems. These are nonspecific signs that relate to many psychiatric problems. However, they may serve as cues for the need for further inquiry.

Emotional signs and symptoms vary according to whether a person is in an acute crisis. They may include depression, anxiety, excessive defensiveness, secretiveness, explosiveness, and reports of suicidal or homicidal ideation. Often, a suicidal plan will be involved that maximizes the possibility that the intention is not detected. Rarely, but possible, are frank delusional and psychotic symptoms. Rapid speed typical of bipolar disorder may also be observed and, in these situations, it is important to supplement a very careful history with a psychiatric referral.

Financial plans that the client has (or does not have) are particularly important to examine for diagnostic purposes. These may include evidence of financial stress, such as increasing numbers of unpaid bills, bills paid late, retirement withdrawals, and selling family possessions. Evidence of unexpected cash infusion that cannot be explained also may be a sign of the windfall gambling profit. Sadly, these profits are usually secured only while obtaining significant losses, which the client might not tell you about!

Similarly, the practitioner may also find that both self report and life data show an indifference to significant financial obligations. The client may not care about the fact that a mortgage is due or the car is being repossessed. This is because the client might have fantasies or plans of making up this deficit through gambling. The client may also have suicidal plans, making financial stresses irrelevant. This may be one of the most disturbing indicators and one that warrants immediate action.

Clinicians also should be aware of *miscellaneous behavioral signs and symptoms* that are not easily categorized. These often include the obvious—a preoccupation with gambling in its numerous forms, excessive secretiveness, a reduction in the number and frequency of previously enjoyed activities, an increased or greatly exaggerated interest in sports, and deterioration in school, work, or home functioning. Be especially mindful of clients who present with vague behavioral and psychiatric problems, apparently suddenly, where there was *no previous or consistent history* of psychiatric dysfunctioning.

Psychiatrists, in particular, may be asked to evaluate a patient who appears depressed, anxious, obsessive compulsive, or bipolar. They may be asked to provide evaluation regarding consultation because there seem to be no known psychological problems affecting this person. These people may present to a counselor and then to a psychiatrist as completely naïve about the potential causes of their problems. Often, they will seek medication to manage symptoms, such as benzodiazepines and antidepressants. Be particularly wary of spotty medical histories and when a patient is reluctant to discuss his or her past. In one case, the client claimed that his 9-month absence from work was due to a history of cancer that, upon further examination, made no medical or anatomical sense.

Sometimes a client can experience such extreme guilt regarding his or her own family's gambling that the client claims to have a problem that, upon screening, actually does not exist. Clinical experience suggests that this occurs most often in parts of the country where there are strong cultural taboos against gambling. Also, people with strong cultural beliefs against gambling may exaggerate their problems, despite showing a history of what is clearly socially appropriate gambling. Often, these people benefit from pastoral referral.

Confabulation is common to all addictive disorders, as are grief, shame, and guilt. Professionals may be frustrated by people who seem uninterested in getting help. But knowing this insight can help a clinician structure the interview to build the client's trust and comfort to feel safe in sharing his or her true reality.

What Spouses or Others May Report

Personality psychologists call this level of data *O Data*, short for reports from others. The strengths of O Data are their detachment from the client and their occasional enhanced objectivity. Counselors need to listen carefully to what spouses, family members, friends, employees, or other important persons are saying for any discrepancies. This is the case with any addiction. However, in the absence of other definitive information that is common in evaluating gambling, this is more important. The people who are close to the client will often present a different picture of reality than that furnished by the client (Ciarrochi, 2002).

Objectivity from *dispassionate* others is not always assured, however. Cases involving the helpful diagnostic information families furnish often vary. Sometimes families are hypervigilant and can furnish detailed information about a member. Sometimes they can tell the clinician nothing useful: On one extreme are spouses, family members, significant others, friends, and other relevant people who simply do not have an indication of what a gambling problem might even look like, much less that their family member has one. Because pathological gambling is so much out of their frame of reference, its existence simply seems extraordinarily implausible. Often, the vague and ill-defined symptoms that they sense in their family are blamed on other causes. For example, spouses frequently believe there may be an extramarital affair or a sexual orientation issue.

On the other hand, some spouses are in (what addictions counselors have been correctly taught) the classic behavioral syndrome of denial. In this case it is usually not helpful to ask why this occurs or to blame the family. Instead, expect that collusion and *codependency* (one of the many definitions of this word) are normal responses to an abnormal family situation.

Table 2.5 shows some useful questions that members of GamAnon, the sister organization of GA, have found helpful in assisting the spouse or others to admit or confront that a family member has a gambling problem. The structure helps people stay focused, which is often valuable during highly emotional periods, such as those of confronting the possibility of the necessity for treatment.

When clinicians state to concerned family members that other people have found these questions helpful, families often open up with honesty and a detailed disclosure. They see themselves as less isolated and realize that their problems are not unique. Their defenses drop and they become partners in treatment.

A questionnaire prepared by the Louisiana Association on Compulsive Gambling, shown in Table 2.6, is often helpful in showing family members that it is likely that there is a gambling problem.

Often, when a diagnosis of pathological gambling is made, the spouse will initially respond in relief. The spouse will say something like, "Thank God! I'm not going crazy after all" or "And the whole time I thought you were having an affair with my brother!" The spouse becomes overjoyed and may underestimate the extent of the pathology. This phase is very brief. It is usually followed by a period of denial or, more commonly, intense and sometimes self-defeating anger.

Table 2.5: Gamblers Anonymous Questions for Spouse or Significant Other—Revised

1. Do you find yourself constantly bothered by bill collectors?

2. Is the person in question often away from home for long, unexplained periods of time?

3. Does this person ever lose time from work due to gambling?

4. Do you feel that this person cannot be trusted with money?

5. Does the person in question faithfully promise that he or she will stop gambling, and yet gamble again and again?

6. Does this person ever gamble longer than he or she intended to, until the last dollar is gone?

7. Does this person immediately return to gambling to try to recover losses or win more?

8. Does this person ever gamble to get money to solve financial difficulties or have unrealistic expectations that gambling will bring the family material comfort and wealth?

9. Does this person borrow money to gamble with or to pay gambling debts?

10. Has this person's reputation ever suffered due to gambling, even to the extent of committing ill to finance gambling?

Source: Reprinted with permission, Gamblers Anonymous.

There are no widely used, standardized assessment instruments for family and concerned others designed to measure the reactions to problem and compulsive gambling. Many of the measures in Fischer and Corcoran's (1994) extraordinarily useful volume are highly adaptable for assessing the dysfunction that accompanies the impact of a gambling disorder on a family system.

Employers and Supervisors

Again, this source of O Data is often valuable. During the last 10 years, there has been an increase in detection of drug and alcohol problems by supervisors and employers. Henry Lesieur, PhD, one of the most influential gambling researchers, has observed many signs that employers or supervisors may notice concerning the possibility of gambling problems. While these signs are often more subtle than with drugs or alcohol, employers may have the first clue that a person has or is developing a gambling-related disorder. Some of these symptoms have been updated to include more recent advances in communication and Internet access and are listed in Table 2.7 on page 52.

Table 2.6: Louisiana Association on Compulsive Gambling Family Questionnaire

- Are you puzzled because you are always short of money?
- Does this person sometimes borrow money to pay ordinary monthly bills even though there has been no known change of income or specific increased expense?
- Has anything of personal or property value mysteriously disappeared?
- Have you sold anything of personal or property value to pay debts?
- Is this person secretive about money?
- Does this person seem to be more reckless about money than other people and not really weigh his chances?
- Have you accidentally discovered secret loans?
- Does this person continue to acquire different credit cards?
- Has this person ever urgently requested you to cosign a loan?
- Do you have any reason to question whether this person has filed an accurate or for that matter, any IRS return?
- Has there been a change in the way this person handles money?
- Has this person reordered spending priorities?
- Has this person let health or life insurance lapse?
- Do you have to resort to subterfuge to get money you need from this person? (i.e., overestimating some expenses, under reporting your own income, stealing from this person).
- Do you suspect this person took money from you?
- Is this person seeking new ways to earn extra money, have a second job or work overtime?
- Is this person gambling with greater frequency?

Source: Reprinted with permission, Louisiana Association on Compulsive Gambling.

Traditional Psychological Assessment

Traditional psychological assessment is what psychologists call *T Data* or test data furnished from a psychometrically and research-based perspective. There is little evidence that traditional psychology tools effectively differentiate people with a gambling problem from others. These tests were not designed to do this, and there is no reason to expect them to have this ability.

Table 2.7: Some Signs That Employers May Notice Regarding Gambling Problems

- Excessive use of telephones (e.g., to call bookmakers, stockbrokers, or to obtain credit)

- Pager or excessive cell phone activity

- Computer time spent reading betting-related sites, exuberant or quirky financial news, sports-related information, or receiving many instant messages that provoke emotional change (e.g., an instant message might signify a large financial win)

- Taking the company vehicle to the race track, card room, casino, day trading facility, etc. (Lesieur believes that parking tickets near gambling locations are usually a "red flag" signal.)

- Unexplained or poorly excused absences from work, often for part of the day (typically after lunch, in areas where there is a race track)

- Arriving late for work (related to all-night card games, casino trips, anxiety-related sleep disturbances)

- Excessive mail or emails received concerning gambling plans or money management strategies

- Excessive investment or "get rich quick" information that arrives for the person

- Bragging about a financial windfall, especially one made on a shaky investment

- Lunchtime alone, on the phone, or at desk with multiple window screens open

- Telephone conversations with intense animation or emotionality

- Vacation days taken on isolated days rather than in logical periods (or vacations taken to gambling locations on a regular basis)

- Failure to take any days off (obsessed with getting money to pay gambling debts or afraid to take a day off because of a fear that embezzlement or fraud will be discovered in their absence)

- Changes in productivity (which seem to be related to gambling-related mood swings)

- Organizing office pools and gambling junkets, often with excessive zealousness

- Borrowing money from co-workers or arguing with co-workers over failure to pay debts, especially vaguely defined debts

- Embezzlement, defrauding customers or engaging in employee theft

Traditional assessment devices may be quite valuable in distinguishing between pathological gambling and other conditions that may be confused with this disorder, such as psychotic thinking or bipolar disorder, discussed in the following paragraphs (McCown & Chamberlain, 2000).

Table 2.8 shows some popular traditional psychological tests, with brief descriptions, and potential usefulness.

Many other popular psychological tests that counselors use, such as the Myers Briggs, do not yet have a clear role in gambling treatment.

As most people who have taken courses in behavioral sciences know, measures can be reliable but not valid. If we labeled everyone who reported they gambled as having a gambling problem, our assessment instrument would be completely reliable in pointing out gambling behavior, but highly invalid in its final diagnosis. Every measure has a similar trade-off between misidentifying people who do not have the problem (false positives) and missing people who would otherwise be found to be diagnosable, using other, more thorough methodology (false negatives).

The National Research Council (1999) identified 25 instruments directly relevant to pathological gambling. Additional discussion regarding measures is available in Petry (2005a) and Coombs and Howatt (2005). Instruments can be divided into two clusters. The first detects problem or pathological gambling; the second detects severity over time. They may be separated also by whether they address teens, adults, or the elderly (where there presently are no instruments). Using a different schema, instruments may be divided by whether they assess the effects that gambling has on the person and/or the person's family and other social systems. No one knows which instrument is best for which population. What we advise is that the practitioner become familiar with a variety of different tools and then choose which one best fits the needs. Then become comfortable administering it and do so whenever needed.

The South Oaks Gambling Screen (SOGS; Leisure & Blume, 1987) is one of the most commonly used screening inventories. Used by a variety of clinicians, it is composed of 20 items that are dichotomously scored. Reliability and validity are quite satisfactory. Cut-offs are used to estimate probable pathological gambling. It may be used to establish present or lifetime rates of symptoms. However, because it is a screening instrument, some people are concerned that it may overestimate the rates of pathological gambling. Furthermore, researchers are concerned that it is not directly keyed to the *DSM-IV-TR*. Petry (2005a) suggests that the instrument be used as a general screen and followed up by a diagnostic interview, and this is a suggestion that colleagues have found most helpful.

The Diagnostic Interview for Gambling Severity (DIGS; Winters, Specker, & Stinchfield, 2002) is an instrument that measures problem gambling and its impact on psychiatric, legal, and financial problems. It is administered through a trained administrator and has good reliability and validity. Only limited data are known regarding its use, although it appears to be a promising tool.

Table 2.8: Popular Traditional Psychological Tests

Test Name	Description	Routine Use	Use in Assessment of Gamblers	Qualifications of Administrator	Disadvantages
Minnesota Multiphasic Personality Inventory, Adolescent or Second Edition	Yes/No test with over 600 questions	Measures a variety of different types of abnormal behavior	Useful for detecting a variety of different psychopathologies; no specific information regarding gambling	May be administered by a variety of mental health professionals, but must be interpreted by psychologist	Very long
Thematic Apperception Test	A measure of response to unstructured picture stimulus	Increasingly used only as an adjunct in testing, though used frequently in research	Primarily research	Psychologist	Long and hard to interpret reliably and objectively
Various Individual Intelligence Tests	Involve response to verbal material and complex stimuli	Measure overall intellectual functioning	Helpful in some situations where gambler has performance deficits that are unexplainable	Psychologist	Long and hard to interpret reliably and objectively
16 PF	Objective multiple choice test	Measures 16 very reliable personality variables	Often helpful for planning recovery	Can be administered by anyone with mental health training and scored by proprietary program	Comparatively expensive to score

Test	Format	Measures	Clinical Use	Administered By	Limitations
Millon Clinical Multiaxial Inventory III	Yes/No items	Measures Personality Disorders	Often very helpful for elucidating client's previous behaviors and predicting future course	Can be administered by anyone with mental health training and scored by proprietary program	Comparatively expensive to score. Notion of Personality Disorder is not keyed to DSM-IV, but is tied to Millon's theory
Rorschach Inkblot Method	Response to 10 ambiguous stimuli	Used to measure unusual aspects of cognitive, personality, and response styles	Occasional use in detection of schizophrenia or tendency for extreme social perceptual deficits	Psychologist	Requires extensive training to score reliably and validly; very time consuming
NEO PI	Questionnaire of about 260 items	Reliably measures five very broad personality traits that are stable throughout life	Often useful in treatment planning, relapse prevention, and in discharge	Can be administered by anyone with mental health training and scored by proprietary program	Somewhat time consuming to complete; interpretive profiles may intimidating
Various intelligence tests	Length depends on quality of test	Measure of general intelligence, which correlates with a number of positive characteristics	Useful in rehabilitation and for cases where a person cannot grasp basic concepts in gambling education	Should only be administered by psychologist	Time consuming; results tend to be vastly over interpreted
Neuropsychological testing	Various lengths	Measure of cognitive functioning related to localized deficits	As above; research suggests certain particular deficits may be associated with gambling dysfunctions	As above	As above

National Opinion Research Center *DSM* Screen for Gambling Problems (NODS) is based on the *DSM-IV-TR* criteria for Pathological Gambling and assesses for both lifetime and past-year problem gambling. This instrument includes 34 items and was designed as an interview tool (Hodgins, 2004).

The Massachusetts Gambling Screen (MAGS; Shaffer, LaBrie, Sclanlan, & Cummings, 1994) was designed for use among adolescents and is structured after the Short Michigan Alcoholism Screening test. It measures past-year behavior. Reliability and validity appear satisfactory.

Complicating Diagnostic Issues

Bipolar disorder is so common that the *DSM-IV-TR* (American Psychiatric Association, 2000) states that episodes of gambling confined to bipolar periods do not receive a diagnosis of pathological gambling. In many cases, a careful psychiatric examination is necessary to distinguish bipolar disorder from pathological gambling. This is especially true for young people, when gambling may have seemed to emerge suddenly.

Bipolar disorder must be treated as aggressively as it usually is, by a psychiatrist experienced in management of complex aspects of mood disorders. Evidence is mounting that many apparent types of gambling behaviors are actually undiagnosed variants of bipolar spectrum disorders. More research is urgently needed regarding this important issue and clinicians are urged to monitor it closely.

Often, however, bipolar symptom reduction and control does not eliminate gambling. It is likely that the client will return to pathological gambling, even if he or she experiences stabilization of mood (i.e., patient may continue to gamble or return to gambling even if showing no signs of bipolarity). Since relapse is usually the rule rather than the exception, people with bipolar disorders and concurrent gambling problems represent a significant therapeutic and assessment challenge.

POINTS TO REMEMBER

- **S** Data are Self-Report Data, or what the client tells us him or herself
- **L** Data are Life Data, or what the client's *life* says about him or her
- **O** Data are data reported by *others*. The strength of O Data can be objectivity, although objectivity is not always assured.
- **T** Data are any data obtained from a valid psychometric *test*
- Reliability is the ability of a test to perform consistently
- Validity is the ability of a test to do what it actually claims
- A test can be reliable, but not valid
- All tests make mistakes
- Mistakes are a trade-off between over- or underidentifying a problem

There also is evidence that people with Bipolar II, a particular subtype recognized by the *DSM-IV-TR,* are not likely to be properly diagnosed. Given the capacity for common antidepressants to induce mood cycling, care needs to be taken in prescribing them to gamblers who may have an undiagnosed Bipolar II condition.

Also, depression and anxiety commonly are found in people who are pathological gamblers. The direction of causality almost always is impossible to determine. Too often, people with mental health training will insist that the depression or anxiety be treated first, with the gambling disorder being treated secondarily, or not at all. The notion is that when anxiety or depression is removed, the gambling also will cease, with minimal intervention. Clinical experience suggests that this may be true for a subset of patients with limited gambling history. After a time, the gambling disorder seems to become *functionally autonomous*, and thus develops a life of its own. On the other hand, people who have pathological gambling problems usually have many reasons to feel anxious or depressed. Sometimes anxiety and depression will lessen when the gambling disorder is in remission.

Of special note is Attention-Deficit/Hyperactivity Disorder (ADHD). People with ADHD are much more likely to have gambling problems. Clinicians tend to avoid stimulants for the treatment of ADHD in gamblers, because many gamblers have another addictive disorder. However, evidence from cocaine addiction suggests that the pharmacological treatment of ADHD does not cause relapse. In fact, aggressive treatment may reduce illicit drug use.

Excluding cigarette smoking, concurrent substance abuse problems are common in as many as 50 percent of people with gambling problems, either presently or by history. It makes little sense to treat only the most serious problem and not treat the coexisting addictive disorder. All addictive disorders warrant treatment simultaneously, regardless of whether there are conflicting bureaucracies involved!

In studying members of Gamblers Anonymous, some data show that at least 70 percent of these people have personality disorders. Most commonly, these involve Cluster B disorders, such as Narcissistic and Antisocial disorders. These disorders may make data obtained from the clinical interview even more unreliable. Clinicians will have to use judgment, experience, and knowledge of clients to design appropriate treatment. There is no algorithm for dealing with the gambler who has a personality disorder or to determine how much of a client's words can be trusted.

Our own experience, supported by a small data set, suggests that, on average, effective gambling treatment reduces personality psychopathology by about half a standard deviation. This is statistically and clinically significant and argues for the fact that some of the increased personality dysfunctioning in people with problem gambling behavior is due to or is maintained by their gambling.

IMAGINE THAT!

A woman with an addiction to alcohol, cocaine, gambling, as well as a problem with bipolar disorder, received treatment from four different agencies. Her psychiatrist for medication was through yet another state agency. Each month the woman had to complete 44 forms. Added to this was the daily attendance at self-help meetings, the effort to work full time, and to take care of her children. She felt as if she had little genuine time to overcome her addictions. Instead, she felt she was a cog in someone else's system. Slowly, over the next several months, her optimistic demeanor about the chances of recovery wore off.

Was this woman being adequately helped?

A good source for the busy general-purpose practitioner is the practical volume by Bauer (2003). This is an evidence-based guide to clinical interviewing that should assist the more general practitioners, who see clients with gambling disorders as well as a variety of other problems superimposed together. The volume by Combs and Howatt is very helpful in providing useful information for diagnosing people with multiple disorders.

Many times, helpful rating scales may assist the counselor in determining the presence of other pathologies. An excellent source for a variety of scales is the volume by Sajatovic and Ramirez (2001). This source is also a useful introduction to rating scales, as well as a compendium of scales available at no charge.

Sometimes there is pressure for clinicians to minimize the existence of Axis I or Axis II pathology. This is because people with dual diagnoses do not fit nicely into existing systems. Treatment facilities that exclude people with co-occurring Axis I or II diagnoses are simply being unrealistic.

TESTING YOUR KNOWLEDGE

1. Level 2 gamblers are included in the *DSM-IV-TR*. True or False?

2. Client indifference to significant financial obligations may indicate the client has fantasies or plans about making up the deficit through gambling, or the client may have _____ plans, making financial stress irrelevant.

3. When obtaining O Data from family members, employers, friends, and so on, it is important to listen carefully for any _____.

4. Evidence is mounting that many apparent types of gambling behaviors are actually an undiagnosed variant of _____.

5. What are two symptoms commonly found in people who are pathological gamblers?

Answers on page 65.

Healthy versus Problematic Attitudes and Behaviors

A person's attitude toward normal gambling done by others does not help diagnose whether that person has a gambling disorder; this is not an appropriate source of O, S, or L data. Even more than with alcohol consumption, people have conflicting attitudes concerning the morality of gambling. Some consider it reprehensible; others consider it a harmless and enjoyable pastime, perhaps even one with financial benefits. A surprising number of people call gambling hotlines and gambling counselors to ask whether their gambling behavior is appropriate. They may want to know, for example, if it is "okay that my girlfriend and I like to spend our time together at the track." It is important that counselors hold their judgments in abeyance. They must not allow feelings regarding the morality of gambling to sway their objective evaluations or suggest the need for treatment when there is really none apparent.

A cross-section of the population has little empathy for problem and pathological gamblers. Recently, a nationally known radio personality said candidly, "I just don't get it. People work too hard for their money to throw it away like that ... Drugs and alcohol, at least they make more sense to abuse." This is a common sentiment. One reason is that gambling is an expensive addiction. A gambler and alcoholic in recovery recently noted, "The buzz from alcohol and drugs are much more cost effective—as long as you aren't wired to be a gambler. If you are, you understand that there is no high like it in the world."

Be careful and do not judge. From the counselor's perspective, gambling is a morally neutral activity. *Do not interpret favorable attitudes toward gambling as evidence of a gambling problem.* This is illustrated in the following vignette.

CASE STUDY

Ginger

Ginger, a 28-year-old woman, was involved in a divorce. She and her husband developed highly adversarial conflicts regarding child custody. One point of contention was whether her husband was "morally unfit for child rearing" because he enjoyed gambling limited amounts of money on a weekly basis at a local casino.

A court-affiliated psychologist interviewed Ginger and her husband. On the basis of these data alone, the well-meaning psychologist stated that he honestly believed the husband was a potential compulsive gambler.

The psychologist involved stated that the husband brought an ethics complaint to the state professional board on the grounds that his attitude about gambling did not substantially influence the likelihood that he was a compulsive gambler. The psychologist was forced to retract his report and attend training on gambling disorders.

Social Settings

If the family of the pathological gambler is sufficiently intact, it is invariably severely damaged and functions poorly. This source of information is included as L or O Data, meaning it is observable from the gamblers' reports or others in their lives, and may be a good indication of the existence of a gambling-related problem. One paradox of pathological gambling is that, although it is physiologically undetectable, it is often more devastating to a client's social system than the abuse of alcohol or other drugs. Perhaps this is because it is undetectable for so long, or because gambling is such an expensive "drug" per "dosage."

The effects of pathological gambling on the family include severe stress, abuse, neglect, and financial ruin. Some common problems are included in Table 2.9.

Typically, the spouse is the primary person who experiences the dysphoria associated with a poor marriage, while the disordered gambler escapes responsibility through wagering.

Less is known about the symptoms and behaviors of children of pathological gamblers. Some clinicians cite examples suggesting that women gamblers may significantly neglect their children. Both fathers and mothers who spend excessive time gambling are neither physically nor mentally available.

By the time a person enters treatment, the person has usually borrowed all of the money possible from family and friends. Acquaintances avoid him or her because they know these people will request only one thing: more money. "She drains me socially and financially," said a family member, "so I avoid her like the plague." This absence of social contact creates another risk for depression.

All these factors combine to make spouses and families potentially important sources of information. However, often the family is fearful or shameful of its member's behavior. It frequently denies the problem or ascribes it to another cause. Family therapists long have noted that denial may have a functional aspect. By making the gambler the focus of attention, scrutiny is diverted from other family behaviors. Because of this, and other reasons, the family may unconsciously resist disclosure of information and may act to impede progress in treatment.

Professional Collaboration, Accountability, and Responsibility in the Screening-Intake Process

Prior to screening, have a ready procedure that outlines the process and methods for who conducts screenings, how they are conducted, and who is available for back up if necessary. The sooner clients are screened, the greater their motivation and commitment will be to treatment, as well as their willingness to begin the process of change. Therefore, strategically, it is of value to have a back-up professional, off-site if necessary, if you and your agency are tied up. Clients often can be screened over the phone if they are highly motivated. However, someone needs to answer the phones that begin the screening process.

Table 2.9: Family Problems Cited in Clinical or Research Literature

- Parentified children
- Neglected children
- Symptoms in members other than identified patients (e.g., anxiety, depression)
- Alcohol or drug abuse of other family members
- Husband-wife problems of many varieties
- Tremendous poverty
- Constant boundary problems
- Physical and sexual abuse
- Childrearing problems involving skills
- Problem solving, and emotional dysregulation
- Anger throughout family system
- Guilt
- Learned helplessness in family
- Emotional insecurity from nefarious figures, such as loan sharks

Counselors who perform screenings need to become familiar with potential environmental triggers that can occur during the screening process. For example, the names of sports teams or discussion about football scores may provoke a strong craving. Once familiar with the clients, it is appropriate to ask if they are comfortable with such topics; however, their possible lack of insight or awareness may limit the usefulness of their answers. Practice restraint and sensitivity during the screening period. According to one recovering gambler, the first mental health counselor he ever saw had a wall filled with sports memorabilia. He promptly left the interview and placed a large bet on an upcoming LSU game! Another client shared that she relapsed after sitting in her physician's waiting room reading a sports magazine. Some of these situations are beyond our control; others we may be able to influence.

Obvious displays of wealth, social status, accomplishments, or egregious flaunting of success may add to resentment over money, which often is rooted in the gambler's history. While this can occur at any time in treatment, clients are likely to be most sensitive during the screening session. This issue often cannot be addressed adequately in textbooks but requires training and supervision to recognize and avoid it in one's self.

Those of us from a recovery background often accidentally blur professional lines during screening. We may say things such as "I had this symptom, so don't feel so bad," or "I was even worse off than you! But I got better." We sometimes forget that screenings are not self-help meetings. Competent and helpful counselors can seek supervision to avoid this problem. They are aware of their own motives and changing needs and avoid interactions that violate the client's boundaries. Remember, only say to clients what you would feel comfortable having recorded and reviewed in a court of law or by an ethics board.

An example: A counselor who is having financial problems due to medical illnesses may be in a poor position to empathetically screen a pathological gambler who has lost hundreds of thousands of dollars from a family trust. The counselor should seek supervision for these difficulties and discuss them with a caring, but realistic supervisor. Counselors often ignore that these problems occur at the screening process and believe they only emerge later during more intense aspects of treatment. *However, it is precisely at screening or intake when the client has the most minimal relationship with the counselor that the counselor is at the most danger of being misunderstood and having his or her motives misinterpreted.*

Be very aware of the tendencies of some addicted people to take statements out of context. Classic *splitting* and paranoid projection may be encountered. The ethical counselor acts genuinely and spontaneously, but also cautiously, in the best interests of the client. Remember, what you say may be misperceived. If you could not defend it in court or to a group of your peers, don't say it. This may make you less spontaneous and genuine, but sadly, this is how it has to be.

There are numerous infractions to dignity and respect that some pathological gamblers face in treatment, especially at screening. For example, a cold, perhaps passive-aggressive, narcissistic, or sadistic counselor can cause extraordinary damage in the name of *screening* and *treatment*. The result of these interactions can leave clients feeling humiliated, insulted, or degraded. No client should ever be treated rudely. The Golden Rule is still a good set of ideals for interacting with all addicted people. It is the responsibility of all professionals to provide empathy and kindness as they begin to support a client's curiosity and interest in recovery.

Summing Up

Gambling progresses on a continuum and there are four categories or levels of severity along that continuum. Level 3 is considered pathological gamblers, whereas Level 2 is considered problem gamblers. Unlike chemical addictions, evidence of problem or pathological gambling is often harder to detect. The counselor must gather all of the data, including signs and symptoms. Data exist

- Note any health signs and symptoms that may serve as cues, including sleep disturbances, headaches, vaguely defined physical ailments, lower back pain, bursts of energy or tiredness, an unkempt appearance, heart palpitations, chronic hypertension, weight change, poor hygiene, sudden moodiness, and gastrointestinal problems.

- Cues that are emotional signs and symptoms may include depression, anxiety, excessive defensiveness, secretiveness, explosiveness, and reports of suicidal or homicidal ideation.

- Financial plans that the client has (or does not have) can be particularly important cues for diagnostic purposes and may include evidence of financial stress, such as unpaid bills, bills paid late, retirement withdrawals, and selling family possessions, as well as unexpected and unexplained cash infusions. Also note any indifference to significant financial obligations.

- A careful psychiatric examination is necessary to distinguish bipolar disorder from pathological gambling, especially for young people, when gambling may have seemed to emerge suddenly.

- Often, bipolar symptom reduction and control does not eliminate gambling.

- Excluding cigarette smoking, concurrent substance abuse problems are common in as many as 50 percent of people with gambling problems, either presently or by history, and warrant treatment simultaneously.

on different levels and come from different sources. In general, the more congruent the data, the more likely the screening is to produce an appropriate diagnosis. A number of tools and screening instruments have been designed to help the counselor. Often, it is necessary to look for evidence of a gambling problem in other sources, such as from family members, friends, and life history.

There are many reasons a counselor may choose to treat a client rather than refer, even if he or she feels a lack of some expertise. On the other hand, there are many circumstances in which referral is not only appropriate but ethically imperative. The counselor or therapist will have to weigh each situation, being careful to fully document decisions.

Key Terms

Winning phase. This is the first of four developmental phases to pathological gambling. It is characterized by positive socialization into the gambling experience.

Losing phase. In this second phase, gambling episodes become more regular, habitual, and integrated into the individual's life. Losses increase and are rationalized.

Desperation phase. The third phase is characterized by increased psychiatric symptoms including frank anxiety, insomnia, depression, avoidance, and even phobic behavior.

Hopelessness phase. In this final phase, the gambler finds there is nothing left. It is very possible this person is homeless and may be living on the streets.

Level 0 gambler. This is the designation for people who have never gambled.

Level 1 gambler. These people may gamble frequently for recreational purposes but show no evidence of problems.

Level 2 gambler. These gamblers have developed some moderate, real, and often persistent difficulties in life that are directly due to wagering.

Level 3 gambler. These gamblers meet the full *DSM-IV-TR* criteria for pathological gambling.

Tilt. A term used by gamblers to refer to the process of losing control over gambling.

Bailout. This is money given to a gambler to pay debts without suffering adverse consequences.

Bad beat. A term used by gamblers to describe a run of bad luck.

S data. Self-report data.

L data. Life-history data.

O data. Reports from others.

T data. Test data.

Recommended Reading

There are ready and available glossaries of gambling terms found at providers such as Gambling-Winning.com at http://www.gambling-win.com/online-gambling-glossary.html.

The North American State and Provincial Lotteries has an informative web site that can be found at http://www.naspl.org/problem.html.

Two helpful resources for therapists are *Gambling Times*, which provides a useful web site with history and insights into a wide variety of games of chance. This site can be found at: www.gamblingtimes.com. To learn more about how a slot machine really works, go to the Safe@play Slot Machine tutorial at http://www.gameplanit.com.

LIE/BET Questionnaire by Johnson, Hamer, and Nora (1988). This is the easiest standardized instrument to use for detection of general gambling problems. It is composed of two questions that are sensitive to the core issues of severe problem or pathologic gambling: "Have you ever had to lie to people important to you about how much you gamble?" and "Have you ever felt a need to bet more money?" Information regarding validity and use can be accessed at The Ontario Problem Gambling Research Centre web site at http://www.gamblingresearch.org.

The SOGS is available many places on the Internet, two being The National Council of Problem Gambling (NCPG) and the Association of Problem Gambling Service Administrators (http://www.npgaw.org). The SOGS is available in English, Spanish, and an English version for adolescents. This instrument also is available in printed format in the volume by Coombs and Howatt (2005). Another Internet site is http://www.addictionrecov.org/southoak.htm.

Both the DIGS and NORC *DSM* Screen for Gambling Problems (NODS) are available at http://www.npgaw.org.

The Helping Interview by Concept Media (three volumes; Video and DVD Series, Concept Media PO Box 19542 Irvine CA 92623-9542). Basic educational tapes, about 20 minutes each, illustrate effective attending skills that many of us temporarily lose during a busy, frustrating day. These are skills that you learned in graduate school and now believe that you are practicing effectively, but may again need to improve.

Clinical and Diagnostic Interviewing (2nd ed.) by Craig (2005). This is a theoretical and practical volume that presents diverse perspectives on interviewing that are helpful for clinicians of every orientation. It is becoming the standard text across mental health disciplines.

Handbook of Addictive Disorders: A Practical Guide to Diagnoses and Treatment by Coombs (2004). This is the single-most valuable tool on the market for professionals who are looking for a comprehensive book that covers a spectrum of addictive disorders. There are two chapters in this book on pathological gambling.

TESTING YOUR KNOWLEDGE

ANSWERS

1. False   2. Suicidal   3. Discrepancies   4. Bipolar Spectrum Disorders
5. Depression and Anxiety

TRUTH OR FICTION

QUIZ ANSWERS

1. False   2. True   3. False   4. False   5. False   6. False   7. True

CHAPTER 3

Utilizing Optimal Professional Resources

TRUTH OR FICTION

QUIZ

After reading this chapter, you should be able to answer the following questions:

1. Gambling Hotlines are a useful tool in your referral network. True or False?

2. Gamblers Anonymous is almost identical to Alcoholics Anonymous. True or False?

3. Most of the variance in therapy comes from nonspecific factors. True or False?

4. Confrontational and judgmental approaches usually work quite well to reduce resistance. True or False?

5. It is usually helpful to confront families about their codependency. True or False?

6. The laws are clear about the duty to warn regarding property threats. True or False?

Answers on p. 106.

Highlights of this chapter include how to optimize professional resources and build an essential network. It discusses some advantages and disadvantages for referrals as well as guidelines to consider when making referral decisions. There are excellent client resources during the screening process as well as how to deal with client motivation regarding treatment. There are suggestions for what to do and not to do regarding referrals and how to best match clients to these referral sources.

Referral Benefits and Disadvantages

One major concern for practitioners is whether they should treat the gamblers themselves or refer them to another professional. Before you conduct an intake interview, you should have some idea where the client will go for treatment, if needed. Be prepared to offer a *seamless transition* to whatever provider is available. Often, this may be you, the solo provider, or you and your colleagues, working in a group. Without experience working with gamblers, this treatment is difficult and ethically tenuous at times.

A good general discussion of this issue applicable to drug addiction is in an earlier book in this series by Blume (2005). It is highly recommended, even if you do not treat drug-addicted people. The following emphasizes some points in Blume's discussion. If you do not feel you are the best person to work with a client, then you should not work with that client. If you think you will do the client harm and your attitude shows this, you will not be helping that client. If you do not match up well as a therapeutic team, then consider referral. Do not see the client if you have an ethical problem that interferes with adequate treatment.

Referrals can be to several sources and can involve varying degrees of collaboration. Optimally, health care professionals should establish working relationships with professionals who treat gamblers, if they do not feel comfortable to provide this treatment themselves. No one feels comfortable treating everyone, and no one has the experience to do so.

Nothing can substitute for *some* aspects of clinical experience working directly with pathological gamblers. In addition to this area of expertise, however, a competent counselor will have a number of other qualifications or experiences. These include crisis management, a background in family systems, a capacity to perform cognitive interventions, the ability to perform psychiatric screenings and to recognize major pathologies, an awareness of limitations of various therapeutic modalities in theories, and clinical flexibility. Perhaps most of all, a competent counselor or therapist will have an optimistic attitude in the face of clients with apparently insurmountable difficulties.

A common mistake is to assume that, because a professional has a background of treating people with alcohol or other drug dependencies, that professional is automatically qualified to treat gamblers. Although the similarities of pathological gambling with other addictions are striking, there may be major differences that affect client management and the client's prognosis. The complexities associated with pathological gambling, including the numerous complicating comorbid conditions, usually demand a history of some supervised experience and treatment flexibility.

The following vignette highlights a situation in which the mental health care provider was qualified on one level to treat gamblers but, through other factors in his life, realized that he would have been an inappropriate provider for treatment.

A Case to Refer

Julius was a small-town mental health therapist who lived in a Northwest state. The nearest psychiatrist was about 80 miles away. There was an uncredentialed "counselor" who operated out of a local church, but he restricted practice to members of a specific denomination. Julius felt he had to help everyone in his community who had a problem. Typically, he worked 60 or 70 hours a week. When he saw his first gambling client, he believed that he possessed the expertise to treat this person without additional reading, supervision, or training. The client left after one session. This pattern repeated with the next few clients. Eventually, Julius began to realize that with his training, experience, and simply with his time demands, he could not be effective.

One variable associated with the desirability of working with pathological gamblers involves whether you can tolerate the potentially slow pace in which they may change. In some ways, their responses to treatment may be as incremental as those of the schizophrenic. Counselors who need client appreciation or the satisfaction of seeing a family system return quickly to a more functional state may be unlikely choices for working with gamblers. Often, when working with addictions such as alcohol, the client may change dramatically, both physically and psychologically, after weeks or even days of treatment. This is usually not the case with gamblers. Following a period of withdrawal symptoms, pathological gamblers frequently experience the onset of other psychological and personal problems. These may include dysthymia, anxiety, and an overwhelming sense of emptiness. There is often a prolonged period in which they mourn lost life opportunities. Treatment is often slow, arduous, and may be unrewarding for counselors and therapists who do not appreciate the process of incremental change.

Table 3.1 discusses other advantages and disadvantages regarding referrals.

Take special care if you are treating a teen, because these people have special needs that involve training in adolescent therapy in addition to gambling treatment.

You may also want to find someone with special experience and training if the client is elderly. Life issues in the elderly are often entirely different from those in other age groups.

Regardless, if you do refer, you must provide adequate reason for your referral. If you do not provide necessary services, state this. If you do not feel you are the right person for the client, it is appropriate to state this also with a brief explanation. You do not need to go into detail. A sentence or so showing that you have considered your appropriateness as a treatment provider may be called for.

Table 3.1: Benefits of Treating the Client Yourself, Even If You Lack Experience

You may:

- Be the only one available due to lack of resources

- Required by your agency

- Be the best person qualified

- Be the most flexible

- Have the best understanding of dual diagnoses, co-addictions, or recovery

- Be the only person willing to see the client for little or no fee

- Be the only person willing to treat gamblers, due to the judgmental attitude of others (presuppositions that gambling is a moral problem, etc.)

- Feel it is necessary to monitor client for change in mental status and that others will not do so as well

- Feel you can advocate for your calling

- Have experience and training

Reasons to Refer Out

You:

- Do not have expertise, and someone in your network does

- Have no time

- Have transferrential problems, meaning the client reminds you of someone from your past

- Have financial problems

- Are scared by this client

- Do not like the client

- Have health or time concerns that may interrupt treatment

- Have administrative or agency problems that interfere with effective treatment

- Cannot provide the intensive treatment the client needs (such as inpatient care)

- Are not licensed or trained to provide medicine the client may need

- Have referred others to providers and have had bad experiences with these providers

- Are worried about continuity of care in systems where providers may be shuffled around and believe that you can provide a better job

Screening Reports, Documentation, and Responsibility

A basic question as a counselor or therapist is whether you are going to treat the client yourself, refer out completely, or refer out for some services. Usually, since no one can do everything, you will probably be in one of the last two groups. It is unlikely, for example, that you are both an expert counselor and a competent psychiatrist. If you are, there are certain types of clients that you probably do not work well with and certainly times when you are too busy. Know your limits and do not overtax yourself. Begin a continuing assessment of yourself regarding this.

In many cases, regardless of your intention, you will make referrals out after having done only an intake screening. The referring source bears the responsibility to make sure that whatever treatment providers are involved are ethical and competent. This is a standard of care that courts and ethics boards are increasingly holding referring professionals to and it now applies to people referring those treated for gambling disorders as well as for AOD. In other words, do not make a referral to a provider that you suspect may be providing substandard treatment. This seems like common sense, but care providers tell colleagues each month that these "innocuous" referrals eventually were highly costly.

Prior to the Health Insurance Portability and Accountability Act (HIPAA), discussed in later chapters, it was common for screening counselors to call the provider with an oral summary of T data, along with conclusions from S and L data. Since HIPAA, there is much more demand for documentation, even at intake. This has resulted in a trend toward longer, formalized intake reports that may be sent to all professionals involved. The problem with this solution is that such intake reports almost always involve integrating objective and subjective material, as well as reporting cut-off or test scores. However, there is also a requirement that *process notes*, or the informal notation of S and O data, be kept in a separate file apart from the official record. What shows up in the client's file is only a formal report that extrapolates quotations, findings, circumstances, and other data that the client does not recall or cannot put together. There are no process notes to accompany the chart to show how the intake counselor might have reasoned through the thinking process.

In this situation, a client may make an ethical complaint to your licensing board that you have insufficient justification for your seemingly bold conclusions. In reality, your copious intake notes fully justify your thinking and work. However, they are not allowed on a HIPAA compliant chart and the client takes offense.

Our solution is more work for the already overburdened counselor. Take thorough notes at intake. Make sure these notes are legible and in a format that shows that they cannot be easily tampered with after the fact. Make sure that your quotations in the intake report reflect what the client literally said. Do not take poetic license as some clinicians often do! Differentiate between the section involving direct client or family quotes and your conclusions from these quotes. Keep all of this data in a separate file.

Standards of care involve your understanding of the rapidly evolving field of client confidentiality, even at the level of the intake. In AOD treatment in the United States, stringent rules exist regarding confidentiality. Federal laws are vaguer regarding confidentiality and gambling treatment. It is not likely that the broad confidentiality protection extended to substance abuse can be claimed, but case laws may be rapidly expanding and exceptions may rapidly emerge.

It is imperative that counselors and other professionals stress the potential benefits of confidentiality at the time of intake. However, clients need to know that some topics, including some past felonious behavior, may not be protected by privilege. Counselors need to become familiar with their jurisdiction's rules *before* they find out through the process of receiving a subpoena.

How to Develop a Professional Referral Network

Whether or not practitioners treat clients themselves or refer, practitioners need a referral network. Optimally, the network goes both ways; clients are referred in for whatever expertise that you have, and referred out when they need a better fit for treatment. Also, networks provide information and resources when needed.

This referral network may be different than the one that typically evolves around drug and alcohol problems. Today there appear to be fewer practitioners prepared to treat problem gamblers. Getting a network in place may be challenging as you are also looking for like-minded professionals who share the same values and are willing to build a professional cooperative relationship. Networks enable you to provide a full spectrum of services. The first question to ask is, "What kind of resources do I need in my network?"

Among researchers, cooperation and cordiality are still the rule; consequently, there is less chance of resistance. Our observation is that the tension that exists between academic research and self-help groups (such as GA, AA, etc.) does not seem to be as problematic in gambling as with other addictions. Nor are there "turf wars" as are common in alcohol and drug research that often pit researchers in psychiatry against psychology, nursing researchers against social work, and other groups into vicious professional rivalries.

To form a viable network, one best practice is to contact others with the skills you have identified for your network and make your intentions known. Drop an email to local groups such as employee assistance groups, local professional associations, and GA. Ask to attend. Observe. Listen. Learn. Getting out and talking to your community is a great strategy. For example, offer to do lectures on areas of your interest and expertise—for free. Of course be principle minded and focus on building relationships, not "trolling" for clients. Volunteer. Give your time away and expect nothing but cooperation in return. It is our experience, and will most likely be yours, that you will be repaid many times over. It is a simple strategy, but it usually works.

What does *not* work for helping establish a network is the following:

- Claiming expertise in an area in which you have none—it will eventually show
- Operating clearly for profit without regard for the clients' needs
- Approaching the problems of gamblers as an *untapped market*
- Being arrogant, especially about your credentials or the incompetent techniques of others
- Being inflexible, insisting that what worked for you once, or for other addictions, will work for all gamblers
- Disregarding the clinical wisdom of GA
- Promising services that you can't provide
- Wanting a lot from others but not willing to give back in return
- Not returning calls from others, because you are too important
- Basing your intervention entirely on a special technique, such as hypnosis or neurofeedback
- Refusing to answer public calls for information about gambling, unless you feel they will *generate a lead*

Remember, when trying to build a network, you are forming a coalition. Be diplomatic and passionate about what you want to do; at the same time, remain self-effacing.

State and National Councils on Compulsive and Pathological Gambling

One of the best national resources in the United States is the National Council on Problem Gambling. Links at this site can facilitate finding both the locations of an inpatient facility when necessary and a certified gambling counselor.

In Canada, provincial governments have assumed the role of regional clearing houses and education facilitators. They also provide outstanding links to current research and treatment options. Canadians are substantially ahead of the United States in linking people who have gambling disorders with appropriate clinical services. Provinces have begun aggressive campaigns for outreach to publicize, prevent, and treat gambling disorders. A research component is also integrated into this service provision, which helps end the gap between researchers and clinicians.

In the United States, many various state councils on problem gambling offer outstanding services. In some states, such as the now cash-strapped and hurricane-ravaged Louisiana, these groups work closely with the state government so that services do not overlap and so that case management is facilitated. This has the advantage because gambling counselors set up immediate appointments, without intermediaries.

In other states, however, specific services may be fragmented and bureau-cratic. The practitioner must attempt to investigate this before the need arises to tap resources in an emergency. Services provided by state councils vary accord-ing to their amount of funding. Their primary role is staffing and administrating gambling hotlines, which are a client's major conduit into treatment. Counselors with training in other addictions often fail to understand the unique role that these hotlines play. Although many groups such as Alcoholics Anonymous have similar services, none seem to be as effective an outreach tool as the hotlines for gamblers in crisis.

Gambling Hotlines

Many gamblers call local or state gambling hotlines during emotional crises, often prompted by financial losses. Clients may be suicidal or feel that someone is out to *get* them, or even kill them. If they owe money to a loan shark, this may be true! Families may be destitute and in total disarray. Often, the reassuring and compassionate voice at the other end of the crisis line is the last social contact in the problem gambler's exhausted network.

Become familiar with these hotlines and what they can provide. For instance, do they refer to you or do you refer to them? Or do you work in parallel worlds, ignoring them as a referral source and resource.

Gambling hotlines often publicized themselves in casinos, on lottery tickets, and in various gambling venues. Although state governments have been reluctant to publicly fund these agencies, they often accommodate by requiring gaming establishments to publicize their presence.

The services of these hotlines may involve referral, crisis intervention, or in some cases they may be able to facilitate brief hospital admissions. The quality and variety of services vary, depending on the level of resources available. Until recently, for example, most of these hotlines were run essentially by volunteers, perhaps with one or two professional paid workers. They may have modeled themselves after Alcoholics Anonymous hotlines and existed primarily to refer people to meetings. These volunteers were usually people affiliated with GA or who had relatives who had pathological gambling problems. The quality and consistency of services were limited by the energy of the core staff.

Increasingly, however, there has been a trend to adequately train and fund hot-line staff. Still, realize the limitations that these enthusiastic, often extraordinar-ily competent front-line clinicians may have. Frequently, they may be simply overwhelmed, handling too many calls at one time. This is especially likely dur-ing highpoints in the gambling season, such as during football playoffs. Clients may also ask for resources, such as immediate shelter or food, which simply do not exist. This inevitably acts to demoralize staff. Through bitter experience, cri-sis lines have often learned to be very careful and circumspect regarding alloca-tion of resources.

Almost all will explain what they can offer and to whom. As in any other serv-ice, it is generally good to be prepared with resources before they are needed.

Liaison with Gamblers Anonymous

Medical and mental health professionals sometimes downplay the value of getting to know a network of recovering gamblers. GA is at least as important a resource for the counselor working with pathological gamblers as AA is for the AOD counselor. For the individual or small group of practitioners, having a GA contact is almost indispensable. Whether or not the client uses GA services and groups, the mere knowledge that they exist with people who are there to help can be therapeutic.

Do not overlook or minimize the differences between GA and other 12-step organizations. Table 3.2 highlights some of these.

The tenet of GA is simple, according to its tradition. What is the first thing a compulsive gambler ought to do in order to stop gambling? According to Gamblers Anonymous it is as follows:

The compulsive gambler needs to be willing to accept the fact that he or she is in the grip of a progressive illness and has a desire to get well. Our experience has shown that the Gamblers Anonymous program will always work for any person who has a desire to stop gambling. However, it will never work for the person who will not face squarely the facts about this illness. (Gamblers Anonymous: Questions and Answers, 1957)

It is helpful for counselors to familiarize themselves with the 12 steps of GA and compare them to those of other 12-step groups. The 12 Steps of GA are shown in Table 3.3.

Table 3.2: Some Differences Between Gamblers Anonymous (GA) and Alcoholics Anonymous (AA)

There are many fewer GA meetings per week and by location.
There are often many more men than women at GA.
Some people believe that GA tends to be more confrontational.
GA meetings tend to be longer, by several hours sometimes.
Most GA meetings are closed.
GA tends to have a much quieter presence in the community.
Many people believe that GA places much less emphasis on spirituality.
Widespread belief that GA does not meet the needs of women, for example, their needs for autonomy and intimacy.
GA meetings tend to be more pragmatic. They emphasize vocation, finances, etc.
Some GA groups are much more open to dual diagnoses than traditional AA groups.

Therapists who have worked with AOD clients and who have not been in recovery themselves often get to know groups like AA through its gregarious and impressive outreach. In general, GA has taken a stance of greater anonymity than AA. It tends to be much more *backstage* and silent regarding its 12-step work. GA may exist in the community for some time and not draw any attention to its existence. There are many reasons for this; one that is most common is that many people with gambling problems could be targets for law-enforcement or criminal elements. However, members of Gamblers Anonymous almost always are open to getting to know professionals who make referrals. A call to the number in the phonebook or an email is all that is usually necessary.

Table 3.3: 12 Steps of Gamblers Anonymous (GA)

We:

1. Admitted we were powerless over gambling, that our lives had become unmanageable.

2. Came to believe that a Power greater than ourselves could restore us to a normal way of thinking and living.

3. Made a decision to turn our will and our lives over to the care of this Power of our own understanding.

4. Made a searching and fearless moral and financial inventory of ourselves.

5. Admitted to ourselves and to another human being the exact nature of our wrongs.

6. Were entirely ready to have these defects of character removed.

7. Humbly asked God (of our understanding) to remove our shortcomings.

8. Made a list of all persons we had harmed and became willing to make amends to them all.

9. Made direct amends to such people wherever possible, except when to do so would injure them or others.

10. Continued to take personal inventory and when we were wrong, promptly admitted it.

11. Sought through prayer and meditation to improve our conscious contact with God as we understood him, praying only for knowledge of His will for us and the power to carry that out.

12. Having made an effort to practice these principles in all our affairs, we tried to carry this message to other compulsive gamblers.

Source: Reprinted with permission, Gamblers Anonymous.

AA and GA Similarities and Differences

Tricia has a gambling problem and is an alcoholic. She attends AA and GA. She is also a mental health professional. She notes the following:

"GA is often criticized for not being like AA. Sometimes, these criticisms are valid, but you have to remember, clients have different needs.

"In AA, people experience change much quicker. By this, I mean that if you quit drinking for a month, you feel better. Your problems start to go away. You're thinking becomes clearer. You become less anxious and less depressed.

"With gamblers, it's often different. There may be a time when symptoms get worse. And once the pathological gambler is stripped of her fantasies, she becomes vulnerable to reality. I'm sure that these problems are there with alcoholics, though they are not as frequent or intense.

"In my experience—as an addictions counselor and recovering person— the meetings seem to have different goals. GA is about basic stabilization of resources and finances.... It's true that in GA there is less talk of 'serenity.' There's more talk about basic survival. GA meetings are much more serious affairs.

"From what I've seen, the low rates of recovery [associated with] GA may be because people have been gambling for such a long time. People's lives are just more damaged by the time they get to GA. Often there is very little to be happy about, at least for a very long time."

It is helpful to remember the following customs about GA meetings, which were obtained from the GA web site:

Closed Meeting—Only those with a gambling problem, or those who think they may have a gambling problem and have a desire to stop gambling, may attend and participate.

Open Meeting—Spouses, family, and friends of the gambler are welcome to attend and observe the meeting.

By tradition and from the necessity of privacy discussed previously, most GA meetings are closed, meaning that they are not open to people who do not believe they have a gambling problem. Sometimes for some groups, rare exceptions are allowed, but only if all group members concur. Again, confidentiality is a paramount concern and open meetings might jeopardize some of this necessary psychological and physical security. However, closed meetings are available without any prescreening to people who honestly suspect that they may have a gambling problem. People *on the fence* are made to feel welcome and not pressured, as they might feel in some other recovery groups.

The ability of GA to welcome new members, though simultaneously not pressure them into joining, is quite remarkable. Unlike other 12-step groups, GA often takes a "Wait and see if we can help you" attitude and does not typically

POINTS TO REMEMBER

- GA meetings are much harder to find than AA meetings.
- GA meetings are usually closed.
- People who believe that they have a personal gambling problem are always welcomed at GA, even at closed meetings.
- GA meetings often have a different characteristic than AA meetings.
- GA and GamAnon have a different relationship than AA and AlAnon.

lobby attendees to immediately begin working a program. Those of us who come from a background of *tough love* in addiction and of client confrontation need to recall that GA does not typically follow this path with newcomers.

GamAnon

GamAnon meetings are for families and friends of compulsive gamblers regardless of whether the gambler attends Gamblers Anonymous or not. It is discussed more extensively in Chapter 5.

GamAnon meetings are usually held on the same nights and physical locations as GA meetings, but in separate rooms.

Unlike AA, the two fellowships do not officially or informally share experiences or information about each other. The wall between the two groups is more formal than it is in other self-help groups and extends on an informal level as well. This may be because many members of GamAnon have had to form irrevocable walls between the family and the member that gambles.

Psychiatrists and Emergency Facilities

Some gamblers require hospital intervention for psychiatric stabilization; consequently, a psychiatrist needs to be part of your network. Psychiatrists whose experiences are limited primarily to AOD (alcohol and other drugs) may fail to realize that, although there are similarities, problem or pathological gamblers are often different from drug addicts. For example, medication for anxiety that might not be appropriate for substance abusers may be indicated for acute use in pathological gamblers. Presently, word of mouth is the best means of finding a competent medical treatment provider.

Psychiatrists who treat gamblers often have to quickly diagnose a number of frankly odd cases that do not easily fit into *DSM-IV-TR* nomenclature. They may find it useful to return to structured clinical interviewing techniques they learned in residency, simply to reduce liability issues and to help clarify diagnostic concerns. An example of practical techniques can be found in the volume by Laney, Rogers, & Phaison (2002). The briefer volume by Bauer (2003) is also valuable for people working with Level 2 and 3 gamblers.

If you have to medicate a number of questionable cases that do not appear to fit into predefined categories, you may wish to add to your network a psychologist who specializes in complex diagnostics and addictive disorders. For example, it may be impossible for the psychiatrist to rule out paranoia, because it may masquerade as a patient's legitimate safety concerns. The judicious use of psychological testing may assist in this diagnostic decision.

Most aberrant gamblers enter treatment when they have serious financial, legal, and/or vocational problems. Many will require crisis stabilization inside a hospital or other facility. Have these resources available before they are needed.

Matching Clients with the Best Professional Options

We could substantially stretch scarce resources if we could match clients with the best professional options. However, we know almost nothing about this hypothetical match.

Unlike in other addictions, where counselors make informal matches based on a variety of factors, there are often too few resources to access for those with gambling problems. For example, in most medium-sized towns, a gay client can be referred to a primarily gay AA meeting. This degree of specialization does not exist for gambling because currently we do not have the diversity of resources.

Among many peer counselors, including certified counselors, there may be a tendency to believe that "What worked for me is what will work for you." Often, this is due to a lack of exposure to other ideas in formal classroom training or in an academic setting. This tendency may be common in all addictions counselors who have gone through personal recovery, although anecdotal accounts suggest that it is particularly common in pathological gambling counselors. An academic background is often helpful for understanding many important factors: contingencies of reward and punishment, cognitive variables associated with relapse, the role of the family in the development and maintenance of addiction, and the relationship of mood and personality with addictive behaviors.

Addictions counselors from a background of recovery in AOD, but not gambling, may err when they assume that the gambling counselor must also be in recovery. There is no evidence that personal recovery is necessary or sufficient to be an effective gambling counselor. There is no evidence that it is harmful, either. Ideally, it is one of several pathways that counselors can pursue.

There is little information regarding cultural congruence and gambling counselors. If the data from AOD are applicable, then the more culturally similar a counselor is, the more effective the counselor likely will be.

A lack of authoritarianism and judgmental style are hallmarks of any good counselor and even more important for the addiction professional. Too often, we ignore rigid or inappropriate interactions and masquerade them as counseling. For example, a counselor stated he was teaching pathological gamblers about *humility* by making them address him as "Sir" with the frequency common in the military. This may have met the counselor's bizarre needs, but it did not help the clients.

Avoid counselors who advocate eccentric, esoteric, or potentially unethical treatments. An example is a gambling counselor who claims to cure by using regression therapy. Holistic and alternative treatments are appropriate when there is a reason for their use and they are within the framework of the cultural context of the client. For example, one Level 3 gambler was successfully treated by a Native American Shaman. However, referral to a nontraditional practitioner without an understanding of the client's needs and desires is often irrational, impractical, and unethical. Focus on what the client needs and what the client is receptive to, not just what you think is best for the client. Our role is to guide and facilitate opportunities, not dictate them.

Keep in mind cultural factors relevant to the client's religious traditions. This requires a good understanding of many common religious traditions that may be encountered. For example, in the United States and elsewhere, some conservative Evangelical Christian groups believe that 12-step interventions are against fundamental biblical principles. Many religious groups cannot accept treatment that occurs on Sunday or Saturday. Other churches promote frequent evening commitments and members cannot attend meetings during those hours. Interpreting this as resistance misconstrues the client's worldview.

Referrals to Counselors under Contract in the Private Sector

Often counselors to whom referrals are made are certified Gambling Counselors or other qualified mental health professionals. Almost always in the United States, these are people working in the private sector. They work on a model called fee-for-service, meaning they get paid for the number of sessions they complete. An advantage of using counselors in the private sector is that they are more available and avoid the inflexibilities of working for a state or provincial agency. A disadvantage is that they are usually only paid by being reimbursed for *billable hours*—not for the amount of time they may have actually put into the client's care. This can have negative effects on therapists. For example, the *no-show* rates of clients can directly affect their livelihoods, sometimes making them resentful or nonparticipatory. Therefore, systems need to be in place to discourage no shows and to provide for some financial security for counselors.

Counselors may be on numerous managed mental health care *panels*, requiring scores of hours of unreimbursed paperwork. This further reduces their effective hourly wage. If you are setting up a program that relies on contractual counselors, please consider that they need to make a living! If you do not pay them, they will opt out of any contract offered. Basically, you will not be able to secure a good network unless you provide a living wage. Similarly, administrators must not exploit the zealousness of peer counselors or young therapists; they do not deserve poor compensation because they have a strong commitment to work with addicted people.

If you are a general counselor or therapist trying to get a gambling specialist to take one of your financially troublesome cases, you should not try to appeal to his or her idealism or to the fact that this would be a great *training opportunity*. Ultimately, these maneuvers weaken your ability to attract and grow a workable professional network.

Referral Do's and Don'ts

The provider needs to keep many things in mind when making referrals to a treatment provider who specializes in gambling disorders. In addition to useful suggestions by Blume (2005) for drug clients, the following may be particularly important for people with gambling-related disorders.

Do remind clients 24 hours before. As in other areas of health care, reminder calls to clients are likely to produce more adherents to appointments. These work better and are less threatening if they originate from the person who has initially seen the client and is the referring source. Most of us can empathize with the often unpleasant feeling of receiving a call from a stranger. For a person with a possible gambling disorder, such calls may be particularly disruptive.

Do show a tolerant attitude if appointments are missed. Often, a referring source will become displeased with a client who fails to carry through with a referral made to a treatment professional. In many cases, the client may reach out again to the referring professional, either because this person is a trusted figure, or because this person provides a gateway for additional services. Frustration and anger at clients is usually transparent, and does not enhance the likelihood of future cooperation. Above all, do not take resistance personally.

Do assess that the client has availability of basic necessities. Often, pathological gamblers will have gone several days without eating and may not have a home. The referring clinician needs to know what to do when this potentially homeless and hungry person shows up in his or her office.

Do make sure that the client can get to the referral. By the time many pathological gamblers get to the stage of requesting intervention, they do not have transportation. Furthermore, they may have exhausted their friends and family. It is certainly appropriate to inquire about this. Often, a liaison with GA will help meet the need.

Do respect confidentiality. This would seem obvious and is emphasized in many places. However, well-meaning professionals often ignore basic guidelines in following up with clients or in providing information to referral therapists. Often, people with pathological gambling problems are especially wary of any information that might be exchanged concerning their status. Consequently, the referring professional needs to inform the pathological gambler of exactly what will be disclosed, why, and in what formats. This is a theme that we reiterate throughout this volume because of its importance.

Do discuss pretreatment contact numbers with clients in advance. People are reticent receiving calls from mental health practitioners. This tendency is often more pronounced for people with gambling problems. The referring clinician needs to inform clients that they occasionally may be contacted prior to the first treatment, unless they specify otherwise. For instance, there might be a change in schedule due to unforeseen circumstances. The client in treatment needs to specify how this contact should be made. Do not attempt to coerce contact permission and do verify that the client is actually comfortable with disclosing this telephone number. A simple phrase is recommended: "Are you comfortable that I or someone else may call on this number?"

Do clarify who is to be called for cancellation. Most professionals do not leave a message without written permission. Due to the level of secrecy that gamblers have in some areas of their lives, take care in this area.

Do discuss the limits of phone and email flexibility. Often, clients may state a request such as "If my girlfriend answers the phone, then hang up. But if my mother answers, it's okay." They may also ask for the referring professional to use a pseudonym. None of these behaviors on the part of the professional are necessarily unethical. However, they may provoke discomfort for the counselor. They may be seen as colluding and therefore as counter-therapeutic. Regardless, they are just strange. Referral sources need to determine their limits of professional comfort. They must stay within these limits, despite clients' excuses or persuasiveness.

Due to confidentiality, we inform clients that we do not answer emails at any email address other than the one that was furnished on intake. We also let them know that we do not answer emails from offensive or questionable sounding addresses, including those that reiterate the virtues of gambling. This is just a personal quirk, but we do not feel comfortable replying to a client at a sexually suggestive address or one such as 4aces4Me@alwayslucky.com (which by the way is fictitious). Nor do we follow their routines for contacting them at multiple emails or Internet locations. ("Between three and six, IM me on Yahoo—after that, try me at MySpace. Or if that fails, sometimes I'm at the Poker chat room. Hunt me down there.")

Do clarify foreseeable treatment costs. Referring professionals often find it useful to do what they can to get the problem or pathological gambler into some form of treatment, regardless of costs. If costs are a concern, the referring professional can state that even though the client has no money, he or she should attend an intake session to find out about other treatment options. In this way, the excuse of no funds is preempted.

Do inspire real hope. While problem or pathological gamblers do not need to be filled with false promises, they need to know that people with similar problems have recovered and have led full, productive, and even joyous lives.

Do leave clients with concrete, written information, if possible. The more information the aberrant gambler has, the better. This includes literature, information regarding GA, and locations of various web sites concerning problem and pathological gambling. Even if referring a client to someone else, with no plans for future contact, leave the client with something in writing.

Do advise clients about the existence of GA and families about options and locations of GamAnon. Even if an abstinence-based treatment is not eventually adopted, GA is extremely useful during the early stages of gambling treatment. For some people, the fit with this group is astounding. However, the questions that may be indicative of denial or resistance may be best answered by the treatment provider later.

Do not keep many phone numbers on file for each client. We have mentioned this regarding emails but the problem in the twenty-first century's wired society is that everyone demands that they be available at all times. For example, a person may have four cell phones and a landline, a work number, and other numbers where he or she can be reached. The client's regular number and cell phone number are appropriately part of the record. Six or seven alternative numbers keyed to specific times are not what you want in your records. People with gambling problems often are worse than most people about this. It is too confusing to keep up with, and we feel it colludes just a bit with the gambler's lifestyle.

Do not ignore potential lethality and suicidal intent. Suicidal ideation may be extraordinarily high among gamblers who are seeking initial treatment. The clinician assesses this, as with any other clients. Emphasis is placed on history and a lethality of method, as well as recent losses, lack of supports, ongoing substance abuse, and with the gambler, an unwillingness or inability to temporarily refrain from wagering. The client needs to be informed that, if suicidal, this will not jeopardize future gambling-related services.

Do not be judgmental in attitude or nonverbal communication. This should go without saying. It should be a commandment placed on every counselor's wall.

Do not be unrealistic regarding the possibility of obtaining treatment. If the client may face a waiting list, the referring professional should be honest.

Do not be inappropriately "cheery." The competent, referring agent will avoid confrontation or labeling; however, when the pathological gambler asks in all sincerity, "Do you think I have a problem?" it is simply wrong to deny the existence or severity of obvious behaviors.

Do not communicate via the Internet if it is the client's current preferred means of gambling. Internet wagering is all too easy. Cases in which professionals have left messages in email have resulted in situations where clients use the opportunity to gamble inappropriately.

Motivation Strategies and Techniques for Getting a Person to Professionals

There are many potential obstacles that may keep someone from seeking help. Ambivalence, anger, shame, and procrastination are a few primary ones that are addressed here with some strategies and techniques that may help an individual stay motivated.

Ambivalence

Addictionologist Howard Shaffer and his associates (Shaffer et al., 2004) believe that, fundamental to every addiction is a core of emerging ambivalence. Gamblers feel both an attraction and repulsion to their behavior. Their sentiments frequently vacillate, or they may simultaneously love and hate what they do, in a confusing blend of feelings. One key to motivating and reducing resistance inherent in change is to capitalize on this ambivalence by gently allowing clients to voice it.

Gentle suggestions are the most useful. It is not necessary to badger or cajole, as previous generations of therapists or counselors were taught. Instead, it is most useful to capitalize on the ambivalence that the gambler sees involved in the failures of his or her life. For example, "You are 34 years old and you live at home with your mother and aunt? Is this related to gambling debts?" The difference between good counselors and great ones is that the latter are able to capitalize on ambivalence by silence and by such phrases as "Tell me a bit more about that."

This does not mean the counselor gains by exploring nebulous feelings at length. A common therapeutic phrase, such as "I bet you feel ambivalent," is not likely to work. Clients may not know what emotions they are feeling and may have problems distinguishing one feel-state from another (Parker, Wood, Bond, & Shaughnessy, 2005). Furthermore, the emotions that they are feeling may be entirely different from your own. Instead, the referring clinician may skillfully sketch a portrait of the goals the client has stated, and then summarize within the client's present circumstances.

Questions and motivational statements are best when the counselor keeps them open-ended and gentle, rather than confrontational (Ciarrocchi, 2002). For example, a 33-year-old former stockbroker inquired about treatment for his pathological gambling from his primary care physician. The physician knew that appearances, clothes, contemporary fashions, and a trendy life were important to this person. She used this knowledge to gently point out the discrepancies between the former stockbroker's present life and his goals and dreams. This in turn acted to motivate him toward the first session of treatment.

A nonjudgmental and optimistic attitude is essential for motivation and for all phases of assessment (Rogers, 2001). The gamblers, perhaps more than other addicted people, may show an emotional *disconnect* between a cognitive or rational state on one hand and an emotional state on the other. This is intensified by the surroundings of the gambling venue. For example, it is not uncommon to see a hard-minded skeptic quickly become convinced that certain slot machines are *due*.

Who Me?

Several years ago at a conference in Las Vegas one of the authors (WG Mc) performed an informal experiment. While not exactly scientifically rigorous, it is useful for demonstrating how influential the surroundings of the casino may be in making rational people behave quite irrationally.

He recruited five volunteers at a conference, all of whom had completed doctoral-level coursework in statistics or probability theory. Three of these people had never been in a casino. Each was instructed on the reality of slot-machine payback: (a) The probability of a payout is independent of each play or spin; (b) machines do not run in hot or cold streaks; and (c) all machines of the same denomination pay at the same rate within the same casino.

He then gave each participant $20 in quarters and instructed them to play for 30 minutes. They could play on any machine that they liked as long as they continued to play the slots. They also agreed that they would not access their own money if they ran out of quarters prior to the end of this time.

At the end of the 30 minutes, he asked the players whether they still believed that the three previous statements were true. All agreed. But on further inquiry, there were some unusual findings. Two people admitted they had briefly developed superstitious strategies for the mechanical timing of coin deposits, in the hopes of priming the machines for payouts. Two other players had independently asked strangers where the "hot machines" were located. One person had accepted advice about where to find the "loosest" slots (those with the highest payout). One person developed a "strategy" based on changing to a new machine following a jackpot. Still another developed a strategy to win based on playing where there were the most people.

In other words, all five of these mathematically literate people were temporarily blinded by the allure of the casino! What does that say about the chances for the rest of us?

Resistance often can be anticipated and successfully thwarted by appealing to gamblers' other needs. An article by Boutin, Dumont, Ladouceur, and Montecalvo (2003) provides concrete advice for attaining these goals.

Using Motivational Interviewing

A variety of motivational techniques may be very helpful for many clients with gambling or other addictions. One very popular technique that is now in use is Motivational Interviewing (MI), which is an *evidence-based* methodology designed to engage and then continue the process of behavioral change and maintenance. This technique (more accurately, family of techniques) was introduced by Miller and Rollnick in 1991 as a brief way of helping people change. The text remains a therapeutic classic and practitioners are strongly urged to read it. It has received substantial empirical support for a variety of addictions, though has not presently been tested as thoroughly for gambling. The goals of this family of techniques include helping the client explore potentially addictive behaviors, helping the client decide whether addiction is worth the costs, and laying the groundwork for the ongoing change process.

Adherents of MI have empirically demonstrated that enhancing the client's choices typically facilitates motivation. Shame and confrontation do not, at least on a consistent basis. Counselors using techniques from MI try to reduce resistance and ambivalence by normalizing it. They introduce the concept that all change is inherently scary and that people normally resist any type of new behaviors. For example, a counselor might say to a client that "If choices for recovery were easy, then you would have already changed. Change isn't easy. That is why you have to see a professional for help."

Table 3.4 highlights suggestions many gambling counselors have found useful from MI. These have been taken from Miller and Rollnick's (1991) book, which is recommended for all counselors. Table 3.5 discusses what to avoid in a client interview and is equally important.

Table 3.4: Suggestions to Enhance Motivation for People with Addictive Behaviors

---

1. *Ask open-ended questions.* Avoid using questions that will elicit a short answer (e.g., "Tell me more about these difficulties" as opposed to "Have you had difficulties with this?").

2. *Ask, don't tell.* Spend far more time listening than you do talking. Allow the client to do most of the thinking for him/herself. (Shoot for a 70/30 listening to talking ratio.)

3. *Practice reflective listening.* Look for the underlying meaning of what is being said and reflect this back to the person. Focus on how the person is feeling.

4. *Use what is known as "double-sided reflection."* Use two-sided reflections in order to highlight ambivalence. For example, "So, on the one hand, you say smoking makes you feel more relaxed, but on the other hand, you know that it upsets your family and it's not good for your health."

5. *Summarize.* Summarize key statements. Connect motivationally relevant material, thus allowing individuals to hear their own words and thoughts again. Try it because it works.

6. *Affirm.* Create the sense that you are supportive. Reinforce important statements with reflective listening and verbal support as well as typical nods.

Table 3.5: What to Avoid for Successful Client Motivation

The question-answer routine. Try to avoid asking a series of questions that demand short answers. This prevents elaboration and exploration.

Confrontation-denial. Confronting someone, by nature, demands a response that is opposite and defensive. Try to avoid arguments, struggles, or one-upmanships regarding what someone should or can do. Optimistically suggest.

The Expert trap. If it appears you have all the answers, the client will feel stupid. He or she will fall into a passive role, and the individual will not work on his or her own to explore and resolve ambivalence. Escape much of this by talking *with*, not at.

Labeling. Many labels (e.g., "sick gambler," "gambling junkie") may be counter-therapeutic. If the issue of a label gets raised. For example, if someone asks, "Do you think I am a 'sicko' like my mom said I am?" it is useful to explain that a label is not what you are interested in; instead, you would like to find out more about this person's behavior and what it means for them.

Shock. Some of us, particularly those raised on various and more dramatic family therapies, were taught that it is therapeutic to be shocked at various aspects of addiction. We were trained to believe that "acting" in this way enhanced a client's motivation to change. This does not seem to be the case, at least according to published studies. As a therapist, be in control of your emotions.

Preaching or excessively instructive. Nobody likes to be scolded or talked down to. Counselors should give useful suggestions and feedback, but not lecture or be pedantic.

In summary, avoid generating negative, defensive-inducing feelings, if possible!

Avoiding Anger and Shame: The Rapid Demotivators

In the past few years there has been a decrease in the emphasis of *shame-based techniques*, once popular in the treatment of gambling and other addictions. It was once believed that, unless a person was publicly willing to admit that he or she was contrite, the beginnings of addiction treatment were impossible. This is a theme of popular accounts in the media and at least one reality television show.

Many counselors are discovering the psychological fact that most people are more likely to change for positive reward rather than for punishment. Furthermore, for any number of reasons, people with gambling and other addictions often have difficulty transferring their intellectual knowledge of punishment to real-life behavioral changes. Gamblers, particularly, are often reward-sensitive and a motivational strategy that is helpful often involves a factual but optimistic view of the life chances associated with gambling cessation.

The initial appeal to GA may be that this group uses the motivational language that is relevant to clients. Perhaps its anecdotes of people in recovery are often more helpful than dismal statistics involving relapse rates, which serve to make the gambling problems seem more uncontrollably present. Experiences suggest that specific GA groups that are more hope oriented, rather than shame oriented, have better long-term outcomes. Again, however, more data are needed.

Recently, some researchers have suggested that shame may act to deplete motivation by reducing dopaminergic circuitry in key areas in the frontal lobes. While that may have had an advantage in the distant past in sorting out caveman relationships, it does not help us in our present-day struggles with addictions. Dopamine suppression would likely be followed by a rebound, thus enhancing dopaminergic activity in other areas of the brain. This might increase reward sensitive to gambling stimulus and later augment gambling cravings. In other words, there may be a biochemical reason that shame eventually triggers a relapse.

Procrastination

Expect procrastination among all addicted people; however, Joseph Ciarrocchi (2002) notes that chronic procrastination is especially common among pathological gamblers. Research has identified two subtypes of procrastinators—the nonanxious and anxious subtypes. The nonanxious subtype does not pick up relevant cues regarding upcoming deadlines and consequently is unmotivated to take necessary steps to complete a task. The anxious type avoids tasks because whenever this individual thinks about them, they are too overwhelming. The groups are orthogonal, meaning statistically independent. You can have attributes of both groups at once.

What is tricky is that the first subtype of procrastinators may sometimes be motivated by cues involving fear and punishment. The second type, already overaroused, becomes more avoidant when faced with a situation in which anxiety is increased. The Recommended Reading section at the end of the chapter contains more information about this topic.

Do not interpret procrastination as denial. Instead, it is part of the personality constellation of many problem and pathological gamblers and may require separate treatment.

The best recommendation is to keep the door open and expect that early referrals to providers will have a low compliance rate. That is reality with many clients, at least until treatment begins.

Overcoming Client Obstacles

Expect client obstacles to emerge throughout treatment, beginning in the very initial phases of referral. Clients generate plenty of their own obstacles through their negative statements and counterproductive thinking. Ciarrocchi's methods also involve the use of Socratic dialogue so that the client generates his or her own self-motivational statements.

Ciarrocchi (2002) reminds counselors that between 25 and 66 percent variance associated with outcome in psychotherapy is related to "nonspecific" factors. These are the "Rogerian" factors of empathy, genuineness, and nonpossessive warmth. However, the usual treatment protocol in addiction therapy is to be confrontational and brash, sometimes with disastrous consequences and no known empirical support for this method. Increasingly, addiction professionals are realizing that this confrontational approach as the first strategy of intervention does not usually work.

Intrinsic motivation comes from within the client. The skillful counselor acts as a fulcrum to facilitate the client's process of seeking change. No amount of logic, cajoling, or reasoning will make clients attend the gambling treatment successfully. Certainly, threats will not work. Ciarrocchi's protocol for overcoming this involves using Rogerian techniques, though using them selectively. The technique described in his book that is very effective is the double-sided reflective statements; this involves a statement that on face value is highly supportive of the client's stereotypic addictive thinking. On deeper analysis, and when pondered more, it stirs up the ambiguous process that underlines addictive thinking.

Common Practical Obstacles

Many client concerns are practical, though may seem exaggerated to people who do not have a background in pathological gambling. This is where training is often most helpful because it teaches counselors what to expect to hear. Client concerns include a myriad of legal problems, difficulties with mysterious underworld figures, loan sharks, and unpaid bills. Sometimes clients will say that they cannot go to treatment because they fear someone will get them (i.e., physically harm them) if they do. Clinical experience has taught that it is not helpful to argue or confront these people. Often, these people will do well if referred to Gamblers Anonymous. At a meeting of GA, fellow gamblers will help them realize that similar people have the same levels of problems.

There are also practical or instrumental concerns such as "I can't get to treatment now, because I don't have a car" or "I need childcare." The counselor's first inclination should be to treat these problems realistically, rather than believe they are some type of resistance. Too often, we have ignored these concerns, believing they were part of the syndrome of denial.

A frequent concern of gamblers is that their problem has been exaggerated by their family, coworkers, or counselor. They often admit that they have some type of problem; however, they want to continue some form of social gambling. Comments during the early stages of treatment may include, "I admit I have a problem, but it is not anything as bad as my mother will tell you." They may seek a goal other than abstinence and ask for a treatment that enables them to control their behaviors, to moderate, but not completely eliminate them.

Responsible clinicians differ at this point regarding intervention. We believe that abstinence is the preferred goal for people who have had significant problems. Therefore, we tell clients that this is how we work. Occasionally the client will only consent to treatment if we promise to allow them to gamble. We tell them that we cannot make that promise, especially in the very early stages of treatment. If they wish to find a counselor who works within another modality, we make efforts to assist them. Exceptions are if the client has failed at this in the past, has immediate suicidal intent, or has a severe problem.

Usually, we are able to frame any options that we want to pursue at the beginning of treatment in a positive framework for the client:

"After you finish treatment, you will be able to decide whether you can safely gamble or not and how much. At that point, the decision will be more yours to make, since you will be more in control of your life."

The "Controlled Gambling Experiment"

Some clinicians suggest that people who vacillate about whether they have a gambling problem should conduct a personal experiment.

In this situation, a counselor states that he or she does not know whether a particular client has or doesn't have a gambling problem. There simply is not enough evidence. Usually the client is denying the existence of the problem as well.

The counselor sets up the "experiment." The counselor and the client agree that the counselor will support the client's inevitable desire for "controlled wagering," usually a fraction of a person's weekly income. Prior to gambling, the client writes out a brief essay concerning why he or she does not believe that he or she has a gambling problem. Next, a variation of the following occurs:

- The counselor and the client set up the amount to be wagered in advance and set up the rules of money procurement.
- Someone must accompany the client to a gambling venue and be with the client at all times. This person must not gamble and must not be a regular gambler.
- The client must not be using alcohol or other drugs while gambling.
- No money must be borrowed from friends or family for gambling.
- No cash advances or trips to the ATM machine are allowed for gambling.
- The client must write down how he or she felt prior to gambling and how he or she felt at the cessation of the gambling episode.
- At the next session, the client discusses whether he or she feels he or she has a gambling problem.
- If the client bets sports betting, this experiment should not be performed at high points during sports seasons, such as the NCAA Finals, the Olympics, the Super Bowl, the Breeder's Crown, and the World Series.

This is often an effective technique at reducing indecision about gambling problems. It clarifies to the client that he or she experiences tension, especially when he or she tries to moderate.

Care needs to be taken because sometimes the failure can be catastrophic. As an example, a client may begin gambling and spend 6 months worth of his or her salary. On the other hand, if mechanisms to limit the client's spending are in place, he or she will usually report back to the counselor that he or she was unable to complete all of the tasks, and will usually have some excuse. The excuse will often focus on the role of emotions or other factors that influenced aberrant gambling patterns ("I swear I could have done it, but I was having a bad day."). These may be used as a motivational device to convince the client that he or she indeed has difficulties in limiting wagering behavior.

Preventing and Dealing with Crisis Situations

The pathological gambler is often motivated for treatment following emotional crises. Consequently, he or she is at a high risk for a number of emotional problems. Extraordinary anger outbursts are common, as well as frank phobic behaviors and appearances of generalized anxiety. Almost always, these can be handled as they would be for any other client. Ventilation, reassurance, and continued therapeutic contact are usually sufficient to diffuse the crisis.

Behavior that resembles hypomania or classic bipolar disorder seems common among gamblers who are beginning treatment. It is difficult to tell at this time whether the bipolar disorder caused the gambling episode. In this case, a person does not warrant the diagnosis of pathological gambler. Too often, gambling behavior acquired during a bipolar episode tends to endure even when the bipolar episode is controlled or remits. Regardless, bipolar episodes need to be treated aggressively by a psychiatrist. *Do all you can to influence the client not to make excuses and delay medical attention for bipolar disorders.* They are literally life threatening.

Many counselors tend to passively collude with clients who discontinue medications for bipolar disorder. When our clients tell us that they have gone against medical advice and discontinued medications, we say something like, "The decision to get off of that drug is between you and your doctor. I'm here to work on your issues about gambling."

At the same time, paradoxically, we don't have much understanding of the subjective feelings of people who have to take mood-stabilizing drugs. In graduate school, we learned that they have a host of unpleasant side effects, a phrase that distances us from the reality that people hate them and do not take them for a reason. Our first hypothesis is to blame the client, "Often people discontinue their drugs because they do not fully grasp the consequences."

The mood stabilizers are often subjectively unpleasant drugs with very nasty side effects. We need to be honest in realizing that our clients have numerous concerns that no one listens to. The official literature that comes as package inserts with prescriptions sometimes grossly underestimates side effects or severity. If there is a problem of denial in mental health, it is the denial of professionals regarding the side effects of many of these and similar drugs. *Warning: Psychiatry Can Be Hazardous to Your Mental Health* by William Glasser, MD, was published in 2004. Dr. Glasser is one of the most influential psychiatrists in the world and is making his research and thinking known about the negative impacts of medications. Medications may have their place but they are not a panacea, and it is important that we as professionals keep our eyes on both the pros and cons of any intervention.

Regardless, in some cases medications are proven to be helpful and bipolar disorders that have been correctly diagnosed appear to be one of these cases. For the treatment of bipolar disorder, they are an absolute necessity, and you will not make any permanent progress with an unstable bipolar client. Fortunately, due to the use of the atypical antipsychotic medications, much more effective treatment is now possible, with substantially fewer side effects.

We need to be empathetic, empowering, yet also therapeutically pragmatic. The more we know about bipolar disorder, the more we understand that it is a chronic and progressive disease that requires aggressive medical treatment. The more we know about bipolar disorders and AODs, the more we realize that aggressive treatment may prevent AOD relapse. Clinical examples suggest that this is the case with gambling-disordered clients.

If the client does not like what a particular psychiatrist tells him or her, do not encourage him or her with your own opinion or own "*issues*" with the attending psychiatrist. Avoid such phrases as "Other clients have told me that Dr. X isn't very good, either" or "I agree, Dr. Z doesn't spend enough time with his patients and switches their medicines way too often." Empower him or her to seek consultation at a university clinic that specializes in bipolar or other relevant disorders.

There is now substantial data suggesting that some people with bipolar disorder may cycle into mania, if maintained on inappropriate antidepressants. Clients who are depressed and treated with medication and who suddenly experience unusual gambling episodes, should be evaluated by a psychiatrist immediately. If this is not possible, they should be seen in the emergency room. Some clinicians are concerned that the liberal use of antidepressants and other drugs, instead of empirically based psychotherapies, may be causing an increase in gambling and other addictive behaviors. While we await more data regarding this important point, it is something to keep in mind.

Homicidal ideation is not infrequent among gamblers requesting treatment. For example, someone might claim that another gambler misled him regarding a hot tip or sports bet. Clinical judgment is necessary. However, it is often legally required and ethically mandated for clinicians to report such threats if they judge them as serious. In most cases, a reality orientation reminding the client that threats are serious and need to be reported immediately to authorities will act to cause an apology.

Homicidal ideation directed toward family may be particularly problematic. Tension often runs very high in family systems of the pathological gambler. It is not likely that this anger intention will dissipate quickly. It is usually helpful for the clinician to have a number of alternative resources for the gambler to investigate regarding lodging. For example, the referring agent might suggest a shelter temporarily.

Suicidal ideation has been experienced by over 80 percent of pathological gamblers. It is not known how many pathological gamblers are actively suicidal when they enter treatment, but the numbers are certainly high. These people need to be handled as carefully as any other client who is potentially suicidal. Clients need to be asked to sign a contract that they will not harm themselves. They also need to be given a crisis line for instant referral if suicidal urges are outside of their control. If clients cannot do this, local police need to be notified and provisions need to be made for hospitalization of the person who is possibly an imminent threat to himself or herself.

> **IMAGINE THAT!**
> "Internet wagering?—It will never amount to much more than a fad. Anyone smart enough to use the Internet is sophisticated enough to want the entire 'gaming experience' that a casino alone provides."
>
> *Source: Noted industry consultant (2001).*

Policies and procedures that meet with established standards of care need to be in place, preferably in writing in several sources. Basic training and crisis intervention need to be conducted as frequently as it is for CPR certification. Practice these procedures until dealing with them becomes routine.

Family and Concerned Others Involvement

It is usually not helpful to establish the motives of a family's interest in helping their member with a gambling problem. Above all, you want the family to be your ally. You do not want to begin a process of blaming them or automatically suspecting them of colluding to help the client continue gambling.

Family members of gamblers become involved in treatment for a variety of reasons. One ostensible reason popular in self-help literature is *codependency*. This term has many meanings but often describes someone who is over controlling of an addicted person's life while simultaneously sabotaging. This is because the family member's status is based on being a provider of an addicted person.

The classically codependent family has assumed roles in response to the pathological gambler's behaviors and identity that are not easily changed. Often these are families who have difficulty with assertiveness and family boundaries. By encouraging the aberrant behavior of a family member, they avoid confrontation and questioning of their own selfish motives.

As in other addictions, family members are frequently enraged at the addict. However, they may also show a passivity and lack of apparent care regarding the addicted person's daily activities. One difference may be that there are fewer small daily victories that family members can celebrate, as compared to those with other addictions. For example, the family of the alcoholic takes great reward that the patient has a few days where he or she does not vomit blood. The downward spiral of gambling does not allow these small points of optimism. Everything looks negative and hopeless.

Family information is also biased because of the financial problems. The family must be counseled to immediately preserve whatever assets remain. GamAnon is extremely helpful in this regard. Failure to do this may devastate the family financially and could potentially be held against a counselor in legal actions.

Risk Management Strategies and Techniques to Protect Cients and Families

Clients should be routinely assessed for suicidal ideation. Clients who are acutely suicidal need to be referred to a professional who can handle this problem. Some clients may require psychiatric hospitalization to stabilize intense feelings of anxiety or depression.

Special care should be taken with clients who are experiencing extreme anxiety. The literature regarding anxiety disorders indicates that people with a diagnosis of chronic, generalized anxiety are more likely to be successfully suicidal than depressed people. Often, these highly anxious people will not show up on a typical suicidal screen, which is usually weighted in favor of depression.

Clients also need to be assessed for evidence that they might do something illegal in the near future. For example, they may have intentions to steal or to hurt people that they believe have been dishonest with them. Ron, 33, was a pathological gambler who was convinced that his bookie had been cheating him for 5 years. He was determined to get even with this person by physical means. A brief psychiatric hospitalization was necessary to allow him to gain more control.

Pay attention when clients believe that someone may be after them. It is much too easy for clinicians to believe that this is simply an example of transient paranoia. However, too often, the pathological gambler owes large sums of money to unsavory people. These people may intend on collecting. Groups like GA are very helpful in teaching clients how to deal with these unique external stressors that the rest of us have no idea how to face because we do not routinely encounter them in our daily lives.

Suicide and Suicidal Ideation

Regardless of where a client is in the therapeutic transition, an emergency treatment plan should be in place on the chart. It should also be part of the policies and procedures of working with all clients. This treatment plan should explicitly address how to manage the risks of suicide or homicidal ideation. It also should address specific evidence by which a more intensive, stepwise approach will be implemented to reduce further risk. For example, the plan might specify that the client who is feeling suicidal will call the counselor on a daily basis. If this fails, then the counselor will contact the client.

Crystal

"I'm 28 years old and I'm a compulsive gambler. When I made my last bet 2 years, 3 months, and 6 days ago, I was in debt $106,000. I was a graduate student. That means I had almost no resources, no credit cards. Basically, I owed some nasty people about $125,000—the increase was due to interest. They intended to collect.

"How I got that far in debt is that I gambled compulsively. I was working in a sports bar, a very classy place, actually. I didn't drink and don't drink. But one of the girls on the floor encouraged me to make small bets with some of the customers, especially those who had been drinking. It kept them around and made the tips bigger. Pretty soon, when my boss made a call about a football wager, I had one too. I won big and lost bigger and there was always someone connected with betting to lend me the money to keep going.

"One day, I think they had enough. It was made clear to me that if I could not come up with the money, then I was going to be hurt or worse. There were also hints that I could make up the money by doing a number of—yeah, illegal things. They were serious and I was justifiably scared. But I didn't think I needed treatment until they cut me off from any more gambling.

"For me, GA saved my life. At my first meeting, I was able to talk about my situation. Not only did people understand, but they knew what to do, with some very basic baby steps. They helped me convince my gambling contacts that I would pay them back. I know it sounds crazy, but these people have a history of good relations with GA. As soon as I set up a repayment plan, which GA is serious about, the threats and calls in the night stopped.

"I had other counseling as well and it was helpful. But for me, what I needed most was someone who had been there, done that, and knew what to do to minimize the damage. There is no way that other types of treatments can help a person who is this far in debt to some very rough characters."

Monitoring can be face to face, but it does not have to be so. Creative options now available include the use of Internet cameras and cell phones with video transmission that are now becoming ubiquitous. Emails also can be used, but for most people the telephone is a much more human interface.

The pathological gambler with suicidal ideation must be told that the law is clear—it is your responsibility to report it to appropriate authorities for action. One possible outcome is that the client be hospitalized. During the previous decade, some professionals believed that it was therapeutic and in the best interests of the client to act heroically and defer hospitalization at any cost. This may not always be the case, and in gamblers who have lost their life savings, family, and so forth, the risk of immediate danger in the desperation stage can be high. The client with a gambling or any other problem that is a danger to self or others, or that cannot be controlled, needs attention, which may be hospitalization.

Sometimes, professionals who accept referrals will be reluctant to take these steps for new clients, because they do not want to appear too eager to use this modality. They believe that they will gain a community reputation as someone who *over-hospitalizes*. However, the practitioner should err on the side of safety. Again, this is good counseling practice.

A common concern for pathological gamblers facing the possibility of hospitalization is the "this will somehow get on my record ... this hospital thing." This thinking is illogical, given the fact that the clients *record* (credit history, employment history, legal status, social relationships, etc.) is already usually very much notable. Furthermore, clients may have more protection of confidentiality in an inpatient unit than they would an outpatient setting, although this varies by states and jurisdictions.

Counselors need to recall traditional techniques associated with crisis management. One of the best resources on the market for dealing with crisis situations is Gilliland and James' (2005) *Crisis Intervention Strategies* (5th ed.). It is a good place to begin for all trauma management. The rationale is that a successful crisis intervention is the result of many little action plans. The number one consideration in crisis is the preservation of life. As a professional who may have to deal with a crisis, the first concern is to ensure the client is safe. Before a crisis management plan can be done, the first intervention may be getting the person to a place of safety.

Six Step Model

Gilliland and James (2005) have developed a user-friendly model that can be used in crisis situations as it provides a dynamic strategy to preserve an individual's safety.

Step 1: Define the Problem

The person's level of functioning will determine how directive the counselor will be with that person. The lower the functioning, the more directive the counselor will be, especially if safety is an issue. One telling sign of recovery is when a person is able to make decisions that are cognitively sound and so he or she can be part of a collaborative process where the counselor is able to be nondirective.

It is important to be mindful of the *intensity, duration,* and *degree* of the crisis. These three variables are indicators of severity. They will help the counselor calibrate the potential extent and damage to the person(s) involved in the trauma.

Step 2: Ensure the Person's Safety

Safety is a major concern; however, counselors must be aware not to put themselves at arms length.

Step 3: Provide Support

Rapport, trust, empathy, and compassion are all important to a person in trauma. Their bodies may or may not be injured; however, trauma can injure their minds and souls. People need this security band-aid to help them gain control of any emotional bleeding.

Step 4: Explore Options and Alternatives

What are the options and what needs to be done? These questions need to involve the person as much as possible. However, the counselor has a role to offer suggestions when the person is lost for direction or is not making healthy decisions.

Step 5: Make a Plan

Make a plan that is realistic and the inroads to long-term health.

Step 6: Get a Commitment

Be mindful of the client's motivation and commitment to the plan. The person may not be able to make the commitment. Again it is important to be very active in an assessment process through this entire model.

These steps set the stage to assist the gambler in crisis. It is important to note that the initial sole focus is a person's immediate safety. Once that is secured, addressing the effects of the trauma is next. Through this model, the professional gets an agreement to help the individual until he or she is physically safe, has cognitive stabilization, and can process his or her environment.

Ask the client about the availability of weapons, methods of suicidal implementation, and potential victims. If working in an agency, it is helpful to have *suicidal client drills*. Then, procedures for these situations can be practiced and later examined for potential flaws.

Most discussions regarding these high-risk situations refer to the need for supervision. A supervisor or colleague can help the clinician double-check his or her thinking, ensuring that any significant aspects of the client's situation have not been missed. Lapses are inevitable when there is an unusual event. Typically, competent emergency room physicians handle thousands of life-threatening emergencies before they work autonomously. Very few of us in the mental health professions see this many suicidal or homicidal clients in our careers, much less in the short period of time it takes to keep our skills active. Even with a helpful protocol in place, we're apt to miss something.

When the client is not cooperative, statutory and most common-law principles indicate that the duty to the client is now superseded by a duty to reduce the client's risk to others. Usually this involves a process of involuntary commitment and the protocol should be in place for implementation. This process is difficult for clients who are in the middle of a referral process, and "handing over" a client who becomes suicidal may seem to sully your reputation. Your protocol should include procedures for clients referred into your services and out for other services so that no one falls between the cracks. You do not want to be liable for a case you believe someone else should have been handling.

Potential victims should be notified as soon as possible, by whatever means are necessary. It is not sufficient to leave a message on an answering machine or an email. Law enforcement must also be called at this point.

Document this entire process. Take concern that this documentation is authentic and reflects the sequence of events, as best recalled. Often, counselors find that they act quite well in emergency situations; however, they feel the full emotional impact when "sitting down to breathe" while writing documentation. Consultation and simple friendship with peers is often the next best step.

The counselor should be especially concerned of suicidal ideation following the client's failure to meet a personal deadline. This might be the payment of a large bill, or even a personal goal the client failed to meet. For example, a medical resident became suicidal after his problem gambling led to procrastination regarding his application for a prestigious fellowship. He had been treated for gambling once before. He noted, "The whole time I was seeing the therapist, no one bothered to ask me if I might hurt myself. I guess they thought someone who had gotten this far in life wouldn't be suicidal."

According to a 1996 report by the National Council of Welfare to Canada's federal government:

- Suicide attempts among pathological gamblers are much more frequent than among the general population.
- Suicide attempts are more common with pathological gambling than with any other addiction.
- Problem gamblers often have other dependencies such as alcohol or drug abuse.
- Problem and pathological gamblers tend to be young (under 30).
- In a Quebec study of college students, 26.8 percent of pathological gamblers had attempted suicide, compared to 7.2 percent of college students who had no gambling problem.
- A survey of Gamblers Anonymous members in the United States found that 48 percent had considered suicide and 13 percent had attempted it.
- No one knows exactly how many compulsive gamblers end up taking their own lives in Canada. The Canada Safety Council believes the number is over 200 a year. For every suicide, five gamblers with self-inflicted injuries could end up in a hospital.

Table 3.6 contains information about suicidal ideation that some clinicians find useful.

Anytime you refer a client who is suicidal, you must follow up. Anytime you receive a consultation concerning a suicidal client, you must make contact with the referring professional. In every case, document and consult with peers.

Clients in transition from one referring source to another sometimes fall through the cracks and may be likely to hurt spouses or other family members. When clients have a counselor or therapist, they are less likely to be volatile because they can be monitored and diffused. Do not refer someone who is at a high risk of violence. Until recently, attempts at ascertaining potential violence were not generally useful.

Table 3.6: Assessment for Suicide After Patterson et al. (1983)

This assessment screening, SAD PERSONS, was originally developed by medical residents, who wanted to identify patients at risk for suicide. It remains popular because it screens better than clinical intuition.

S = sex

Clients who are male are more likely to act out dangerously to self and others.

A = age

Older clients are more likely to hurt themselves.

D = depression

Clinical depression increases suicide potential.

P = prior history

As with assessment for violence, risk increases when there is a history of attempts.

E = ethanol abuse

We would add other drug abuse as well.

R = rational thinking loss

Potential psychosis: "A voice told me to kill myself ..."

Other rational thinking loss might include the notion that "I am completely unlovable." For the gambler, include brief rational thinking losses due to extraordinary bills, family rejection, or extreme social humiliation.

S = support system loss

Decreased support system indicates increased risk of suicide. In the Patterson et al. (1983) article, this was underemphasized. In working with pathological and problem gamblers, the anticipation of support loss from shame may prompt suicidal attempts.

Pathological gamblers may be also likely to attempt to hurt themselves to avoid subjecting their support systems to the shame they are feeling.

O = organized plan

As with violence assessment, this is usually very clear, despite a client's occasional denials.

N = no significant other

No meaningful significant other in the client's life.

S = sickness or chronic physical illness

Has the person or a loved one recently been diagnosed with an illness or disease that has made this person want to end his or her life?

Award one point for each yes answer above. Then assess risk, based on the following chart.

0–2 points	No real problems, but use your judgment for keeping watch.
3–4 points	You might send the client home, but check frequently.
5–6 points	Consider hospitalization depending upon your level of assurance that the client will return for another session.
7–10 points	Definitely seek hospitalization for the client, either voluntarily or involuntarily.

These studies did not involve people specifically with known gambling disorders, nor was the violence prompted by situations in which gambling was the trigger. However, it may be possible to extrapolate findings from this half decade of research for the important task of protecting clients, families, and the community. The clinician may wish to look for the following:

1. The stereotype that men are more violent than women appears to be vanishing. Men are more likely to be violent, although women are more likely to demonstrate violence at home.
2. Violence of any type, whether aimed at self or others, is a powerful predictor of future violence.
3. Being physically abused as a child predicts future violence.
4. Having a father who was a substance abuser is a predictor of future violence.
5. Threats of violence from a person with a personality or substance abuse disorder are much more likely to result in the violence, as are those made by someone with an affective or anxiety disorder.
6. On the other hand, there appears to be a negative relationship between schizophrenia and affective violence.
7. The much believed relationship between race and violence (e.g., African Americans are more violent) disappears when socioeconomic and relevant community factors are considered.
8. People who have certain relevant Axis II disorders are much more likely to be violent (psychopathy is a strong indicator of violence).
9. Delusions are not important per se, unless they breed suspiciousness.
10. Hallucinations are only important if they *command* specific violent acts.
11. Violent thoughts and feelings are associated with violence, especially if they are persistent.
12. Anger also is predictive of violence.

While these are not weighted in a multivariate fashion, the clinician may use them to obtain rough estimates regarding the various risks at stake and options for the family, such as restraining orders and/or alternative shelter. Clients who have a history of aggression, who have threatened others, or who have fantasies about hurting others, need to be closely monitored. Good counseling techniques usually allow for feedback if the client's suspiciousness or hostility is increasing. A phrase such as the following is often helpful: "Right now, I'm sensing that we are both uncomfortable with these questions. Do you feel like coming back to them later?" This shows empathy and also respects the client's wishes and rights. Also it reiterates the importance of the information that is gathered.

Remember, when it comes to suicidal or homicidal thoughts or feelings, it is okay to be direct! In fact, it is the standard of care. You have to ask phrases such as, "Are you feeling like hurting yourself now, after that last big loss at the casino?" They are entirely appropriate and are keeping within good counseling practice.

Risk Management Strategies and Techniques to Protect Counselors

There need to be policies and procedures in place that are modeled after the AOD requirements that exist in most states to protect counselors who work in agencies. For example, in Pennsylvania, there is an elaborate set of contingency plans that must be in place to qualify as a treatment provider of AOD services. People who treat nonpharmacological addictions need to plan to this level of contingency.

It is rare that referring or treating professionals are physically assaulted by problem or pathological gamblers. Some assaults may occur at intake or when the issue of termination is discussed. However, danger to counselors also includes problems from verbal or other escalating threats. The counselor or agency needs to decide *in advance* what constitutes threatening behavior and what the responses will be.

To avoid litigation and ethical complaints, take care regarding disclosure to Employee Assistance Programs (EAPs). These often are sources for referrals or treatment providers. The counselor may encounter legal problems without advanced documentation of what will and will not be disclosed to the EAP. Often, this is clearly detailed in the services agreement. Do not assume. Be sure!

Duty to Warn for Property Damage

A common, but difficult, situation occurs when the counselor is informed by the client that he or she is going to commit a crime to finance future gambling or to pay gambling debts. For example, in one case, a client told a psychiatrist that she was about to steal a large amount of money from her trusting employer, and that this would not become evident for several years. No one could possibly get hurt. That part was absolutely certain from the details, as the psychiatrist would have to agree.

"And no one will miss it for a couple of years ... By then, I will have made it all up gambling and I'll have paid it back."

What do you do?

To add a bit of dark humor to the situation, the client stated that she could not afford the psychiatrist's fee, but would pay him after she *borrowed* from her employer!

In this situation, the psychiatrist first thought of what *not* to do. Do not call the police and ask for the appropriate next step. Police are trained for one type of intervention. More usefully, the psychiatrist called his risk manager at his malpractice insurance agency and then employed the help of a supplemental attorney. Finally, he sought peer review. This was a complex case, and the appropriateness of his action depended on a number of factors.

Everyone knows what they would do regarding duty to warn under the Tarasoff case. The wrong time to prepare for a crisis is when it is happening, such as a client threatening nonviolent property crimes. We recommend the following:

- Prior to any critical incidences, talk to a local attorney with expertise in mental health to find what is relevant where you live.
- Prior to any critical incidences, discuss this with the risk management attorney at your malpractice insurance provider or liability underwriter. They often are helpful, because it is in their interest to reduce your liability.
- Formulate a written policy and set of procedures.
- Have them peer reviewed and incorporate comments.
- Revise them and submit them to a second attorney for *approval*.
- *Use them when you need to and use them every time.*
- Document that you have used them, as quickly following the incident as possible.
- Perform all duties to warn that are legally or ethically required under the law and under your policies and procedures.
- Discuss the specifics of the situation with your risk manager and your liability underwriter.

TESTING YOUR KNOWLEDGE

1. People are more likely to change for positive reward rather than for punishment. True or False?

2. A good resource for the family of a disordered gambler is _____.

3. The number ONE consideration in crisis is

   _____.

4. Potential victims of violence from clients should be notified as soon as possible, by whatever means necessary. True or False?

Answers on page 105.

Referral Follow-Up and Cautionary Notes

Counselors usually may not release confidential information without the adult client's or minor client's legal guardian's signing such a release. Exceptions include legally mandated duty to report suspected child abuse or to protect identifiable people who are in imminent danger of harm. An excellent volume by Luepker (2003), *Record Keeping in Psychotherapy and Counseling,* helps clarify some of these concerns.

It is not clear whether people with gambling problems are afforded the degree of confidentiality that routinely is granted other mental health problems. Clinicians often are very sloppy with confidentiality, as they were in the alcohol field 40 years ago. Regardless, all follow-up regarding referrals should not sacrifice confidentiality, unless there is an imminent danger requiring the necessity to warn others.

This seems to make good clinical sense. But we are aware of one county agency that insists that practitioners contact treatment counselors to make sure that the client made the transition from the referral source to the provider successfully. Unless very explicit details are designed so that a client's rights to privacy are not violated, this may violate ethical standards and HIPAA regulations, which are described later.

Often, referrals may be from a group therapy modality to another modality, such as to individual therapy or to medication management. Therapists, who work with groups where any one member may be a pathological gambler, may prefer to keep an individual record for each group member, so that anyone who is referred has clearly appropriate records.

Do not release information simply because someone calls and says that he or she is a lawyer or is from a District Attorney's Office. Consult with an attorney, even if the person claims to have a subpoena. Be prepared that if child custody is involved, there may be attempts to circumvent confidentiality by professionals.

Summing Up

The theme of this chapter is how to stretch your resources and to protect them—and your clients. Counselors interested in treating gambling disorders need to develop a professional network, not for purposes of marketing, but for offering something, learning, or giving something in exchange. Hotlines, state contacts, and GA are excellent resources for the counselor's network.

We do not yet know how to match clients with appropriate resources. Strategies to enhance motivation should focus on providing information and addressing ambivalence, not *classic* confrontation.

Clients in the transitional phases of treatment are at high risk for suicidal or other security threats. Policies, procedures, and training need to be in place to address these concerns prior to their occurrences. These seem at first like good clinical practice or even common sense, then we realize that, too often, we fail to practice them consistently.

- Having a background in treatment of alcohol and drug addictions does not automatically make a professional qualified to treat disordered gambling. There may be major differences that affect client management and prognosis.

- Counselors need to become familiar with their jurisdictions' confidentiality rules before the screening or intake process.

- Use Motivational Interviewing to facilitate motivation and attempt to normalize resistance and ambivalence.

- People who vacillate about whether they have a gambling problem can conduct a personal experiment.

- Suicidal ideation has been experienced by over 80 percent of pathological gamblers. Clients need to be asked to sign a contract that they will not harm themselves and be given a crisis line for instant referral. If clients cannot do this, local police need to be notified and provisions need to be made for hospitalization.

- When the client is not cooperative, statutory and most common-law principles indicate that the duty to the client is superseded by a duty to reduce the client's risk to others.

Key Terms

AOD. Alcohol and other drugs.

GA. Gamblers Anonymous.

GamAnon. This is a group for families and friends of disordered gamblers regardless of whether the gambler attends Gamblers Anonymous or not.

Closed meeting. (For a GA meeting.) Only those with a gambling problem, or those who think they may have a gambling problem and have a desire to stop gambling, may attend and participate.

Motivational interviewing. This is a motivational technique that is an evidence-based methodology designed to engage and then continue the process of behavioral change and maintenance.

Open meeting. Spouses, family, and friends of the gambler are welcome to attend and observe the meeting.

Process notes. These are the informal notations of S and O data, to be kept in a separate file apart from the official record.

Recommended Reading

The National Council on Problem Gambling (http://www.ncpgambling.org). This site also features an interactive screen to state affiliates, as well as numerous useful links to treatment and research resources.

The Addiction Progress Notes Planner (2nd ed.) by Berghuis and Jongsma (2005) and *The Addiction Counselor's Documentation Sourcebook* by Finley and Lenz (2005). These resources collectively will assist you in streamlining all of your work, from intake to termination. They will facilitate transfer and collaboration of clients and communication between providers and are worth the investment the first day you purchase them.

Counseling the Procrastinator in Academic Settings by Schouwenberg and colleagues (2004). Although written about college students, this is an excellent book for anyone who works with procrastinators of any type. It offers many practical suggestions that gambling counselors can use in motivating people to begin or continue treatment.

Pathological Gambling: A Clinical Guide to Treatment by Grant and Potenza (2004). This book covers a number of useful topics including screening and assessing. Chapters on special populations are outstanding.

The URL for GA meetings worldwide is http://www.gamblersanonymous.org/mtgdirTOP.html.

DSM-IV-TR Gambling Assessment Tool (http://www.no-dice.com/dsmiv.htm). This site provides a computerized version of the *DSM-IV-TR* criteria for pathological gambling that people can take in the privacy of their homes. Slight changes were made by the well-known clinicians and researchers Richard Rosenthal, MD, and Henry Leisur, PhD, to reflect "probable compulsive gambler" and "is compulsive gambler." It also provides computerized versions of other assessment tools.

A study funded by the National Institute of Mental Health employed the public assessment data from the MacArthur Violence Risk Assessment Study to develop violence risk assessment software, and it also validated that software on independent samples of patients. The results of this validation study have been published by Monahan and colleagues (2005) and are available as a software package. The software, called the Classification of Violence Risk (COVR), is commercially available from Psychological Assessment Resources, Inc., 16204 N. Florida Avenue, Lutz, FL 33549. Phone: 800 331 8378. Web: www.parinc.com.

An outstanding link about ongoing research involving assessment of dangerousness can be found at http://www.trowbridgefoundation.org/docs/arguing_future_dangerous.htm.

TESTING YOUR KNOWLEDGE

ANSWERS

1. True   2. GamAnon   3. Preservation of life   4. True

QUIZ ANSWERS

1. True   2. False   3. True   4. False   5. False   6. False

CHAPTER 4

Developing an Effective Treatment Plan

TRUTH OR FICTION

QUIZ

After reading this chapter, you should be able to answer the following questions:

1. Clients rarely drop out of treatment until they have met their counselor and decide whether they can work with him or her. True or False?

2. Some clients apparently improve prior to contact with a therapist or counselor. True or False?

3. Effective treatment begins only after the intake is completed. True or False?

4. Informed consent requires *full disclosure* of treatment. True or False?

5. Federal confidentiality rules for alcohol and other drugs apply to the treatment of problem gambling. True or False?

6. Action plans are cognitive concepts that measure commitments to change. True or False?

7. It is usually not a good idea to negotiate with the client over any aspects of treatment. True or False?

Answers on p. 141.

Highlights of this chapter include some of the therapeutic benefits of treatment; and why some clients do not follow through with treatment, despite the benefits. The chapter provides models for the client intake, what tasks and information are needed, as well as tools for conducting an intake. There are suggestions for what to do and what not to do during an intake and issues around confidentiality, fees, and insurance coverage. Also provided are a few recovery contracts.

Therapeutic Benefits of Treatment

Screening often occurs within the context of discussing possible therapeutic benefits of treatment. When asked about the presence of gambling symptoms, sometimes clients will stop and inquire about what treatment can actually do for them. This is a good sign. Often, clients will reveal more when they realize that treatment can offer something tangible in life.

Clinicians need to remember that gambling treatment is a *good bet*. The lives of severe Level 2 and Level 3 gamblers are full of anxiety and depression. Suicidal ideation is often common (Potenza et al., 2002). Life is full of broken promises and missed opportunities. Family relationships are tattered and grinding loneliness is the norm.

The following client handout in Table 4.1 summarizes some possible benefits to treatment and may be useful in presenting helpful possibilities to clients who are ambivalent about receiving help.

Table 4.1: Benefits of Treatment for Pathological or Problem Gambling

---

Treatment for a gambling-related disorder can result in the following positive events, thoughts, situations, and emotions in your life:

Ability to reach your potential

Acceptance of responsibility

Better physical health

Better sleep, naturally

Capacity for wisdom

Control of paranoid thinking

Enjoyment of family and friends

Experiences of more pleasurable activities

Financial solvency-savings

Formation of new friendships

Increased leisure interests

Increased rational thinking

Less domestic violence

Maturity

More positive life attitude

New achievements in life

Pursuit of active lifestyle

Reconnection with your moral values

Reconnection with spiritual values

Reduced procrastination and greater goal attainment

Reduction in anxiety and stress

Reduction in depression

Reduction in other unhealthy activities, such as smoking and alcohol abuse

Reduction or elimination of homicidal thoughts (if present)

Serenity

These are only a few of the many possible benefits of gambling cessation and the recovery process.

Many clients are motivated by increased social interactions, the possibility of resumed family ties, restoration of parental roles, and, generally, of enhanced social functioning. In the past, these clients have tended to be *relief* gamblers, women, and those who developed gambling problems later in life. Presently, the demarcation between gambling subtypes seems to be blurring. Table 4.2 is a client handout that appeals to those who are motivated by taking care of the needs of others—classic *codependents*. Often, these people will not admit to gambling problems, because they feel the guilt and shame might interfere with their roles in being perfect parents or spouses.

Clients' concerns for the negative aspects of treatment must also be addressed. In the screening process, treatment providers need to be realistic and not expect complete honesty or insight. Typically, upon cessation of gambling, clients may experience an increase in anxiety and a pervasive sense of extreme boredom that is hard to describe. In response to gambling-related cues, there may be an acute craving for gambling and memories of successful wagering. Fantasies and dreams are apt to be dominated by *gambling talk*. Pathological gamblers have been found to experience withdrawal symptoms, including irritability, restlessness, depressed mood, obsessive thoughts, poor concentration, anxiety, and sleep disturbance. Treatment acts to normalize this process, guiding the gambler through the beginning stages of a new life.

Table 4.2: Client Handout: Benefits of Gambling Treatment

When people get a grasp on their gambling problems through treatment, they usually make improvements to many areas of their lives. If these areas are important to you and you believe that you might have a gambling-related disorder, you might be interested in participating in a screening or seeking treatment, if it is appropriate.

Treatment for problem or pathological gambling can result in:

Better relationship with children and other family members

Better relationship with spouse or significant other

Deeper capacity to experience love and affection

Deeper spiritual life

Enhanced ability to help others

Fewer crises in your daily life

Greater serenity

Better home life for your kids

Improved health

Less anxiety, depression, and manic symptoms

Less stress, tension, moodiness, unevenness in life

Less worry and heartbreak

More effectiveness at work

More friends and better times with friends you already have

More opportunities to date (if you are single)

Reduced tiredness, exhaustion,

And a chance to reclaim the real "you" that people like to be around

---

Initial Attrition

Rapid initial attrition is termination from counseling or therapy after one session or less. Typical reasons are that the client loses interest, cancels, doesn't show, or otherwise changes his or her mind about treatment.

Ironically, many who experience early attrition may be helped by their counseling experiences. If psychotherapy studies can be generalized, some clients begin to change prior to calling a counselor, perhaps because they have already committed to the change process and believe that they can overcome their problems. Other clients drop out but seek treatment elsewhere or later. Nonetheless, if we believe that gambling treatment is effective, we should do what we can to reduce rapid attrition.

The specific numbers for rapid initial attrition vary according to the client's severity of problems, social supports, demographics, and other factors. I have concluded from my own clinical research that approximately two thirds of gambling clients drop out of counseling before the second session. This number was lowest for people seeing private counselors and for those whom the first counselor or therapist contacted was ultimately the treating therapist (without an additional referral). The number was highest in agencies with a waiting list and for clients who were referred to people they did not know. Attrition is another reason counselors may consider treating disordered gamblers themselves, rather than referring them to others.

Our belief is that, under most circumstances, practitioners should do whatever they reasonably can to discourage early attrition. Sadly, a system that is not responsive to client needs does just the opposite. Clients encounter frustration, indifference, obstacles, and difficulties and are likely to take a better-known path of lesser resistance. The smoother the transition from client screening to active treatment, the more likely the client will accept our services. A focus of this chapter is to provide strategies for engaging clients in the treatment process as seamlessly as possible.

It is helpful for counselors to realize that client motivation for change will vary; different people will have different degrees of motivation. Moreover, the amount of motivation that any one person has may vary at any particular time, due to an assortment of factors, most of which we cannot predict or control. Treatment programs designed primarily for highly motivated people are unrealistic. Programs that require clients to overcome impractical hurdles in order to access those program services are not likely to be successful. These hurdles include costs, geographic limitations, unrealistic time commitments, and extraordinary exclusion criteria.

Sometimes clinics, managed care groups, and successful demonstration projects have innocent-sounding requirements to ensure they have highly motivated clients. In this way, their statistics look impressive. Clever screening requirements have included the following:

- Clients must pay a reasonable fee for services. Most gamblers cannot afford it.
- Families must participate in treatment. More severe clients may have alienated families.
- Clients must have local residency. Gamblers tend to wander and be mobile, perhaps even homeless.
- Clients must not have a substance abuse diagnosis. What about nicotine? What about the fact that over one-third of gamblers have a drug or alcohol problem?

- Clients cannot be on psychotropic medication. Why? Many Americans take antidepressants or mood stabilizers effectively and no one denies them any health care services.
- Clients cannot have another *more primary* psychiatric diagnosis. This excludes almost all gamblers.
- Clients must not have been treated previously. Anyone ever heard of relapse?
- Client must be employed. This requirement reduces likelihood of problem severity.
- (Our favorite) Clients must not have had any exposure to GA or AA.

Telephone Contact and Crisis Intervention

Effective telephone contact and crisis service can substantially reduce treatment attrition. As mentioned in Chapter 3, many pathological gamblers make initial contact with a counselor through telephone help lines. Many states and provinces have a toll-free number that provides this initial contact. In ideal situations, these are staffed 24 hours a day, 7 days a week. These help lines typically do not provide intakes, since this usually occurs in face-to-face settings. Instead, telephone crisis and help lines often are to set up appointments for professional contacts. In addition, they provide a variety of crisis-related services, as appropriate, within the limits of their resources.

Often, gamblers will call help lines following an initial screening or other contact with a community agency. They are often between systems or even between treatment modalities within your own office and do not know who else to call. The number they call may be a number that they have called previously or may be one that they received from a local agency when they refused additional services.

Sometimes people will call crisis lines and help lines following an unsuccessful entrance into treatment. They may have been reticent for treatment until recently, but suddenly they feel the need for immediate help. They may have missed an appointment and suddenly are concerned. Perhaps they are calling because they admit that when they were first screened, they were not honest and now want to talk with someone further. Facilitate these requests and do not move these people to the back of any priority line.

Many clients will seem inappropriate for services because they are requesting information other than direct and immediate help for gambling problems. For example, the experiences of the Louisiana Compulsive Gambling Help Line are that a high percentage of clients call to find out about the winning lottery number, casino hours, or what's on the buffet at specific venues. In Louisiana, the best practice adopted is to respond to these requests professionally and courteously and provide information, if it is available. This is because the same caller may be testing out the service provision or may call back with *more serious* needs in the future (sometimes in a few hours). The *test* may be to see whether "you counseling types" are good and helpful people. Furthermore, kindness and courtesy for all requests are an excellent way to advertise services.

Crisis calls during this period often are very severe. Typically, the problem or pathological gambler screened previously may call a toll-free number and show a much more volatile side than he or she showed the screening therapist. Previously, he or she may have been cooperative and subdued. Now, this individual is quite upset, sometimes in desperation, often calling after a large financial setback. This client is likely to be feeling extraordinarily stressed, guilty, and perhaps suicidal. His or her thinking is likely to be severely impaired and there may be frank psychotic symptoms associated with the intense stress. His or her affect is subdued, judgment is impaired, and constant themes of remorse and guilt are often superimposed on restlessness and agitation. The client also may have been using drugs or alcohol.

Regardless of their point of entry into the system, clients in crisis need to be seen by a treatment counselor as soon as possible. We encourage professionals to implement risk management protocols (much like an Emergency Room) to handle these clients right away. For instance, if the client happens to be on a waiting list or has a scheduled future appointment, do not allow the politics of the day to make this person wait—because when a client hits this stage of desperation, there may be *no* future.

If there is a Gamblers Anonymous available, clients screened and waiting for services or further evaluation may need to be referred to it in the meantime. GA does not work for everybody. On the other hand, attending even one GA session may have some intrinsic motivational value. People become remotivated when they feel they are not alone and when they understand there is an international group that shares the same problems. However, clients also need to understand that GA is only one of several treatment options. They need to be reminded that, for some people, GA works remarkably, though there are other treatment possibilities if it does not *click* for them.

Give explicit directions for GA locations and information about hours. The client may lose these directions; do not interpret this as resistance. Many factors for this can include: anxiety, inattention, general distractibility, depression. Counselors may include a standard phrase such as, "If you lose these directions, and people often do, don't feel bad. Just call back and we will give them to you again."

Client Intake

Almost all gamblers receive some form of formal or informal screening, as previously described in Chapter 2. When engaging a new client and you suspect the client has a gambling problem, you may be comfortable performing this screening yourself. If the client has been screened and is appropriate for gambling treatment services, an additional assessment may be performed by either you or the person to whom you refer the client. This is usually referred to as a specialized gambling intake or, simply, an intake. This more detailed inquiry is not to duplicate what is already on the client's chart, but instead to determine unique information relevant for the treatment of the client's gambling problems.

Effective treatment plans can begin with an effective client intake into the system. An intake should assess the client, certainly, but it also should be the beginning of treatment, providing motivation. More than 30 years of addiction treatment has shown professionals that the longer it takes to develop a treatment plan, the more likely that clients will slip through the cracks or otherwise fail treatment. A successful intake can be the process by which a client begins to feel hope. This contrasts with the counselor-centered intake, where the client completes the process to satisfy the counselor's paperwork requirements. Clients surmise this attitude and react accordingly.

There are two models of intake procedures for addiction treatment. One is the *rational model*, which virtually every agency uses. Emphasis is on dates, documentation, order, efficiency, and compliance. The strength of this model is its accountability and that minimally competent counselors can deliver standard care in a reasonably satisfactory fashion.

The *humanistic model* emphasizes the client-counselor relationship and usually ascribes therapeutic aspects to this relationship. This model is not found in many publicly funded clinics, partly because counselors often are unaccountable for what happens in treatment. The strength behind use of this model is that good counselors can be more influential than they can in rational models. The weakness of this model is that bad counseling is difficult to detect and a mediocre counselor can be therapeutically ineffective or worse.

An intake is often most effective when it taps into the humanistic tradition of mental health services and allows clients to feel that someone cares about their problems. This occurs when clients feel they have spent valuable time meeting a real person, not simply completing more paperwork. An effective intake does more than fulfill bureaucratic obligations and supply answers to questions about basic client information. It presents the possibilities of something better, while allowing the intake counselor, or other screener, to lay the groundwork for a comprehensive treatment strategy. This involves a caring professional who believes that change is possible.

On the other hand, the intake must have specific structure. When the initial point of contact into the system is a licensed professional, the standards of care are much higher than when contact is made through a help line. The intake counselor needs to obtain detailed information and get beyond the tendency to talk about recovery options and merely discuss feelings. One of the skills of mental health counseling is how to incorporate the strengths of these two traditions into a brief session with the client.

A Client's Comments on Intakes

Byron, 27, had received intake services from three different clinics for his gambling problems. He notes:

"Up in _____, they asked me so many mean questions on the intake that I felt too ashamed to continue. I already knew that I was the lowest form of humanity in their eyes, even before they knew me. I just felt they didn't understand.

"When I was out at_____, the counselor looked like he was bored. He reminded me of one of those people you see at the motor vehicle office. I'm here all shaking and scared and he's looking at the clock. I said 'Screw that' and gave up.

"After a couple of more months, I tried again at _____ [a different place]. This time someone listened to what I had to say. Maybe I was ready this time, but I think it was because the counselor looked like she cared. For me, that is what mattered and that is why I took treatment seriously on the third time."

Client feedback reminds us of the following: Do not be rude, do not be judgmental, and do not be angry or apathetic. You may be a *pro* at this, performing so many intakes that the process is tedious and monotonous. *However, for your client, the experience of meeting you and finding out about your services may be one of the most important events in his or her life.* Long after you have potentially forgotten your client's name, he or she will remember yours, as well as remember your demeanor and whether you treated him or her with the self-respect that a caring professional can bestow.

The Counselor's Tasks During the Intake

Clinicians are responsible for a clinical chart that, depending on jurisdiction, must include very detailed information. The clinician has to collect this information while maintaining rapport, motivating the client, further assessing information about the gambling disorder, and finding out other relevant client data.

For counselors who work in a free-standing setting, there are a number of commercially available intake forms for collecting psychosocial history. Colleagues seem to like those in the *Addiction Desk Reference* (Coombs & Howatt, 2005). Other intake forms can be found in the very useful (though not inexpensive) package TheraScribe® (John Wiley & Sons), available with various modules that include treatment planning, intake, and documentation. Although it does not contain a module specifically for gambling, it contains a treatment package for substance abuse that is recognized by many people as quite good. Useful client homework assignments also are generated and save the clinician time. They act as a template for peer review, providing expert opinion on treatment options.

Typically, completed intake forms include information similar to that in Table 4.3.

Table 4.3: Typical Intake Information

- Demographics, education, employment
- The present problem
- History of assessed problems and previous treatment
- What forms of gambling the client participates in
- Evaluation of environment and home situation
- Psychosocial history—as much as you can obtain
- Evaluation of past or present addiction issues and treatment
- Medical history, including date of last medical exam and any current medications
- Family history of gambling and of mood disorders
- Evaluation of past or present mental health issues and treatment
- Religion or spiritual association, if appropriate
- Ethnic or cultural issues, when appropriate
- Financial status and health insurance, if appropriate
- Legal and vocation needs
- Social and peers group supports
- Current relationship status (family and peers)
- History of prior treatments for gambling and other addictions
- Evaluation of safety issues and overall assessment of risk
- Short- and long-term goals
- Diagnostic impression based on the *DSM-IV*
- Global Assessment of Functioning (GAF), if required

Make sure the intake information includes vital emergency information in case the client is suicidal or homicidal.

Questions That You Might Need to Ask Yourself

1. The counselor needs to find as much *pertinent* information as possible regarding the presenting problem. This can often be assessed by questions that inquire along the following lines:
   a. Why is the client seeking treatment *now*?
   b. How severe is the problem at the present time?
   c. Was it worse in the past? Why did it go into remission?
   d. Are there underlying motives for treatment at this time that were not present a few hours or day ago? For the pathological gambler, this is critical because treatment may be sought following a catastrophic loss, which may also result in suicidal feelings or actions. Are you, as a clinician, comfortable dealing with someone who is potentially suicidal? Many people are not.

2. At the intake, counselors must also ask themselves whether they are the most appropriate treatment provider for the client. Be honest with yourself here!
   a. Is it possible that seeing this client would involve an unethical relationship?
   b. Are your credentials and training appropriate?
   c. Do you have countertransferral issues that preclude effective treatment?
   d. Do you have the needed experience and expertise? Imagine where you will be if this case goes wrong. Can you live with the results? If not, then you may need to make plans to refer the person to someone else.

3. Then there is the taboo subject of finances, which is so important for practitioners in the United States. Ethically determine whether you can provide services, despite the fact that you may not receive the fee you expect to receive.

If the client has chosen the counselor, the counselor has to ask, "Why me?" This may tap into your therapeutic narcissism that we all possess at times, so be careful! Do not be swayed by stories such as, "I heard you are the best." These say nothing and usually indicate a desire to ingratiate. Are you holding yourself out as a *specialist* to the client? Care is needed, since specialists are usually held to a higher level of expertise than others. Legal implications may be involved in these claims.

Helpful Information Before the Intake

Cut down on time spent asking routine intake questions by having background information in writing from the client.

Table 4.4 suggests one format that is useful to obtain background data *before* the intake interview. It includes questions regarding gambling and other addiction history, severity, and psychiatric history, and it suggests the basic steps toward a treatment plan. We do not use it for clients who cannot read well, lack education, are suspicious, or are likely to view completion of this form as an uncomfortable process.

For people who are at least marginally computer savvy, this intake form can be electronically sent as a locked self-encrypting attachment to be completed on their machines. We transfer it to an encrypted database, reducing paperwork and providing maximum security. Currently, we use commercial programs with a high degree of encryption because it may assist some clients in feeling more comfortable and secure. Clients also have the option of writing directly to our machine via an encrypted form through the web, thereby reducing any potential evidence on their computers that they are seeing a therapist.

Informed Consent and Limits of Confidentiality

An informed consent is typically obtained when the client agrees to the treatment, after hearing about the specific possibilities that the treatment might involve. This differs from a release of information, which merely allows you to forward records. Counselors and therapists often obtain informational releases quickly. Informed consent, however, is a serious process that follows disclosure concerning fees, orientation of the therapist, and limits of confidentiality. Explain what you are going to do, what the expected outcome will be, and what the client will have to do to get this outcome.

Any information must be presented in a language that the client can easily comprehend. If the client's native language is not English, then provisions need to be made to ensure that the client can understand. Excellent copies of consent forms are available in the volume by Coombs and Howatt (2005) and in Jongsma and Berghuis (2005). Written informed consent is mandatory by statutory requirement and ethics boards.

Be mindful if the client is participating voluntarily, or whether there is some degree of coercion. When treatment is court-ordered, there may be different statutory and ethical concerns regarding what is considered confidential.

Be careful what you can disclose to family members, employers, employee assistance programs, and various legal authorities. Presently, pathological gambling is not afforded the same protection by the U.S. federal government as drug and alcohol records.

The limits of confidentiality have been discussed in several texts. However, it is not clear to what extent the counselor must act to advocate for the client when confidentiality is threatened. Federal guidelines regarding substance abuse are very clear and delineate what can be revealed under which conditions. At this time this protection is not available for nonpharmacological addictions.

Table 4.4: Preintake Form

Your completion of this form will help us focus more effectively on your problems.
Thank you very much for your cooperation.

Name:_____

Maiden and/or Married Names:_____

Nickname/Alias Names used:_____

Date of birth:_____-_____-_____

Age:_____

Sex/Gender: _____

RESIDENTIAL INFORMATION

Current address:_____

Length of time at above address:_____

Home phone:_____

Work phone:_____

Cellular phone:_____

E-mail address:_____

If renting, are you named on the lease as a resident?_____

Permanent address:_____

PLEASE LIST ALL THE PEOPLE WHO ARE PRESENTLY LIVING WITH YOU:

Name	Relationship	Date of Birth
_____	_____	_____
_____	_____	_____
_____	_____	_____
_____	_____	_____
_____	_____	_____

(continued)

Table 4.4: Preintake Form *(continued)*

MARITAL INFORMATION

Current status **(circle one)**:   Single   Married   Separated   Divorced   Widowed

Number of times married:_____   Date of most recent marriage:_____

Date of most recent divorce:_____

Number of children:_____

Number of children you are supporting:_____

CHILDREN (Please list any additional children on the back side of this page)

Name:_____

Date of birth:_____

Address:_____

Phone:_____

Sex/Gender:_____

Child lives with:_____

Amount of court-ordered financial support:_____

EDUCATION INFORMATION

CURRENT SCHOOL STATUS: Are you currently enrolled in school?_____

HIGHEST GRADE COMPLETED:_____

EMPLOYMENT STATUS

Current employer:_____

Address:_____

Occupation/Title:_____

Hourly wage/Salary:_____

Annual income:_____

FINANCIAL INFORMATION

Your monthly income (approximate):_____

Spouse/Partner monthly income (approximate):_____

Other (public assistance, trust fund, etc.):_____

Sources of income **(check all that apply):**

_____Salary from job

_____Investments

_____Other (list):

Estimate the total amount of your average monthly living expenses:_____

HOW MUCH DO YOU OWE TO THE FOLLOWING SOURCES?
(Indicate if this is per month or total.)

Parents or other family:_____

Friends:_____

Boss or employer:_____

Bank (other than credit card):_____

Credit card companies:_____

Auto loans:_____

Merchant loans (e.g., furniture stores):_____

Healthcare providers:_____

Government or back taxes:_____

Probation or parole fees:_____

Child support:_____

Alimony:_____

Attorney fees:_____

Bookies:_____

Student loans:_____

Mortgage:_____

Second mortgage:_____

(continued)

Table 4.4: Preintake Form (continued)

Other:_____

_____

Summary total month cash flow:_____

Have you talked to a Financial Planner or Bankruptcy Specialist? _____

PHYSICAL AND EMOTIONAL HEALTH

Please rate your current physical health (check one):
___Excellent ___Good ___Fair

Please list any history of medical problems any current medical problems/conditions:

_____

_____

Allergies to medication? ___ or other allergies?___

Are you taking any prescription or over-the-counter medications at this time?
  If yes, please list names of medications:

_____

Name of your family doctor, if any:_____

When was your last physician appointment?_____

What was it for?_____

Have you ever had contact with a counseling service or mental health center?___

Have you experienced any of the following? **(circle one):**

  Severe anxiety/panic attacks

  Depression (lasting more than two weeks)

  Thoughts of suicide

  Attempts at suicide

  Anger problems

  Anger outbursts

  Paranoid thinking

  Sleep disturbance

  Long periods of fatigue

Feelings of hopelessness

Weight changes (unplanned)

Tendency toward violence

Thoughts of homicide

Have you ever attended meetings of Gamblers Anonymous?_____

Have you ever attended meetings of Alcoholics Anonymous or Narcotics Anonymous?_____

Do you feel you are in need of treatment for substance use or any other type of addictive behavior?_____

Do you have any guns or rifles in your house?_____

If so, what kind? _____

_____

It is recommended that clinicians who are going to treat problem and pathological gamblers find out what their state allows them to disclose or not disclose, in case records are subpoenaed. Find a lawyer prior to the need for one and invest in money up front to reduce risks. Gambling cases may involve situations that include vast amounts of money. The ability to claim privilege may be tested in ways clinicians never knew existed by very sharp, extraordinarily aggressive lawyers.

HIPAA, Intake, and Client Records

The Health Information Portability and Accountability Act (HIPAA) requires that counselors follow federal guidelines regarding the confidentiality and security of client records. Requirements cover informed consent, security, and electronic transmission. Basically, in the United States, if you use a computer for *transmission* or *storage* of client records, you now are required to be HIPAA compliant. Any agency that receives direct or indirect federal funds is also required to be HIPAA compliant.

When HIPAA was first introduced, many clinicians predicted that it would have substantial negative impacts on clinical practice because it produced rules that were difficult to follow. As mentioned in the last chapter, one concern was the insistence that clinical process notes, or informal session comments and analyses, common in counseling, be kept in a separate folder from the official chart. The questions of who owns these informal records and whether they can be subpoenaed do not have clear answers. Because there may be many emerging crises with gamblers, process notes often are an important part of the clinical process. Some legal experts suggest that courts will rule that practitioners own the physical contents of these informal records; however, the verbal content may be owned by the client. Whether the client will have access to the practitioner's interpretation of his or her statements and actions in the process notes is unclear. In cases in which practitioners have been asked for their notes and are unsure of the best thing to do or even their professional rights, it is important they ask other professionals or a lawyer in their network.

Clinical process notes are important; be careful with them. Do not write down anything that you would be uncomfortable discussing with an ethics board or in court. As the old adage goes, "just the facts," is sage advice for note taking. Even if kept separate, if these notes exist, practitioners may have to turn them over if requested to do so.

Intake Do's and Don'ts

Don't keep it too long. Establishing rapport and encouraging the client to attend the first treatment session should be the first goal.

Do a test run with someone who has been there. It is often helpful to obtain a volunteer consultant, such as a member of GA, to evaluate the intake procedure for loopholes or roadblocks. For example, an intake that requires a client to furnish a Social Security number may cause the client to be suspicious and leave. Ask the consultant to role play as a desperate pathological gambler and then determine any *holes* in the system and its capacity to deliver services.

Do tailor procedures to fit the clients' needs. Intake procedures should be tailored and fine tuned to clients' needs, rather than the counselor's or an agency's. Treatment programs are likely to fail when they emphasize their own interests above their clients. Examples occur when they collect excessive client information or have unrealistic hours available for intake.

Do go where the clients are. To help elderly patrons, set up and do intakes at a bingo facility, where these people may often frequent. If the desired focus is minority male gamblers, increase contacts at the sports bars where they congregate. There is no rule that says intakes have to be in some cold office. They will come to your office once they know you can offer a legitimate service.

Don't delay seeing clients. Among some agencies, a waiting list is a sign of the need to justify the addition of more staff and increased funding. Intakes should be first priority. Clients need to be seen as soon as possible.

Do maintain confidentiality. This goes without saying.

Don't neglect the fact that people often present with a hidden agenda. For example, a disordered gambler may decide to seek treatment because creditors are after her or loan sharks are trying to strong arm him into payments. This person might be seeking hospitalization to hide from these people and might be disappointed that the practitioner suggests that outpatient treatment is more appropriate. From the practitioner's perspective, the suggestions are less intrusive—from the gambler's perspective, they are unacceptable.

Formal Assessment Processes

Formal assessment processes such as biopsychosocial assessment are used in a structured clinical intake to gather the most reliable and valid data for design of the client's treatment plan. The clinical intake aligns and uses all relevant materials, such as screening materials as well as screening tools and clinical measures findings. Our philosophy is to screen clients to determine whether they might have a gambling problem, which is then corroborated by a clinical interview.

Caution: Lengthy diagnostic procedures employing multiple formal instruments are not compatible with most clinical treatments, unless the intervention is being performed as part of a clinical trial. Assessment that takes several sessions probably interferes with the need to begin prompt treatment. Again, a key element to success is to get a treatment plan in place as quickly as possible.

An article by Pallesen and colleagues (2005) found more than 40 measures used to assess the severity or the progress made in gambling treatment. Some of these lacked validity or the demonstrated ability to measure what they claimed to measure. On the other hand, formal procedures that provide objective data are useful for the following reasons:

They provide a baseline for measuring change. If, later in the counseling process, a client feels he or she is not progressing, present scores can be compared to earlier levels.

They provide a better and more objective view of the client. Every client is different. It is often difficult to assess the effects of pathological gambling because complexities of individual clients may obscure the damage done by gambling and we may also overlook their strengths.

Furthermore, objective data allow practitioners to avoid hopeless staff arguments. In virtually every addiction treatment facility, the staff disagrees regarding clients' prognoses. One of the most common phrases used at case conferences is "He just reminds me of a former client." The reliability and validity of this type of assessment is not high. Another reason is that counselors possess different information regarding clients. To some counselors, the client may have presented a worse picture than to other counselors. Objective measures may clarify this.

Objective measures help us begin to understand what might work. To determine types of treatment for clients who have received treatment before, it's imperative to understand to what degree the client was actually helped. Subjective arguments ("I know he didn't get a lot out of this treatment, but I just feel he'll change later on") are not as useful in determining which modalities work and which are counterproductive.

When assessing levels of functioning, the following Client Placement Criteria from the American Society of Addiction Medicine, found in Table 4.5, may not exactly fit for a gambler. However, we believe what does fit are the criteria listed for which all clients must constantly be assessed within the following six dimensions. For example, the wording of dimensions 1 and 2 may not fit gambling, but the risk a gambler may have can be aligned, such as: suicide, angry loan shark, criminal behavior for money, loss of family support system, and even a dual-diagnosis issue that requires medical intervention.

Table 4.5: Client Placement Criteria

---

1. Acute Intoxication and/or Withdrawal Complications.

   A. What risk is associated with the client's current level of intoxication?

   B. Is there significant risk of severe withdrawal symptoms, based on the client's previous withdrawal history, amount, frequency, and recency of discontinuation of chemical use?

   C. Is the client currently in withdrawal? To measure withdrawal, use The Clinical Institute Withdrawal Assessment of Alcohol Scale (CIWA).

   D. Does the client have the supports necessary to assist in ambulatory detoxification, if medically safe?

2. Biomedical Conditions or Complications.

   A. Are there current physical illnesses, other than withdrawal, that may need to be addressed, or that may complicate treatment?

   B. Are there chronic conditions that may affect treatment?

3. Emotional/Behavioral Complications.

   A. Are there current psychiatric illnesses or psychological, emotional, or behavioral problems that need treatment or may complicate treatment?

   B. Are there chronic psychiatric problems that affect treatment?

4. Treatment Acceptance or Resistance.

   A. Is the client objecting to treatment?

   B. Does the client feel coerced into coming to treatment?

   C. Does the client appear to be complying with treatment only to avoid a negative consequence, or does he or she appear to be self-motivated?

5. Relapse Potential.

   A. Is the client in immediate danger of continued use?

   B. Does the client have any recognition of, understanding of, or skills with which he or she can cope with his or her addiction problems in order to prevent continued use?

   C. What problems will potentially continue to distress the client if the client is not successfully engaged in treatment at this time?

   D. How aware is the client of relapse triggers, ways to cope with cravings, and skills to control impulses to use?

6. Recovery/Living Environment.

   A. Are there any dangerous family members, significant others, living situations, or school/working situations that pose a threat to treatment success?

   B. Does the client have supportive friendships, financial resources, or educational or vocational resources that can increase the likelihood of treatment success?

   C. Are there legal, vocational, social service agencies, or criminal justice mandates that may enhance the client's motivation for treatment?

Source: The American Society of Addiction Medicine, Client Placement Criteria for the Treatment of Psychoactive Substance Use Disorders, *Second Edition (PPC-2; 1998). A copy of the criteria can be obtained by contacting The American Society of Addiction Medicine, Inc., 4601 North Park Ave., Upper Arcade, Suite 101, Chevy Chase, Maryland 20815.*

Assessment Measures and Instruments Commonly Used and Why They Are Useful

Many practitioners spend much energy worrying about what assessment instrument they use. Rather than develop comfort with a particular instrument, they read technical criticism that academics usually generate in the journals, and they have a pervasive sense of insecurity. They go to conferences to learn about the newest assessment measures, primarily because they catch the hint that some obscure studies suggested that the methods they use are not valid.

We don't recommend that clinicians operate this way. We do encourage them to make a commitment to stay current, but not paranoid. For example, we coach professionals to find a set of proven and reliable instruments that work for them and their populations, and then learn to use these instruments well. If the instruments do not work, or the bulk of the scientific literature shows they are faulty, then it is time to try something else. However, do not be insecure because a particular scale worked better in a particular study than the instrument that you are presently using. It doesn't say anything at all about your use or current clinical need.

However, take care to use normative data appropriate for women and minorities, young people, and people with *special interest gambling*, such as those who gamble on high-risk stocks.

The *Diagnostic Interview for Pathological Gambling* (Ladouceur et al., 1998) is an exceptional instrument that can form the starting point of a comprehensive treatment. This interview is keyed to the *DSM-IV-TR* but also solicits important information regarding cues in the environment that prompt gambling urges and behaviors. You can incorporate this interview immediately following screening or into a first session. It is strongly recommended.

The Addictions Severity Index (ASI) is favored by some researchers in the United States and is often required for programs that receive federal funding. It is brief, relatively unobtrusive, and takes only 20 minutes to complete. It can be scored in less than 10 minutes.

The Christo Inventory for Gambling Services is a brief structured inventory inquiring about location, social, financial, and other resources that the client has in order to develop information for a treatment plan or discharge summary.

The Maudsley Addiction Profile (MAP) is a public domain research instrument and may be used free of charge for not-for-profit applications. The MAP has been designed explicitly for outcome-research purposes. All of the problem measures can be repeatedly administered at points during and after an index treatment episode. Changes in these measures can then be attributed to treatment or other processes over the intervening period. A key principle behind the MAP is that, as a core instrument, other measures and items can be added as required according to clinical, operational, or research requirements. For example, a measure of drug dependence could be included, as well as questions concerning drug use history. Although this instrument is designed for AOD, it is easy to alter it (with permission) for gambling.

Other instruments that are applicable for drugs and alcohol can be modified for gambling and are described in Coombs and Howatt (2005). Additionally, several very promising instruments have been published and are being cross-validated in additional populations at this time.

Diagnostic Processes and Determinations

The diagnostic determination is based on whether a person reaches the criteria in the *DSM-IV-TR* (2002). People who score high on measures that correlate with the *DSM-IV-TR* criteria but do not meet the exact definition are referred to as *subclinical*. Subclinical people often receive the term *problem gamblers*. However, the term *subclinical* is not an official diagnosis.

There is no *DSM-IV-TR* equivalent of problem gambling (Petry, 2005a). Consequently, if you treat a person who is subclinical, you will be treating them without a *DSM-IV-TR* diagnosis, even if they have all but one of the necessary criteria for the diagnosis of pathological gambling.

All diagnoses must be keyed to the *DSM-IV-TR*. In the case where screening instruments were not constructed to measure *DSM-IV-TR* criteria, diagnoses must be clarified with an interview.

Additionally, a diagnostic interview must be performed to rule out bipolar disorder, since the *DSM-IV-TR* requires that the diagnosis be restricted to patients whose symptoms cannot better be accounted for by a manic episode.

The Division on Addictions, Cambridge Health Alliance, and Harvard Medical School have created a series of self-change toolkits that can be found at http://www.1800betsoff.org/PDF/gamtoolkit.pdf.

These toolkits are designed to help people do three things:

1. gain information about addiction-related problems
2. evaluate their own addiction-related behavior
3. develop change strategies, should they decide that change is the best course

Because people struggling with one addictive substance or behavior often struggle with another, we have designed these self-change toolkits to complement each other and have structured them similarly so that they are easy to navigate. These self-administered online toolkits provide resources to help guide a person's journey to change. Individual toolkits will identify other treatment resources for participants who decide they need additional help.

Our experience suggests these tools often are helpful in getting people motivated for treatment, as well as in being a complete treatment by itself for some people.

Treatment Planning

As we have been saying, what works in gambling treatment may not always work in AOD treatment. But the clinical process and best practices used in AOD very often have utility in gambling treatment. The end goal of treatment planning is to line up goals and direction of treatment. This treatment plan will provide the road map for treatment, which is called the recovery contract (explored in more detail later in this chapter).

The ATTC National Curriculum Committee (1998) points out that the main goal of a treatment plan is to help clients overcome their addiction disorders. The plan addresses areas of the client's life that need to be put back in order, such as family, employment, health, and finances.

All treatment plans need to include long-term goals in order of priority (primary, secondary, and tertiary) with short-term action steps for achieving each goal. It is important to include the following three elements for all action steps:

1. interventions—defined recovery tools
2. timeframe—defined period of time
3. measurement devices—defined criteria for success

Short-term action steps need to be SIMPLE—meaning the client has the Skills to implement them; Immediate action can be taken; they are Measurable; are Plausible, so the client's chance of success is positive; and are Legal and Ethical.

Fees and Insurance Coverage

Ethics and pragmatics demand that fees be set in advance. Sadly, people in most need of gambling treatment are usually the ones that can least afford payment. Discuss your fee and help the client make alternative arrangements for treatment if he or she cannot afford it. Be honest and, if no resources are available, let the client know that.

Finances are difficult for most clinicians to discuss. Counselors often feel guilt regarding how much they are charging per session, especially when clients are financially burdened. However, counselors in private practice have to make a living. When you are experiencing cash-flow problems from a lack of insurance provider payments, one or two non-paying clients can be exasperating.

Pathological gamblers often are ambivalent regarding money. They adore it and yet, like remembering a lover who has badly betrayed them, they also feel resentment and anger toward it. This attitude may encourage counselors to further avoid discussing fees. But the client should leave the session knowing how much each treatment session is going to cost and, if possible, how long treatment is likely to be.

Until recently, insurance coverage was virtually nonexistent for the treatment of pathological gambling. A general rule is that the fewer than 10 percent of people who have mental health insurance coverage generally have coverage for any type of gambling-related services. While these concerns are usually irrelevant, because many gamblers are unemployed or underemployed, the concern is often relevant for spouses and dependents.

The practice of billing for alternative psychiatric diagnoses, such as "Adjustment Disorder" rather than a gambling disorder is unethical and may violate statutory rules. Questions concerning insurance coding for clear cases of psychiatric comorbidity should be addressed to a specialist familiar with the counselors and jurisdictional requirements.

When there is comorbidity or a dual diagnosis involved, insurance companies seem to respond with an algorithmic inability to process requests. Some claim that they do not recognize the second diagnosis. One *infamous* group denies services for pathological gambling because it states that it is not a disorder that is serious enough to warrant treatment. However, if a client has pathological gambling and another diagnosis, all services are denied because the client has a combination of disorders that do not respond to treatment and cannot be treated with counseling or therapy!

Others claim that a gambling diagnosis excludes the possibility of other diagnoses. It seems they make these rules up as they like. In these situations, the best bet is to appeal loudly. Expect to be rejected on two or three rungs of the appeal process. We've had luck getting the gamblers interested in the process and focusing their enormous energies and talents in securing the insurance rights for themselves and others.

Managed Care

In the United States, the majority of the population who has mental health coverage has *behavioral health coverage*, a euphemism for highly rationed mental health benefits. Practitioners know that some managed care companies are good and generally honorably, while some are seemingly without ethics and are insensitive.

Our experiences vary, but generally they are unsatisfactory. For instance, colleagues who ask to be authorized for approval to treat a client with a gambling disorder may be excluded because they are not *certified gambling counselors*. On the other hand, referring counselors who request referral to certified specialists are told that the referring counselor should have the training to provide appropriate treatment. Often, you cannot win.

The practitioner who specializes in gambling clients and affiliates with managed care is also at their mercy. Often, these counselors are on 20 or more behavioral healthcare panels, each one requiring extensive paperwork prior to receiving referrals. All of this occurs with no promises of receiving clients. Juxtapose this with requirements that records conform to HIPAA and it is an arduous task. Therapists may feel there is a conspiracy to drive them from the market. Be aware of the problem, but there is no immediate solution.

Filing for Insurance: The Practice of Responsible Client Billing

There are basic principles to maximize effective billing and collection that have been identified in the literature. They are usually appropriate whether a person has a managed care or another type of care provider.

- Wherever possible, try to require payment at the time of the session.
- Maintain meticulous accounting records so money does not *slip through the cracks*. If this is not your strength, hire someone.
- Render statements to patients in a timely manner at specified and regular intervals.
- Issue appropriate reminders regarding unpaid bills, with clear procedures explained in advance regarding unpaid accounts.

- Try to openly and undefensively discuss with clients a resolution of payment problems prior to accounts becoming overdue.
- Be very careful in bartering for services, which is usually an ethically questionable procedure under the best of circumstances. Seek consultation here.
- Do not negotiate a bartering-for-services-fee arrangement if there are financial problems that are looming.

Ethics of Insurance: Modeling Financial Responsibility for the Pathological Gambler

Clients learn that financial responsibility includes paying for services legally. The therapist also must follow insurance guidelines, even if he or she considers them insipid or bureaucratic. If the requirement is that a therapist attempt to collect an amount of money, (i.e., the co-pay), then the therapist needs to attempt to collect it. While this is generally the ethical requirement of most professional mental health groups, sometimes therapists believe that they are doing the patient good by ignoring this or other fees.

In reality, all this is doing for the client is modeling another example of how laws are meant to be broken. The client is getting the message that financial rules and concerns really do not matter to smart and talented people. These are exactly the messages you do not want to send your clients.

Family and Concerned Others Involvement

The family may be an ally or foe in the early days of treatment. The family is a system and gambling affects all parts of the system. The counselor's dilemma is in knowing whether the client is the *individual gambler* or the *family*. Usually, the gambler is the client, not the family. You will be required to work with the client, whether the family agrees to treatment or not.

Family or concerned others responses typically fall into four patterns. The first pattern involves family members who are in a *semiengaged system*. Usually there is some degree of intimacy and sharing, though the family is clueless about the extent of the gambling problem. As mentioned in earlier chapters, often their initial reaction is disbelief or even relief, because they have sensed that "something was wrong." Then, they respond with anger. These families may be appropriate treatment allies. However, counselors ethically may need to make sure that the people in these families get their own needs met first. The book by Berman and Siegel (1992) describes self-help steps for these families. Every therapist should read this book, even if he or she does not treat families.

A second pattern of families involves those that are *psychologically disengaged*. They have previously cut ties or are in the process of cutting ties. These families may be unwilling to work with pathological gamblers because gambling is so financially devastating. These people usually will not be helpful in treatment. There is no value in attempting to force these people to cooperate with counseling at this stage. They are likely to be pessimistic and cynical, if they feel anything at all.

A third pattern of families shows *collusion* or *denial* about the extent of the gambling problem. These are usually over-involved families that are included under the classic description of codependence. These family members remain remarkably unphased when they hear about gambling losses, often citing aphorisms like, "Well, it's only money." These families may interfere with treatment, especially during the early periods.

A fourth pattern of family, common in a variety of addictions, is the *oscillating* family. This pattern fluctuates from over-involvement to under-involvement and occasional neglect. The patterns shift abruptly, sometimes periodically, sometimes seemingly randomly. The unpredictability of these families makes them very difficult to treat. These families may respond to gambling by *acting out* or engaging in their own pathology. As soon as the gambler appears to make progress, someone else in the family system appears to deteriorate, as family therapists have long realized.

In a family system where there is less impairment or less severe pathological gambling, the family's stance may be that they want the Identified Patient (IP) to be *cured*. Families may resist involvement because they believe that a brief rehabilitation somewhere can successfully treat their family member, with minimal effort from all. Sadly, television and popular media accounts support this belief, just as addictions professionals have rejected this notion.

Family members often seek affirmation of their narrative stories and symptoms. As GamAnon has found, many families primarily want to discuss their bitterness regarding the member who gambles. While this is certainly normal, it is not a useful part of therapy for a client with pathological gambling. Hostility and shame from this type of repeated encounters are not therapeutic. Individual counseling or referral to a self-help group is most helpful for families that cannot get beyond this stage.

The counselor's primary allegiance is to the pathological gambler—the client. This spreading of alliance is often very difficult to handle, especially for people who entered the field primarily because they had a significant other who had a gambling problem. Clinical supervision may help clarify some of the difficulties when they emerge that the counselor or therapist may not see.

IMAGINE THAT!

"It's hard to be sympathetic to a Diagnostic Disorder whose patron saint is Liberace."

Source: Attributed to a Keno-playing psychiatrist in Las Vegas (2005).

Recovery Contracts

Once the treatment plan has been determined the next step is to put it into a meaningful document that assists the client in being clear about the game plan. A written recovery contract is a strategy to help clients develop ownership and responsibility for their treatment plans. This is a measurable and definable agreement that outlines the actions and commitment of a client over a determined period of time such as attendance at GA, financial counseling, weekly counseling, bibliotherapy, spiritual activities, volunteering, and other therapeutic pursuits.

Recovery contracts are constructed for the good of the client and not the convenience of the agency or for obligations concerning documentation. They first need to emphasize the safety of the client and the safety and financial well-being of the family or other contacts. Following this, they should address commitment to treatment and other approaches at reducing or eliminating unplanned or uncontrolled wagering.

An example of a recovery contract includes the following:

1. A client wishes to cease gambling and the counselor asks that she commit to treatment to further this goal.
2. She agrees to see the counselor, attend GA to see if she likes the modality, and to undertake financial counseling.
3. In exchange and as part of her *contract negotiation,* the counselor offers her 12 sessions of cognitive therapy, the requirement of weekly GA, and the additional stipulation that the client be evaluated for depression by a psychologist.
4. The client agrees, with the stipulation that regardless of what the psychologist finds, she will not take medications.
5. The counselor responds as part of the negation that she will not *interfere* and these results are placed in writing.

The client's action plan includes:

1. Specific instructions for the hours in which she will receive cognitive therapy.
2. The location of the local GA meeting.
3. The appointment times available for the consulting psychologist and how to make an appointment with him.

The last step is to do a detailed review to ensure the client understands the contract and is motivated to honor it. Have the client sign the contract and give him or her a copy. Let the client know this is not a legal agreement and what will happen if it is broken. It is important that clients know that if they break the contract, they can feel safe to come back to pick up the plan and refocus.

Action Plans

In the development of a recovery contract, provide the client with a clearly defined action pan. This is a set of actions a client will do to stay safe and to prevent risk and attempts of suicide. If the client feels that suicidal ideation is out of control, he or she is usually instructed to call the counselor, an emergency number, or the police. It is common to need to write a *no suicide* contract for the pathological gambler. In order for the gambler to be treated in a location other than the hospital, he or she must consent to this. It is often helpful to give the person some concrete ideas regarding how to manage suicidal thoughts.

Table 4.6 is an acute action plan for a gambling client who is suicidal. Action plans may be written to be educational and motivational. One counselor helped a client construct an action plan to combat anxiety, which was one of the cues that led to his episodic gambling binges. By reducing his chronic anxiety, which has plagued him since childhood, he had powerful motivation to continue in treatment. Table 4.7 is an example.

POINTS TO REMEMBER

- Pathological gamblers have been found to experience withdrawal symptoms including irritability, restlessness, depressed mood, obsessional thoughts, poor concentration, anxiety, and sleep disturbance.

- The longer it takes to develop a treatment plan, the more likely that clients will slip through the cracks or otherwise fail treatment.

- An intake is often most effective when it taps into the humanistic tradition of mental health services and allows clients to feel that someone cares about their problems.

- Informed consent is a serious process that follows disclosure concerning fees, orientation of the therapist, and limits of confidentiality. Explain what you are going to do, what the expected outcome will be, and what the client will have to do to get this outcome.

- Do not write down anything that you would be uncomfortable discussing with an ethics board or in court.

- Action plans are a set of actions that a client will do to stay safe, and to prevent risk and attempts of suicide.

- For all action steps, include interventions, timeframe, and measurement devices.

Table 4.6: Action Plan for A Suicidal Gambler

I _____ agree that I will do the following.

I will:

1. Stop thinking about my ex-wife, because she makes me want to kill myself.

2. Arrest fantasies of death by not dwelling on them for more than three seconds in a two-minute period.

3. Realize that these sad feelings will pass, as they always have before.

4. Empty my home of all firearms, potential poisons, and medications that could be used for suicidal acts.

5. Arrange to have supervision through my friend _____ or if necessary through the Internet.

6. Pour out all alcohol and avoid drinking while I feel suicidal.

7. Avoid driving, because I stated that I have fears that I will try to hurt myself with a car.

8. Avoid watching sad stories on television.

On the positive, I will:

1. Maintain a regular schedule, even if I am not sleeping at night.

2. Shampoo the cats, because they need the attention and I do not need to dwell on me.

3. Go to church this Sunday.

4. Clean out my shed that I have been too busy to work on.

Table 4.7: Action Plan for Anxiety-Related Gambling

As a gambler, I realize that anxiety, once diagnosed, spawns
many different symptoms, including:

- sleeping troubles

- specific obsessions over stressful topics

- difficulty thinking about anything besides a stressful topic

- feeling tense, restless, jittery, or dizzy

- having trouble concentrating

- fluctuations in appetite

- being overly cautious

- being startled easily

- having an omnipresent feeling of impending danger or disaster and the desire
  to gamble

I _____ realize that I gamble when I am anxious. Therefore,
when I am anxious I will do the following:

1. I will take a deep breath.

2. I will ask myself whether I am responding to the situation, or whether I am
   responding to a faulty perception of the situation, based on a misunderstanding
   of it.

3. I will recognize that some anxiety is normal and that everyone gets nervous in life.

4. I will find other activities to distract me, such as television, but I WILL NOT
   GAMBLE.

5. I will exercise, such as walk or do yard work.

6. I will reach out and ask friends for help when I am feeling anxious.

7. I'll avoid beer, wine, Valium, and Xanax, because my experience has taught me
   that they make me gamble more and ultimately don't help my anxiety for very
   long.

1. After initial screening, an additional assessment may be performed by either you or the person to whom you refer the client, and is referred to as a specialized _____.

2. In the United States, if you use your computer for transmission or storage of records, you now are required to be _____ compliant.

3. A measurable and definable agreement that outlines the client's actions and commitments over a determined period of time is a

   _____.

4. A recovery contract must be signed by the client indicating that, if the client breaks the contract, future treatment may be jeopardized or terminated. True or False?

5. It is therapeutic for the gambler to have an opportunity to hear other family members express their bitterness regarding the gambler's actions. True or False?

Answers on page 141.

Summing Up

Many clients drop out of treatment before their first session, even before they have met with a counselor. Gambling services need to be arranged to reduce this attrition. Telephone help lines and effective intake procedures may reduce this attrition. On the other hand, nothing destroys client motivation faster than carelessness or ineptitude during the intake process. Intake therapists should remain optimistic and positive.

Intakes involve technical aspects as well. The client must sign consent to treatment, which must be placed on the chart. HIPAA places restrictions on what may be included in the client's charts. Rules regarding confidentiality are unclear and constantly changing. Counselors must be up front with fees and honest with filing for insurance. After clarifying diagnostic issues, clients and counselors must negotiate a treatment strategy, with the goal of developing a broad recovery contract and a more specific action plan.

Key Terms

HIPAA. The Health Information Portability and Accountability Act requires that counselors follow federal guidelines regarding the confidentiality and security of client records.

Humanistic intake model. Emphasis is on the client-counselor relationship and ascribes therapeutic aspects to this relationship.

Informed consent. The client agrees to treatment after hearing about the specific possibilities that the treatment might involve, including disclosure concerning fees, orientation of the therapist, and limits of confidentiality.

Rapid initial attrition. Termination from counseling or therapy after one session or less.

Rational intake model. Emphasis is on dates, documentation, order, efficiency, and compliance.

Recovery contract. A written, measurable, and definable agreement that outlines the actions and commitment of a client over a determined period of time. This is written after the treatment plan has been determined.

Release of information. Allows you to forward records.

Recommended Reading

Resource for General Paperwork

The Paper Office by Zuckerman (2003). This book will save you time because it has the forms you need. The documentation is there to help you improve the quality of your services, including keeping them HIPAA compliant. The wealth of information in this book may be overwhelming. Most of it is not usually directly applicable to the treatment of gambling. However, if you spend some time with this book, you will start to work more carefully and more effectively. We heartily recommend it as a resource and as an antidote to the *shock ethics* approaches that attempt to get you to comply with regulations by reciting horror stories.

HIPAA

The best current information regarding the impact of HIPAA for all mental health professionals can be found in various updates, including those by the American Psychological Association, found at http://www.apapractice.org. At this time, this site is only opened to APA members, unfortunately. Relevant information is also obtainable at http://www.hipaa-101.com/hipaa-faq.htm. To review details of this act go to http://www.cms.hhs.gov/HIPAAGenInfo/.

An assessment tool directly relevant to gambling is available at the Evaluation Instruments Bank of the European Monitoring Center for Drug and Drug Addictions (http://eib.emcdda.eu.int).

The Christo Inventory for Gambling Services is available at the previous URL. This is a brief structured inventory inquiring about location and social, financial, and other resources that the client has in order to develop information for a treatment plan or discharge summary.

The Division on Addictions, Cambridge Health Alliance, and Harvard Medical School has created a series of self-change toolkits accessible at http://www.basisonline.org/changetools.htm.

Addiction Counseling Competencies: The Knowledge, Skills, and Attitudes of Professional Practice (http://www.nfattc.org/uploads/TAP%2021.pdf). Addiction counselors who are doing treatment planning may review this document. This publication was prepared under the Addiction Technology Transfer Center's cooperative agreement from the Center for Substance Abuse Treatment (CSAT) of the Substance Abuse and Mental Health Services Administration (SAMHSA). We recommend this site, pages 36 to 42, for treatment planning.

To review 13 core principles for treatment planning set by the National Institute on Drug Abuse research, go to http://www.nida.nih.gov/PODAT/ PODAT1.html.

We highly recommend the *Treatment Addiction Planner* (hard copy and electronic treatment planning tools; John Wiley & Sons), progress notes, and treatment planning homework resources. These tools may be viewed at http://ca.wiley.com/WileyCDA/WileyTitle/productCd-0471725447.html.

The Drug Addiction web site provides information on recovery contracts at http://www.drug-addiction-information.com/drug-addiction/.

Dual-Diagnoses Clients

Addiction Counseling Review: Preparing for Comprehensive, Certification and Licensing Exams by Coombs (2005). This is a practical tool for professionals that covers a wide range of addictive disorder treatment considerations and is a must for a professional library for those who work with people with addictions.

Behind the 8-Ball: A Recovery Guide for the Families of Gamblers by Berman and Siegel (1992). This is a practical book, helping family members know when to take concrete steps, such as how to secure assets. It also addresses the emotional concerns of families. Counselors should read it to understand some of the pain that families encounter. This is *not* one of those volumes that believes that with hard work, it can always end happily!

The Complete Adult Psychotherapy Treatment Planner (4th ed.) by Arthur E. Jongsma, L. Mark Peterson, and Timothy J. Bruce, PhD (contributing editor; 2006) and the accompanying package of clinical notes. For writing intake and treatment plans for clients with co-occurring diagnoses, we like both of these (available from John Wiley & Sons as e-books). These provide a very effective way of maximizing the likelihood that all aspects of a client's likely behaviors are treated in an interdisciplinary fashion, while being documented in a manner congruent with current profession peer, third party, legal, and HIPAA standards.

TESTING YOUR KNOWLEDGE

ANSWERS

1. Intake   2. HIPAA   3. Recovery Contract   4. False   5. False

TRUTH OR FICTION

QUIZ ANSWERS

1. False   2. True   3. False   4. True   5. False   6. False   7. False

CHAPTER 5

Recovery Theories, Programs, and Tools

After reading this chapter, you should be able to answer the following questions:

1. The Principals of Effective Treatment point out the single best practice for treating gambling. True or False?

2. Most addiction professionals now realize that confrontation is used to break through the wall of denial. True or False?

3. Counselors should avoid discussions with gambling clients about such things as food and shelter. True or False?

4. Family therapy often is effective as an adjunct for the treatment of gambling. True or False?

5. Cognitive and cognitive-behavioral techniques have received the best empirical support to date regarding their effectiveness for treating problem and pathological gambling. True or False?

6. The Disease Model of Compulsive Gambling has been largely influenced by AA. True or False?

7. Prochaska's Stage Model of change may represent an alternative to the popular models of recovery from addiction. True or False?

Answers on p. 179.

Highlights of this chapter include principles of effective treatment and various recovery theories and models. A client's state of change is explained as are strategies for client motivation. The chapter also discusses details of different therapy and behavioral models, along with client support systems to use throughout this process.

An Overview: What We Know from Other Addictions

The National Institute of Mental Health has established general Principles of Drug Addiction Treatment, extrapolated from a variety of scientific studies.

These principles should form the guidelines for planning and implementing comprehensive treatment strategies for gambling disorders, as they do for other addictions. They are displayed in Table 5.1. (They have been abridged slightly to make them relevant for gambling addiction. For example, sections regarding the medical treatment of opiates have been removed.)

Table 5.1: Principles of Effective Treatment

---

1. **No single treatment is appropriate for all individuals.** Matching treatment settings, interventions, and services to each individual's particular problems and needs is critical to his or her ultimate success in returning to productive functioning in the family, workplace, and society.

2. **Treatment needs to be readily available.** Because individuals who are addicted to drugs may be uncertain about entering treatment, taking advantage of opportunities when they are ready for treatment is crucial. Potential treatment applicants can be lost if treatment is not immediately available or is not readily accessible.

3. **Effective treatment attends to multiple needs of the individual, not just his or her drug use.** To be effective, treatment must address the individual's drug use and any associated medical, psychological, social, vocational, and legal problems.

4. **An individual's treatment and services plan must be assessed continually and modified as necessary to ensure that the plan meets the person's changing needs.** A patient may require varying combinations of services and treatment components during the course of treatment and recovery. In addition to counseling or psychotherapy, a patient at times may require medication, other medical services, family therapy, parenting instruction, vocational rehabilitation, and social and legal services. It is critical that the treatment approach be appropriate to the individual's age, gender, ethnicity, and culture.

5. **Remaining in treatment for an adequate period of time is critical for treatment effectiveness.** The appropriate duration for an individual depends on his or her problems and needs. Research indicates that for most patients, the threshold of significant improvement is reached at about three months in treatment. After this threshold is reached, additional treatment can produce further progress toward recovery. Because people often leave treatment prematurely, programs should include strategies to engage and keep patients in treatment.

6. **Counseling (individual and/or group) and other behavioral therapies are critical components of effective treatment for addiction.** In therapy, patients address issues of motivation, build skills to resist drug use, replace drug-using activities with constructive and rewarding nondrug-using activities, and improve problem-solving abilities. Behavioral therapy also facilitates interpersonal relationships and the individual's ability to function in the family and community.

7. **Medications are an important element of treatment for many patients, especially when combined with counseling and other behavioral therapies. Addicted or drug-abusing individuals with coexisting mental disorders should have both disorders treated in an integrated way.** Because addictive disorders and mental disorders often occur in the same individual, patients presenting for either condition should be assessed and treated for the co-occurrence of the other type of disorder.

8. **Treatment does not need to be voluntary to be effective.** Strong motivation can facilitate the treatment process. Sanctions or enticements in the family, employment setting, or criminal justice system can increase significantly both treatment entry and retention rates and the success of drug treatment interventions.

9. **Recovery from drug addiction can be a long-term process and frequently requires multiple episodes of treatment.** As with other chronic illnesses, relapses to drug use can occur during or after successful treatment episodes. Addicted individuals may require prolonged treatment and multiple episodes of treatment to achieve long-term abstinence and fully restored functioning. Participation in self-help support programs during and following treatment often is helpful in maintaining abstinence.

These principles can form the framework for effective and scientific treatment of gambling disorders. They summarize the necessity for a variety of treatment options to meet diverse clients' needs. Treatments may include biological therapies, as well as a variety of psychosocial interventions. Emphasis is placed on therapies that address behavioral or cognitive changes, though other modalities also may be useful. In addition to counseling or psychotherapy, clients may require family therapy, case management, and ancillary social and legal services. The goal of this chapter is to discuss various types of gambling therapy and broader theories of treatment, especially as they relate to these principles.

Levels of Traditional Gambling Treatment

More traditional treatments have struggled with ways to measure the degree of services that they provide. One useful approach is to incorporate the terminology of the American Society of Addiction (ASA). These criteria are popular for physiological addictions. They attempt to furnish objective criteria for when a person should be hospitalized and what appropriate level for aftercare he or she should receive. Four levels of care are described and they are purportedly applicable to every physically addicted person. They do not necessarily apply to non-pharmacological addictions, yet may be a useful framework, nonetheless. They are described in the following, as they hypothetically refer to people with gambling problems. Don't confuse these levels of care with levels of *severity* discussed in Chapter 1 (e.g., Level 2, *problem*; Level 3, *pathological*).

Level 0.5: Early Intervention. This is for clients who do not meet the criteria of a gambling-related disorder, but who are at high risk. These are low intensity, problem gamblers that otherwise do not fit into treatment. Intervention is designed to reduce risk factors so that they do not transition to a further level of addiction.

Level 1: This level involves outpatient treatment. Traditionally, the setting is face-to-face interaction, although now this may occur over the telephone or Internet. The modality (group or individual) is not important. Most problem gamblers and many pathological gamblers would receive services at this level.

Level 2: Intensive outpatient/partial hospitalization. This has been divided into two subclassifications:

1. Intensive outpatient program: This is a structured program of 9 or more hours per week.
2. Partial hospitalization programs: These programs are highly structured and involve treatment for 20 or more hours per week.

These programs are rare for gamblers, although they may be expanding, as there is certainly a need in some areas.

Level 3: Involves hospitalization, occurring either:

1. Briefly, or
2. In a structured or therapeutic community for an extended period.

In some cases, Level 3 services have been overused. In others, Level 3 services are not available, despite their need.

Applying ASA Levels of Care to Gambling Treatment

Petry (2005b) notes there is little research regarding early treatment of people at high risk for developing gambling problems. These people might qualify as *habitual episodic excessive gamblers,* a phrase borrowed from the binge-drinking field. In ASA criteria, they probably fall under the classification of requiring the 0.5 Level of services.

Most empirical research has been conducted on people with Level 2 or mild Level 3 severity in a Level 1 setting. The treatment modalities usually involve individual or group therapy administered to clients, generally for a limited duration. A typical protocol involves a few or up to 20 or so sessions. Often, the literature does not differentiate between the different severities of gambling disorders, so that some of the clients treated in Level 1 modalities may not have met diagnostic criteria for pathological gambling.

Programs that treat more severe gamblers may decide that it is necessary to provide services more than once a week. Level 2 services are probably underutilized.

Criteria are not clear for when people need to boost the number of sessions from one a week to more than one. A few progressive gambling treatment facilities run day programs for Level 3 severity gamblers. These are similar to partial-hospitalization programs for chronic schizophrenics or more severely psychiatrically impaired people. This level of treatment is appropriate for clients who are available for treatment in the daytime and who need this level of care. Usually, the number of days per week and the length of treatment are both flexible, based on the needs of the client.

Brief hospitalization for stabilization is rarely practiced for gambling treatment in the United States. On the other hand, there is some evidence that traditional psychiatric hospitalization may be more common than it is realized.

Comprehensive inpatient treatment remains popular and is often an overused option. Inpatient treatment is available in abundance to people who do not need it but can afford it; and it is scarce or nonexistent for people who desperately could use it. Inpatient programs that simply copy treatment from alcohol or drug modalities are no longer seen as likely to be effective. Inpatient treatment is more necessary when someone has a number of risk factors (Griffiths, Bellringer, Farrell-Roberts, & Freestone, 2001). There are no standards of care to determine when a person needs this level of treatment.

Long-term therapeutic communities correspond to the final ASA level. Some of these, such as CORE in Shreveport, are successful for severe gamblers, including people with few resources. Experience from other addictions suggests that a subgroup of clients will need intensive, long-term treatment.

Recovery Theories and Models

Theories of recovery are different from specific interventions, described earlier. Many clinicians become technically proficient at interventions, but just are not able to be effective because they cannot articulate a coherent and meaningful theory of recovery. When you ask them what they are doing in therapy, they are very accurate in describing their moment-by-moment techniques. However, they are not able to link any of these together to form a more effective and *natural* style of intervention. As a result they are not able to explain why they chose to do what they did in therapy.

Theories of recovery involve the way that techniques are merged to change the causes of pathological gambling. Action Identification Theory (Vallacher & Wegner, 1985) serves as a useful framework for discussing how we should choose our therapeutic model. This theory posits that identical behaviors or beliefs can be labeled from an infinite number of descriptions. When we first learn new behaviors or concepts, we identify our tasks on a low level, usually involving motor skills and sequencing. For example, when we are learning to drive, we must pay rigid attention to such things as how far to turn the wheel and how far to depress the brake pedal. After some competence, we are able to move beyond specific requirements and perform actions more automatically, without thinking.

Once mastering the constituent technical behaviors, we have to be able to think more holistically in order to develop a deeper expertise. We then are able to identify our behavior by a higher level. We no longer think of ourselves as turning the wheel or putting on the break, but instead we see ourselves as *driving*. At that point, thinking about specific behaviors will usually interfere with performance.

The implications of Action Identification Theory are that we should not decide which theoretical orientation we like until we have mastered the various techniques associated with it. We can't fully understand it until we do. This is not the way training typically proceeds—graduate students and others find a model they like and then learn its techniques.

Models of gambling disorders have been reviewed in the series by Aasved (2002, 2003, 2004). Essentially, in North America, these can be reduced to two megamodels of recovery. The first is the *Disease Model* that was adapted from that of Alcoholics Anonymous to Gamblers Anonymous. It is so pervasive that it is part of the American mythology concerning how people should recover from addictions. Secondly, is what should be called the *Alternative Model,* which basically is anything other than the Disease Model.

The Disease Model

In the Disease Model, disordered gambling is assumed to be progressive, chronic, and often fatal. Adherents generally believe that gambling is largely determined by biological factors, though rehabilitation usually involves psychosocial intervention. The *DSM-IV-TR* promotes a *softer* variant of the Disease Model, sidestepping the important question of whether the purported disease is chronic and requires intense treatment for the duration of the patient's life.

Proponents of total gambling cessation generally support a Disease Model. This includes members of GA. Controlled wagering or a return to gambling in any form is assumed to be a sign of an inevitable and severe relapse (Ladouceur, 2005). The assumption is that treatment has to continue for life. The outcome associated with this recovery modality, even according to its proponents, is often poor.

Many members of GA believe that deep psychological problems (rather than spiritual issues, as is the case with AA) are often at the root of the disease that causes compulsive gambling. Biological factors also are important in many members' minds. These must be addressed in a group context, through contact with other recovered gamblers. Emphasis is placed on honesty, financial restitution, strict budgeting, management of legal affairs, fulfilling family obligations, and service to other compulsive gamblers. However, members generally do not believe that it is necessary to get to the root of the problem in order to recover successfully from pathological gambling. Many frankly note that although they are still quite "sick," they are presently "off the bet."

People who ascribe to the traditional Disease Model do not usually reject other treatments, as some people believe. In fact, most support advancements in whatever therapy works. However, Disease Model adherents are skeptical of behavioral and cognitive-behavioral techniques that use gambling stimuli as cues for treatment. They believe that these are too dangerous and that the potential efficacy of the treatment does not outweigh the potential side effects.

Most Disease Model adherents believe that eventually, empirical research will demonstrate that total abstinence is necessary for cessation of gambling, especially for a particular class of the most severe pathological gamblers. Many will admit that this does not apply to everyone with a gambling problem. To some extent this becomes circular thinking. The only way an outsider knows how to determine if a person has a *true* compulsive gambling problem (compared to a bad habit) is to see if GA worked for them. For those that it did not work, then perhaps they were not truly compulsive gamblers.

As stated previously, many adherents of the Disease Model believe that a biological basis will be found that distinguishes compulsive gamblers from everyone else. Presumably, problem gamblers share more in common with the biology of people who can wager without difficulty. There is evidence that this may be true. Level 2 gamblers may represent people who do not have the same genetic or biological predisposition toward extreme aberrant wagering that more severe Level 3 gamblers have. Other researchers believe that the experience of gambling may permanently alter the brains of Level 3 gamblers, in ways similar to the manner in which Post-Traumatic Stress Disorder also affects the brains of some patients.

The Alternative Model

The strongest empirical evidence exists for interventions based on what can be called the *Alternative Model*. This model assumes that many factors can cause problem and pathological gambling. These include genetic or deep psychological problems. They also include proximity, conditioning, cognitive distortions, stress, lack of social support, cultural norms, and many other variables. Advocates of this alternative perspective believe that treatment needs to be more individualized, as indicated in the *Principles of Effective Treatment,* discussed at the beginning of this chapter.

The Alternative Model is controversial among advocates of the Disease Model and the general public. Some proponents argue that an abstinence from gambling may not be the best or only desired outcome for people in recovery. The Alternative Model also stresses that some people spontaneously recover, although for whom this recovery will occur cannot be specified in advance (McCown & Chamberlain, 2000).

Some of us still tend to side for total abstinence, although we admit that there is insufficient scientific evidence to justify our belief that people who vigorously pursue the goal of a wager-free life are ultimately happier. We are concerned when someone comes into treatment expressing the goal to return to social gambling. It is almost tantamount to a hypertensive and obese person who insists that a prerequisite for entering treatment is that he can continue to eat cheesecake! We believe that longer-term studies are necessary and because of this, we do not recommend controlled gambling. We recognize that *zero gambling* may be an elusive goal, similar to an attractive lipid profile. Not everyone can reach this end. The behavioral steps may prove too great. However, we feel that the best treatment is to seek the initial goal of gambling abstinence and we encourage clients to meet this goal.

The Transtheoretical Model of Change (Prochaska, DiClemente, & Norcross, 1992) was developed to allow counselors and therapists to understand change as a process, rather than as a larger, specific event. In doing so, this model helped lay a framework for a counseling process directed toward reducing blame and facilitating readiness to change. It also enables us to look at change as a *phenomena occurring over time.*

Many common clinical interventions are variations of these models, Prochaska and his associates claim. For example, traditional psychotherapy is often a mixture of change through helping relationships aimed at dramatic relief or insight. Not everyone agrees with the correctness or usefulness of these classifications defined in Table 5.2. However, many counselors find it advantageous to use these labels. This system helps us categorize what we are doing on a moment-by-moment action.

This framework may also help elucidate the intake process by emphasizing what the goals of the session will be and what the referral is likely to be. It also enables us to maximize our efforts to clients who are in greatest need. When resources are scarcest, we may target clients who are most sensitive to change, which are those in the Preparation and Action stages, described in the table.

A strength of the model is that it avoids stigmatizing clients as *resistant to treatment.* Instead, these people are seen as functioning at a Precontemplation level of change readiness. According to this model, Precontemplators are unwilling, for whatever reason, to attempt change—perhaps because they have been unsuccessful before. Traditional disease theory may also assume that they have not *bottomed out.* Regardless of their reasons, their thoughts and behaviors are not congruent with imminent behavioral change. Precontemplators are not moved into action by shame or guilt, though they may be nudged along by information. The treatment goal is to expose them to the possibility of change and to show them that when they want to change, you may provide some necessary tools.

The next stage, Contemplation, has been aptly described as a period of ambivalence. Contemplators might think about aspects of change, but they are aware of both the positive and negative aspects of their behavioral shifts. They are weighing the costs and benefits, often many times a day. Traditional programs that demand behavioral change while people are in the Contemplation stage are usually less effective. These people are not usually ready for programs that demand insight or action. However, they may respond well to key additional information that helps increase their ambivalence and forces them to recognize that they have a problem that demands behavioral changes.

Table 5.2: Prochaska's States of Change

Precontemplation Stage

- The client has no intention to decrease or discontinue gambling

- The client may feel ambivalent about his life

Contemplation Stage

- The client intends to change gambling behavior within the next 6 months

- The client is thinking about these changes, though with trepidation

- The client feels ambivalent about his life

Preparation Stage

- The client intends to change gambling behavior within the next 30 days and has taken some behavioral steps in this direction

- The client is thinking of what life will be like after changes are under way

- The client's ambivalence is moving toward the direction of action

Action Stage

- The client has changed gambling behavior very recently or for less than 6 months

- The client is involved in thinking about how to cope with the changes

- There are many crises during this stage

Acute Maintenance Stage

- The client has changed problem gambling behavior for more than 6 months

- The client is beginning to think about life without gambling and enjoys the results of his change

- While there may be relapses, they are less likely to be incorporated into the client's self identity as time goes on

Termination Stage

- The client's gambling behavior may not recur

- The client has confidence that he can maintain changes

- The client looks for alternative activities to define his life

- Some people do not reach this stage

Unlike those who try to quit smoking or exercise more to lose weight, the gambler during this phase struggles with the concept of dosage. How much benefit can I accrue if I merely cut down? Do I have to quit completely? Could I possibly have any kind of enjoyable life? People in this stage may ask many more questions than at another stage, primarily because they are seeking information. Most of the clients a counselor sees, who call on a hotline or in a crisis, will generally be in a Contemplation stage. The general techniques of motivational interviewing, discussed in Chapter 3, may help to increase the disparity between their perceptions of themselves and what they want to be. This facilitates transition into the next stage of Preparation.

In the Preparation stage, people are planning to make some significant changes in the near future. They recognize that their ambivalence is too great and is tilted in a negative direction. They are motivated, though lack direction. In other areas of behavioral change, researchers believe that people in this stage are planning to take action within the next month. Ambivalence at this point may result in a situation in which people perpetually *sit on the fence* about making commitments and never take the final steps toward change.

In the Action stage, people more actively begin the process of doing what they must do to make change occur. Taking action—any action—is important. In other areas, researchers have found that people who try and fail are more likely to try and succeed than people who do not try at all. These are the rare people that show up to intake interviews ready to change. Therapists talk about them as being *no longer in denial*.

In Maintenance, people are consolidating the new behavior and struggling to prevent lapses and relapses. The main task at this stage is to establish a richer, more satisfying way of life as well as to undo the damage from the addictive behavior. For some people, maintenance becomes a constant struggle and therapy must continue to address it. For others, continual therapy at this stage becomes a hindrance and may be counterproductive. It is rare to see people at this level seek an intake, but it does happen occasionally. Clinical experience suggests that when people who are in this stage seek an intake, they usually have experienced a relapse or are requesting additional services that they might access through you.

Termination is the sixth stage of change. It is the stage at which change has happened and the former problem presents no threat. For many addictive behaviors, the number of people who reach this stage is small, perhaps a quarter or less for some addictions. Some people require formal treatment to go through all of these stages. Others do not and make changes on their own.

Progression through these stages is not necessarily linear. People can progress repeatedly from Contemplation to Action and back to Contemplation. This kind of nonlinear progression may feel like *going around in circles*, but data suggest that people may actually be spiraling upward, perhaps better modeled by an illustration from chaos theory.

Miller and Rollnick (2002, pp. 201–216) point out examples of interventions that can be used, depending on the client's state of change:

Stage of Change	Goal	Intervention
Precontemplative	Increase awareness; focus on cognitions rather than behavior	• Acknowledge/support client's feelings • Explore self-concept • Reinforce client's internal locus of control • Suggest self-monitoring tasks • Provide objective feedback
Contemplative	Work through ambivalence	• Decisional Balance process • Self-monitoring
Preparation	Assist clients to formulate their treatment goal and match the need with appropriate treatment	• Identify strengths/coping supports • Select appropriate recovery tools (e.g., individual counseling)
Action	Assist client in the treatment process	• Assign recovery tools and put into client recovery contract
Maintenance	Assist client in maintaining treatment	• Relapse prevention and preparing for the future (e.g., developing new skills)
Relapse	Assist client in returning to change strategies	• Assess motivation and focus on getting back on track and aligned to a treatment plan.

As a process of developing this model, Prochaska identified many of the common techniques of effective therapy and counseling that exist in a variety of *schools* of psychotherapy. These are listed in Table 5.3 and counselors often find them helpful descriptors of what occurs within typical counseling sessions.

This recycling is seen by adherents of this model as an opportunity to learn, gain missing information, redefine plans, and take action again. This is a very optimistic model. One implication might be that, given enough time, most people would quit problem gambling. This may actually be supported by the literature.

Table 5.3: Prochaska's Techniques of Effective Therapy and Counseling

---

Consciousness Raising involves increasing a client's awareness about causes, consequences, and management of gambling or other behavior that the counselor or society may wish to change. Psychoeducation and public health campaigns are examples of consciousness raising.

Counter Conditioning involves learning actions that are antithetical to the undesirable behavior. Relaxation training is an example, as are self-statements that remind the person about the dangers of an addictive experience.

Dramatic Relief tends to produce emotional elevation which may motivate a person to change behavior. Examples are the frequent testimonies that people give in self-help groups or in church.

Environmental Reevaluation is an assessment of how one's behaviors affect others. An example of where this occurs is in family therapy. Often, people will change because of the impact that they have on their surroundings. This may also be a key aspect in prevention and in natural recovery through methods, such as through the church, synagogue, or other important group.

Helping Relationships seem to work through providing trust, acceptance and openness. In counseling, we label them as therapeutic alliances. Helping relationships may also be informal, such as social support that we get from friends during crises.

Reinforcement Management provides consequences for taking steps in a particular direction. This may include punishment. However, an overwhelming amount of literature indicates that people are more apt to change because of rewards. Competent counselors try to mimic the processes by which people naturally change, therefore they emphasize rewards. Reinforcement management may occur many times during the addicted gambler's day when she tries to substitute alternative behaviors for wagering. She might, for example, reward herself with trips to her favorite Internet site for every hour that she remains wager free.

Self-liberation is both the belief that change is possible and the commitment and a public or private commitment to act on this belief. For example, the gambler who publicly declares his faith in God at church is one example of self-liberation. The ability to try on a new identity at self-help groups that is often such a powerful motivator is also a form of self-liberation.

Self-reevaluation is the examination of one's life and learning how one's self image is incompatible with reality. Shaffer and his associates see this as one of the key components in the process of addiction change and it may be especially helpful in the treatment of gambling.

Social Liberation occurs when people realize that they have other options. A person who is in an abusive relationship and who gambles to distract himself experiences social liberation when he realizes that he does not have to tolerate this abuse.

Stimulus Control removes cues for behavior and adds prompts for the behavioral alternatives which are more desired or preferred. Many of these techniques are commonly taught in behavioral and cognitive behavioral texts. Personal avoidance of dangerous stimuli and participation in self-help groups can provide stimuli that support change and reduce risks for relapse.

Prochaska's model allows us to think differently about gambling and other addictions. Once a client is in the Action phase, the model makes intuitive sense to most clients and helps explain why past efforts at change were often hard. We can think of the Action phase as a point in which clients are able to conceptualize all of their past prechange behaviors from a new perspective. This theory also helps clients understand the rough road that they will face in the future. Finally, it helps them realize that there is hope and a resolution to their problems.

Motivational Therapies

In Chapter 3 we highlighted the importance of motivational interviewing (MI) in encouraging clients to consider the possibilities of change. Similar techniques now are replacing the confrontational interventions found in the past *folklore* period of addiction treatment from a few years ago (Isenhart, 2005).

A common factor in successful addiction treatment is enhanced self-efficacy. You can help obtain this by motivating the client through positive means (Miller & Rollnick, 2002). No longer can therapists or counselors simply pass blame to clients, if clients are unwilling or unready to change (Wahab, 2005).

Client motivation was typically seen as the key element in treatment success. This may be based on what psychologists label as *personal attributions*. We attribute success in many daily life tasks to our personal levels of motivation. When we succeed, we take credit ourselves, highlighting our own efforts. When we fail at a task, we escape responsibility by pointing out that we really were not trying as hard as we could or that we had some other excuse. Therefore, the failures of others must be due to the same processes that motivate us, namely a lack of sincere effort.

Applying this *reasoning* to the recovery process, anyone who failed to improve was seen as unmotivated or not trying hard enough. Counselors were quick to pass off blame to their clients, rather than to look for other treatment methods that would be more effective. This odd type of reasoning does not occur in the treatment of any other disease. Fortunately, many counselors now realize that this view is usually not productive (Joukhador, Blaszczynski, & Maccallum, 2004).

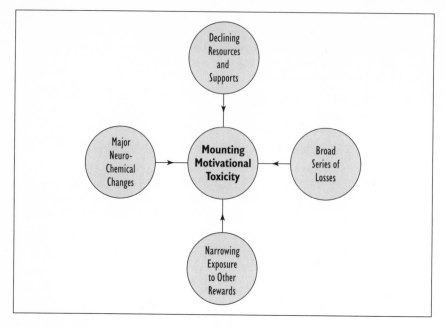

Figure 5.1: Motivational toxicity: A multicausal phenomenon.

An insight from a variety of disciplines has been that the process of addiction tends to destroy many aspects of motivation. It does so through several ways involving direct biochemical action, an exhaustion of social resources, a narrowing of daily activities, exhaustion of physical, financial, and spiritual resources, and other causes. This combined effect results in *motivational toxicity*—a loss of ability to be motivated about anything other than the addicting experience. This is illustrated in Figure 5.1. When faced with an addicting stimulus, the person may demonstrate *abulia*—an inability to make choices.

During the past 15 years, the responsibility for motivating clients in addiction has gradually been assumed by treatment providers. Providers are now recognized as key in facilitating the addicted person's motivation (Wulfert, Blanchard, & Martell, 2003). Techniques that foster shame, accusations, or blame are not congruent with maintaining motivation. Counselors should try to avoid them.

Social Interventions

By this term, we mean the broader concepts associated with case management, rather than counseling or psychotherapy.

Social interventions, including comprehensive case management, often are useful for people treated for other addictions (Borkman, 1998). Research with alcohol and other drugs suggests that comprehensive, client-centered case management (not bureaucratic paper shuffling or *program design and evaluation*) has a significant and positive effect on all types of addiction treatment outcomes in a variety of populations.

The needs of the gambler may include legal problems, vocational rehabilitation, job counseling, leisure counseling, social skills training, housing, and welfare assistance (Juniper, 2005). Offering gambling treatment alone, without providing for basic needs, such as food and shelter, violates what we know about human motivation. Particularly, clients with comorbidities may be very difficult to treat and may require extensive ancillary services.

Clinicians need to remember Maslow's well-known *Hierarchy of Needs* that posits that there is a universal sequence of needs that have to be met. Shelter and food are much lower—and therefore more important—needs. Hungry clients are not going to have time to worry about their gambling problems. If we want clients to stay in treatment, sometimes we have to help them find a place to live and something to eat, despite the fact that those duties might not be on our job descriptions.

Medical Treatments

We recommend all people with gambling problems have a medical evaluation. Regardless, there is still no magic medication for gambling, although there are a number of promising agents (Hollander, Sood, Pallanti, Baldini-Rossi, & Baker, 2005). A good review of available medications may be found in Rosenthal (2004). Medication studies have demonstrated the *short-term efficacy* of various selective serotonergic reuptake inhibitors (SSRIs), opioid antagonists, and mood stabilizers.

The selective serotonergic reuptake inhibitors (SSRIs) and other serotonergic drugs may be effective because they reduce the tendency for people to behave impulsively. They also reduce anxiety and depression, which are cues for gambling. The exact role of serotonin in problem and pathological gambling remains unclear.

Drugs that modify opioid sensitivity may be therapeutically useful. Naltrexone is a pure opioid antagonist, usually devoid pharmacological activity without the ingestion of narcotics. It has been mildly helpful for the treatment of alcoholism and may be of benefit for aberrant gambling. Very high doses may have toxic effects on the liver, so further study is needed. Nalmefene, a selective opioid receptor antagonist, is under testing specifically for gambling disorders. Purportedly, it inhibits the effects of endorphins in the brain, reducing the craving and subjective high associated with gambling.

Bupropion, a dual-action antidepressant that is also used for smoking cessation, has also proven promising in at least one study (Dannon, Lowengrub, Musin, Gonopolski, & Kotler, 2005). Bupropion is notable because it is devoid of serotonergic activity. With the exception of concerns regarding seizure thresholds, bupropion is usually well tolerated.

The limitations of the drug treatment trials published to date are that they are short-term in nature. They frequently exclude a broad spectrum of clients, including some of the most severe, those with physical problems, people with coaddictions, ethnic minorities, the elderly, young gamblers, and too often women. Also, studies typically have small or moderate sample sizes and statistical effect sizes are generally moderate or less. Still, any effective medication is welcomed into the therapeutic arsenal.

Occasionally, some clients will say that they plan on continuing gambling until a pill fixes their problems. Clients need to be reminded that a medical *cure* for disordered gambling is not likely in the near future.

Findings suggest a role of latent or atypical bipolar illness in causing or exacerbating excessive wagering (Dell'Osso & Hollander, 2005). If this is the case, then some clinicians believe that treatment with SSRIs may make a person worse (Kawa et al., 2005). There is also some evidence that abnormal gambling is common in mixed episodes of bipolar disorder, in which a person has dysphoric symptoms associated with mania and depression. Often, these patients are hard to diagnose and many may use alcohol and other drugs to mask their symptoms.

Epilepsy needs to be ruled out for gamblers who report fugue-like states or who have a history of head trauma or other significant injuries. For reasons that are not understood, seizures may be more common among pathological gamblers. The most famous example is the Russian author Dostoevsky (Hughes, 2005). Soft neurological signs, a history of multiple head traumas, developmental problems such as Attention-Deficit/Hyperactive Disorder, neural pathologies due to substance abuse, and other neurological problems are commonly found in people with a history of chronic gambling. These deserve evaluation by a neurologist and are often treatable.

Attention-Deficit/Hyperactivity Disorder and problem or pathological gambling often appear together, though no one knows why for sure (Petry, 2005b). There is no evidence that treatment with stimulant medication, such as Ritalin, is associated with relapse. On the contrary, evidence from AOD studies suggests that proper treatment of ADHD may help clients to experience fewer relapses.

Responsible Gambling

There is a school of thought that points out the importance and value of educating people who want to know what is responsible gambling and what is not. Often, as a professional you may be asked this question.

Dr. David Hodge, University of Calgary (2006), provides some insightful research results for therapists to coach clients of potential risk in his presentation in Alberta entitled *Using Population Health Data to Develop Responsible Gambling Limits.* Following are notes from his presentation that provide some guidelines for helping a person understand how to gamble responsibly and when to stop gambling based on his research.

Note: The following recommendations are only intended for individuals who choose to gamble and want to avoid developing gambling problems. These recommendations apply to all forms of gambling (lottery, bingo, casino games, VLTs, poker, sports betting, etc.).

- Don't borrow money to gamble.
- Gamble with discretionary income only, not money for everyday expenses. Limit your gambling expenses to no more than 1 percent of your gross income.
- Balance gambling with other leisure activities.
- Set a gambling budget and stick to it. Limit your gambling expenses to no more than $1000 per year (about $80 per month).
- Do not use cash machines to get more money for gambling than you intended to spend.
- Gamble for entertainment, not as a way to make money.
- Do not *chase* losses; accept losses as the cost of entertainment.
- Set a time limit and quit when the time is up. Do not gamble more than 3 times per month.
- Recognize that some types of gambling have a higher risk of causing harm than others.
- Continuous-play games (electronic gaming machines, slot machines) carry a higher risk of addiction than other forms of gambling.
- Research shows that gamblers who stay within these limits are less likely to experience problems.
- Gamble less or not at all if you:
  - Have a gambling problem or suspect you have a gambling problem.
  - Are currently depressed or have a serious mental illness.
  - Are experiencing financial difficulties.

Teaching How Video Gambling Works

For assisting clients in increasing their ambivalence about gambling, which, in turn, may assist in increasing their motivation, there is no better medicine than the truth. Problem or pathological gamblers still have cognitive functions and are able to draw conclusions the majority of the time, provided there is not other AOD or mental health issue. Researchers now have created powerful tools that teach clients how a machine really works, pays, and the real odds of winning. This can help crack a gambler's mythical thinking about his or her power over the machine. Since video gambling has taken its hold in North America, the following research and tools are helpful for gamblers to explore and learn when appropriate.

The following provides information that is useful for the person who is helping a gambler stop gambling:

- The payout of the slot is determined by the mathematical structure of the game, not by how recently the machine has paid out.
- Payout and game randomness are two separate issues. Randomness refers to how the symbols are selected. Payout is how much you get paid for a randomly displayed combination.

- Players lose in the long run because the amount the slot machine pays out for wins is insufficient to make up for the times players lose. As an illustration, suppose you were running a dice game in which you asked a player to bet $1 on any specific number (one to six). The probability of rolling a specific number on a die is one in six (1/6). Thus, the player wins one out of every six rolls on average (a hit rate of 16.6 percent), but he or she might win 8 times in a row or lose 60 times in a row. Suppose you paid the player $3 for a win. On average, the player is winning back $3 for every six rolls, which means losing $6 for every $3 he or she wins. This would be a payback percentage of 50 percent of what the player bet (payback = $3/$6 = 50%). After a few games, the player realizes that it's a bad deal and is about to walk away, so you now offer $7 for a win. That would be a payback of $7 for every $6 bet or 116.7 percent. You start to go broke, but you think the player will walk away if you cut the payback. In desperation, you change to an eight-sided die, so now the hit rate is 1/8 or 12.5 percent and the payback is $7 for every $8 bet (a payback of 87.5 percent). At this point, the player may no longer notice that he or she is losing money, because the wins most often seem to make up for the losses. The point is that the only difference between these three games is the amount the player is getting back relative to the chance of a win. In each case, the game is random. However, with $3 won for every $6 bet, or $7 won for every $8 bet, the house is making money; but, with $7 won for every $6 bet, the player is making money. Of course no casino would offer a game with a payback of 116.7 percent, but this example illustrates how it is the amount of the win relative to the probability of the win that determines the payback percentage. Payback has nothing to do with randomness per se.

Family Therapy

Family therapy encompasses a variety of techniques, with varying degrees of empirical support in the scientific literature. There is considerable evidence that family therapy is effective for substance abuse problems; however, there is no current evidence that family therapy should be the primary treatment for gambling disorders. It may be *extraordinarily helpful* to the family in setting appropriate boundaries or in forgiving the gambler. In Chapter 4 we discussed whether the family may be useful in the earliest stage of treatment. The same typologies and concerns apply regarding whether the family is an appropriate focus of intervention for longer-term treatment goals.

Ciarrocchi (2002) sees many reasons for using family therapy as a treatment modality. Family therapy may help obtain more objective data, which is important because the clinician cannot rely on physiological tests to determine the occurrence of a gambling addiction. Families may motivate clients and help reduce dropout. Furthermore, family therapy may reduce the financial bailouts by other family members, which are a frequent cause of slipping and relapses. Relationship counseling may also enhance other aspects of the families' functioning that emerge after gambling cessation, such as sexual dysfunctioning.

Bütz, Chamberlain, and McCown (1997) argue that there are two situations in which family therapy may be especially valuable. One is the family system that is constantly in crisis, but resists outside intervention. The dynamic of these families is that, as soon as one member gets well, another member becomes ill. Furthermore, the family becomes increasingly

---

IMAGINE THAT!
"By request of patrons, this machine no longer dispenses money."

Source: Sign on a malfunctioning ATM machine in a Baton Rouge casino.

---

insular as pathology becomes more rampant; consequently, the health of any member is met by an opposing force of other family members to induce an equal amount of psychopathology. As an example, the mother with a gambling disorder might quit gambling, only to have a son or daughter develop a drug problem.

The second type of family system, observed by Bütz et al. (1997), has been labeled the *nonlinear family*. These are families in which members are intermittently enmeshed and the system behaves *chaotically*. The family acts like an unstable weather pattern and may amplify or dampen any pathology, depending on the state of its aggregate members. The environment provided by these families is incredibly inconsistent. For a day or two the family might celebrate the pathological gambler's early abstinence. Then, due to factors related to the family's internal dynamics, members of the same system will suddenly align against the gambler's new behavior and try to sabotage him or her. Colleagues believe that a series of *shocks* to these family systems, much like what a physician performs to an erratic heart, may serve to synchronize family members into a degree of role-appropriate interactions.

Classic formulations, such as structural and strategic family therapies, have been blended into multimodal and eclectic techniques that many practitioners find useful. The behavioral and cognitive-behavioral traditions have received substantial empirical support in alcohol and drug research. A review of the varieties of family therapy and their strengths and weaknesses can be found in the volume by Coombs (2005).

Many family therapists have an overriding concern with keeping families together, despite the wishes of family members. After all, this is what we were trained to do and this is how we measure our successes! Early literature (Custer & Milt, 1985) often assumed that families wanted to stay together in even the most scarring situations. This may be an inappropriate goal when a family has been devastated by severe pathological gambling. Forgiveness and behavioral change are only two facets of therapeutic complexity that must be considered in family therapy-related treatment of pathological gambling. The uncertainty that a person may return to gambling, with the ensuing devastating financial consequences, cannot be denied and should not be minimized.

We suggest having different strategies for working with families in different stages of their recoveries. During the first stage, the goals are primarily empowerment and behavioral limit setting. The family works as closely as it can to limit the pathological behaviors. For example, family members work to stop enabling or to put limits on the gambler. This may involve temporary or permanent separation and, if this is the case, the therapist works with members to help them make this decision.

The decision to leave a spouse or to not allow a spouse (pathological gambler) to return home does not have to be permanent. The decision may be made on the basis of behavioral goals. For example, a spouse may be allowed limited contact with the family if he or she attends GA. He or she is allowed weekend visits upon continuing counseling and follow-through on treatment for bipolar disorder. He or she may be allowed to stay overnight if he or she avoids gambling for specific periods.

During the second stage, the goals involve cognitive and spiritual concerns. The family has shown that it can make decisions. Now it must decide whether and how it will encourage the gambler back into a social system that has been changed by his or her absence and that usually cannot return to its previous system. This second phase of therapy may also involve pastoral counseling because deep ethical and spiritual issues are involved during this decision-making process. On the other hand, some family members consider the return to *normal* as a part of the treatment process and find it impossible to imagine that there could be any other choice but to welcome the pathological gambler back into the family system and immediately forgive him or her.

The third stage of family therapy involves more structural and strategic methods and goals. This is not necessary if the family decides it cannot incorporate the gambler back. If it can, the family works with a therapist to facilitate the day-to-day integration of a *new* family member into a functioning household. Therapy at this stage is not unlike introducing a step-parent into daily rituals of a functional unit.

Psychosocial Therapies

Psychosocial therapies can be considered from two useful perspectives. We can discuss individual actions that occur in counseling. This is called microcounseling. Examples include the common techniques of ventilation, relearning, interpretation, punishment, supportive listening, and successive approximation, to name a few of the hundreds of terms that make up some aspects of counseling. Examination of behavior on a microcounseling level is a useful way to make sure that you know the basic skills and are paying attention to what you are really doing *now*. Psychosocial therapies can also be discussed more holistically. This occurs when we discuss the broader classes of intervention, such as behavioral therapy, cognitive therapy, and psychodynamic therapy. The reader is referred to Howatt (1999) for a hands-on discussion of basic schools of therapy and therapeutic techniques associated with each school.

Insight and Psychodynamic Therapies

Therapies from this tradition are considered *classical* and are usually what most people expect when they consider seeing someone about a problem. They often believe that there will be many sessions, in which judicious interpretations will finally help them understand themselves. Eventually, they will gain insight and experience symptom reduction or even a cure. A variation of this approach occurs in the context of group therapy, in which confrontation may help provide insights about gambling.

There is not much evidence that traditional insight-oriented therapies are particularly effective in the initial phases of treatment. Although there are some case studies that show promising results, more controlled studies are needed before this form of intervention can be routinely recommended for early treatment. On the other hand, insight-oriented approaches may be of particular value later, when a client wishes to make sense of his or her addiction and tries to place a meaning on his or her experiences.

CASE STUDY

Tiffany

The family systems perspective has been useful for cases in which there are multiple and different addictions within the same family. Tiffany, 31, an "exotic dancer," relates the following story about her family's multiple addictions:

"My husband and me [sic] have a relationship around our addictions. He wants to gamble. I want to use meth [amphetamine]. We worked out a kind of crazy lifestyle. We take turns staying straight. For about 2 weeks I stay clean. During that time, he gambles. After he spends his paycheck, he stays home at night, on weekends. He's just an unpleasant person ... just nasty to me. Then I send the kids to live with his mother. She is really cool with this, because she knows I'll use, but I guess she knows that I'll leave if I don't go through this routine.

"That's when I go back to using again and things are okay. I have a hundred little projects to do, to keep me occupied. Then he gets another paycheck and starts gambling and everything starts again.

"I think I would stop using if he wouldn't be such a jerk when he runs out of money."

Grief Counseling

People who have lost everything—job, spouse, respect, to name but a few—may grieve once they stop and look back at what they have done over the past few months or years. It is important to keep in mind the stages of grief and be mindful how sadness, which may report as depression, may be a natural part of the healing process. Kübler-Ross (1969) describes that people can go through five stages: denial, rage, bargaining, depression, and acceptance. Be mindful to support a person to grieve naturally in order to move through his or her change process; meanwhile, do not dwell on what cannot be controlled or changed. In some cases it may be helpful to teach the stages of grief.

Behavioral Therapies

Behavioral techniques focus on what clients do, while cognitive-behavioral techniques, which are usually developed later, focus on what they do and think.

Many behavioral techniques for the treatment of gambling have been cited in the literature. In general, the punitive behavioral therapies, such as aversive therapy, have not proven to be consistently helpful. Table 5.4 summarizes some popular interventions. They may be integrated into existing counseling or other modalities. There usually is insufficient justification to use them as the sole treatment for problem or pathological gambling, unless you have special training as a behavioral psychologist.

Behavioral treatment for gambling disorders may be reviewed in more detail in Ladouceur, Sylvain, Boutin, and Doucet (2002) or in Petry (2005a). More general descriptions of behavioral interventions can be found in the comprehensive volume by Hersen and colleagues (2005), which is also listed in the Recommended Resource section at the end of this chapter.

Cognitive and Cognitive-Behavioral Models

Cognitive and cognitive-behavioral methods for aberrant gambling are the most thoroughly researched methods of treatment to date. Cognitive models try to change a person's thinking, while cognitive-behavioral models change a person's thinking and teach the person to closely modify his or her own behavioral feedback. (This is an important distinction for people in graduate school, but for most practitioners, it really does not mean much!) These general treatment strategies usually are based on several different techniques that now have broad empirical support. Some specific techniques have been carried over from other cognitive therapies, while clinicians also have developed unique treatments specifically for gambling disorders (Tavares, Zilberman, & el-Guebaly, 2003).

A review of cognitive behavioral models and methods relevant to addiction may be found in Howatt (2003). The counselor treating the gambling client may use a complete treatment package or individual techniques. The Recommended Reading section at the end of the chapter contains sources for cognitive therapy that practitioners have found most helpful in describing specific cognitive-behavioral techniques.

We recommend that the counselor try to use a more integrated treatment package, because these are more theoretically sound and have a higher degree of empirical support. Typically, these represent *unbundled* treatments, meaning that they offer several interventions, and the practitioner does not know which ones are likely to be particularly effective. This is why they should be used as a package. These programs are easy to use and promise some consistency, yet they do require skill. Practitioners who believe that cognitive techniques can be performed without adequate clinical training and experience make a serious mistake (Freeman, Felgoise, Nezu, Nezu, & Reinecke, 2005).

An elegant and integrative treatment package that employs cognitive and behavioral techniques has been described in detail by Petry (2005a). The treatment package can be completed in as few as eight sessions, involves techniques that motivate a client (both inside and outside a therapy session), and does not require therapists to have unusual training.

Table 5.4: Common Behavioral Interventions

Technique	Description	Effectiveness
Systematic desensitization	Experience of gradual reduction in winnings	Mild benefit in most studies
Aversion therapies	Unpleasantness or punishment paired with gambling	Conflicting data; generally seen as ineffective
Imaginal desensitization	Training in imagining imagery associated with absence of success at gambling	Mildly effective in some situations
Relaxation techniques	Learning to relax on cue, either at the thought of gambling or during anxious situations	Effective as an adjunct in many situations
Skills rehearsal	Practicing alternative skills and activities instead of gambling	Effective as an adjunct in many situations; a major part of a variety of therapies
Flooding	Not quite the same as in other uses of flooding in behavioral therapy; has been used to present sudden negative stimuli associated with gambling	Experimental only; positive results, but not for routine use

1. A common factor in successful addiction treatment is
   _____.

2. Nalmefene appears to inhibit the effects of _____ in the
   brain, reducing the craving and high associated with gambling.

3. Prochaska attempted to find common methods of change that were
   practiced by _____.

4. Insight-oriented psychotherapy is or is not especially effective for gambling problems?

5. Behavioral techniques focus on what clients do, while cognitive-
   behavioral techniques focus on what clients do and _____.

Answers on page 179.

Another outstanding presentation of two different methods is available in
Ladouceur et al. (2002), *Understanding and Treating the Pathological Gambler.*
This book illustrates examples of brief cognitive and behavioral approaches. Use
the methods *as is* or adapt them into another treatment protocol. The thrust of
Ladouceur and colleagues' research and treatment is a cognitive methodology
that teaches clients that they have serious flaws in reasoning regarding the probabilities of winning. These fallacies involve an ignorance of independence of
events in wagering, negative expectancies over the long run, and a belief in super-
stition.

Actually, these are errors that all gamblers make, not just people with wagering problems. However, for some reason, social gamblers are able to limit these
errors and apparently suspend rationality at times for the sake of amusement.

The practitioners are encouraged to examine these volumes. If the choice is
to work in a cognitive-behavioral modality (which literature suggests is usually
the treatment of first choice), these two volumes offer what is very close to *off-
the-shelf* treatment manuals.

Existential and Spiritual Interventions

Ciarrocchi (2002) discusses a framework for integrating spirituality into a variety of alcohol- and drug-counseling experiences, especially gambling. He argues
that self-regulation theory provides a psychological basis for understanding some
12-step traditions focused on overcoming self-centeredness. Drawing on an
influential paper by Baumeister and Exline (1999), he argues based on the Aris-
totelian tradition of virtue as a transcendent agent of the narrow focus of the self

and selfishness. Gambling treatment, it is argued, is actually training in virtuousness. Ciarrocchi's (2002) framework can be described as eclectic or multimodal. He offers an integrative treatment package that employs a variety of different techniques.

More distinctly, spiritual counseling occurs among pastoral counselors and attempts to remotivate people to change within church-based settings, as an alternative to traditional treatment (Neff, Shorkey, & Windsor, 2006). We do not know how effective these approaches may be. However, there are many anecdotal accounts suggesting they are helpful for particular people, who may be culturally congruent with receiving assistance from church rather than from mental health practitioners.

Issues of self and identity have been hard to measure but are important in the addictive process (Larkin & Griffiths, 2002). Existential and spiritual approaches can be helpful in the early stages of recovery. Counselors would need to feel comfortable in this orientation. People struggle to find a meaning for their addiction and a reason why they have an addictive disorder; this cannot be the task of a secular psychotherapy and demands expertise that is outside of science. Sometimes, 12-step groups are able to provide this missing spiritual component (Laney, Rogers, & Phaison, 2002).

Holistic and Alternative Treatments

Descriptions of holistic methods that have been useful in other addictions can be found in (Coombs, Howatt, & Coombs, 2005). Popular holistic recovery methods haven't yet caught on for the treatment of gamblers.

Financial Counseling

Financial counseling is not an alternative method in the traditional sense. It is discussed at length in Chapter 7. Finances are an impetus for relapse, as members of GA have long realized. Financial concerns may be addressed through GA and through nonprofit credit counseling services. It is important to have several of these professionals in your network for client referrals. Look for a Better Business Bureau approval, since it may be meaningful in this situation.

Support Groups

As mentioned, the consensus seems to be that GA is helpful, but is often incomplete as a treatment modality and may be more effective if combined with other interventions. GA was loosely founded on the principles of Alcoholics Anonymous, by most accounts in the 1950s. Like AA, GA has no formal criteria for membership, other than a desire to quit gambling. Total gambling cessation is seen by GA members as the only appropriate goal. Unlike AA and NA, much of the time in GA is devoted to counseling members in legal difficulties and financial problems. Partly because of the confidentiality involved in legal issues, most GA meetings are closed, meaning that they are not open to people who do not admit to a gambling problem.

The 12-steps of GA have been presented earlier. The Unity Program of GA is similar to AA's 12-Step Traditions, though with a few differences (Finley, 2004). A principle difference is on the understanding of God, or Higher Power.

In order to maintain unity, our experience has shown that:

1. Our common welfare should come first; personal recovery depends upon group unity.
2. Our leaders are but trusted servants; they do not govern.
3. The only requirement for Gamblers Anonymous membership is a desire to stop gambling.
4. Each group should be self-governing except in matters affecting other groups or Gamblers Anonymous as a whole.
5. Gamblers Anonymous has but one primary purpose—to carry its message to the compulsive gambler who still suffers.
6. Gamblers Anonymous ought never to endorse, finance, or lend the Gamblers Anonymous name to any related facility or outside enterprise, lest problems of money, property, and prestige divert us from our primary purpose.
7. Every Gamblers Anonymous group ought to be fully self-supporting, declining outside contributions.
8. Gamblers Anonymous should remain forever nonprofessional, but our service centers may employ special workers.
9. Gamblers Anonymous, as such, ought never to be organized; but we may create service boards or committees directly responsible to those they serve.
10. Gamblers Anonymous has no opinion on outside issues; hence the Gamblers Anonymous name ought never to be drawn into public controversy.
11. Our public relations policy is based on attraction rather than promotion; we need always to maintain personal anonymity at the level of press, radio, films, and television.
12. Anonymity is the spiritual foundation of the Gamblers Anonymous program, ever reminding us to place principles before personalities.

Compared to AA, GA is run on a pittance. Even its web page is minimal. Its central office is sparsely staffed, efficiently fielding requests, however faithfully maintaining anonymity. While some of the veneer regarding anonymity is slipping from AA members, GA members are careful to remain circumspect.

The *pressure-relief group* is a feature of GA that other self-help groups do not have. These groups are composed of people who have a longer history of recovery and who volunteer to assist newcomers with legal and financial problems. These problems are often severe. Usually, the group will work to set up a repayment schedule for the newcomer and request that the person inform the group regarding adherence to the schedule. Most pressure-relief groups suggest that finances be turned over to someone else, preferably a family member, if one is available. They generally are staunch advocates of total repayment to creditors, even to unsavory characters. Often the group may provide informal advice regarding previous illegal actions and suggest appropriate lawyers and a course of action that does not compromise moral principles.

Usually, GA meetings begin with the reading of the *Combo Book*, which is similar to the *Big Book* in AA. Following this, members share stories, much as they do in AA. Since discussion tends to be very lively, some meetings restrict *cross comments*, in a manner that many members of AA find stifling. Perhaps because there are fewer meetings, or perhaps because of the subject matter, emotional intensity can occasionally become dramatic. For some reason, however, it is rare to see conflicts spill *out of the rooms* as they sometimes tend to do at AA, and especially at NA.

An advantage of GA is that it offers an immediate set of alternative peers, a strong group dynamic for change, and structured time for the compulsive gambler. On the negative side, the spiritual side of recovery that is common in other 12-step groups has been noted as lacking. There may be less emphasis on feelings in GA and more confrontational rhetoric.

Another problem with GA cited in official literature is the high attrition. By some accounts, less than 5 percent to 10 percent of people who initially participate in GA achieve gambling abstinence at a 5-year period and are still active in the group. It is not known how many people are helped by GA and drop out or are helped by GA and reduce, but do not eliminate their problem or pathological gambling.

Generally, members of GA are willing and eager to work with other treatment providers. However, like Alcoholics Anonymous, they remain entrenched in the classic Disease Model of addiction, described previously. They believe that if gambling is not treated, it will only become worse. Abstinence is seen as a major component of effective treatment. Any type of gambling by the compulsive gambler is bound to result in a return to ruinous wagering.

The beliefs of GA may be different than those held by some more empirically oriented counselors. However, the goals are the same: to help gamblers in trouble. GA members are much more pragmatic than it might seem. The *medication aversion* that is sometimes found in other 12-step groups is rarely encountered. The content of GA can usually be seen as complementary to cognitive therapy modalities (Petry, 2005a). In GA groups in larger cities and where members have regained affluence, it is not rare to find more experienced members undergoing psychoanalysis or other insight-oriented treatments.

The frequency of cooccurring substance abuse in aberrant gamblers suggests that many would benefit from attendance at two self-help groups. Substance abuse rates tend to be two or three times higher than the general population, with at least half of GA members having had a history of alcohol problems. As of 2006, there were few smoke-free GA meetings, partly because many gamblers are addicted to nicotine.

Little is known about GA and women. At one time, GA was largely a male organization. In some areas, this is beginning to change. The culture of GA is starting to reflect values that are often more common among some women, including a respect for family, a need for community, and a desire for continuing nurturance. Regarding ethnicity, even less is known about whether GA is effective for minority members. Until recently, there have not been enough minorities in GA to know this.

GamAnon is a complementary fellowship to GA. GamAnon, like GA, runs on a shoestring budget and keeps a minimal profile. It often meets at the same time as GA and has many conjoint activities.

A quotation from the site sums up GamAnon's role in recovery for the family:

None of our members are here to give you specific advice which you should take as gospel. And we cannot dilute our principles to a point where we perform as marriage counselors, psychologists, members of the clergy, vocational guidance specialists or as a representative of the legal profession.

The Suggested Welcome, which is read at meetings, is unlike similar greetings in other 12-step organizations. The tenth suggestion explicitly states that "Gamblers Anonymous is a program for the compulsive gambler. Loved ones should not interfere."

There are very few studies of GamAnon and few published accounts of how well it works. Experience suggests it is extraordinarily supportive and much less confrontational than might be expected, given the toxicity of some gamblers' behaviors. GamAnon is very practical, with members offering advice about real situations, rather than more emotional insights that often accompany other *coaddictions*.

A weakness of GamAnon as a resource is its lack of availability. While meetings sometimes are scheduled to occur with GA, usually there are just not that many meetings. Furthermore, practically all attendees are heterosexual women who are married to men with gambling problems. Men may attend for a session or two, but usually feel uncomfortable with the mixed format of sharing of intimate feelings and soliciting practical advice. There are also no dedicated gay or lesbian groups that we are aware of. As stated previously, in our experience, there are too few minority participants, though this is changing, in some areas.

There are not any other nationally known groups directly associated with treatment or maintenance of pathological gamblers. A brief review of the Internet showed 60 alternative groups to Alcoholics Anonymous! A few of these groups involve people with particular interests, for example alcoholics and drug abusers who are fans of specific rock bands. Many of these other organizations advertise proprietary *secrets* of sobriety or abstinence for a fee. Some seem reminiscent of the tout sheets that promised to pick racing winners or lottery tickets. Perhaps because they have this flavor and because gamblers have tended to be very cynical, there are no consistent national rivals for GA at this time.

In local areas, there may be support groups for people who were affiliated with specific forms of gambling (e.g., one group in a western state, composed largely of retirees with gambling problems). Many of these people became addicted to recreational bingo following the death of a spouse and came together to seek additional leisure activities. Similarly, on some racetracks there are groups, often run through chaplain services, which are deliberately not based on 12-step programs. Their aim is more preventative and to provide more long-term maintenance rather than to be traditionally recovery oriented. Perhaps as gambling addiction becomes more openly accepted, alternatives to GA will become more common.

Internet Treatment

Internet treatment for clients with gambling disorders has been tried by various practitioners. So far, there are no controlled trials. Clients who use this resource seem to like it. The Internet is readily accessible, is available regardless of geography or of a client's physical or other handicap, is more anonymous, and allows the client to gradually transition into the role of moderation or abstinence.

The Internet delivery program that we have used involves weekly group counseling based on a didactic method outlining some of the common principles of addiction. Clients have no face-to-face contact, though they are encouraged to contact each other, as appropriate. Because this treatment program is new, there are no costs and only a limited number of clients have been treated.

Being free of charge and on an experimental basis, we do not believe, at this time, that Internet services come close to taking the place of traditional counseling or therapy. They are helpful for people who otherwise cannot or will not go to treatment; although they may be risky for people who gamble on the Internet. Additional research is needed to determine who this type of treatment can help.

Formal Treatments

By formal treatment, we mean an organized set of services delivered by professionals. Practitioners need to remember that few gamblers find formal help through traditional sources (Cunningham, 2005). Less than 20 percent find help from outpatient services. We do not know how many people reach out to GA. Only about 1 to 4 percent of pathological gamblers seek inpatient or residential treatment. Expansion of formal treatment opportunities could increase this number substantially.

Formal treatments vary on a continuum of nontraditional interventions, discussed in the following paragraphs, to those of traditional formal treatments. The latter also vary according to treatment acuity, or intensity.

Very Minimal Treatment

Very brief, minimal treatment can involve motivational interviewing, as brief as a single session. It can also involve informal counseling by a physician or other health care provider. For someone contemplating change and ready to undertake the process, this type of degree of intervention may be effective and cost efficient. Recently, some physicians have begun assessing patients for gambling problems and this is a welcomed step. Petry (2005b) illustrates brief and motivational interviews, reviews research support for these interventional modalities, and offers useful concrete examples.

Other researchers believe that very brief and minimally invasive outpatient therapy is important because it emphasizes a person's community ties and present life circumstances. Rosenthal (2004) argues that early intervention may help because it may delay the onset of worse gambling episodes, just like early intervention in depression seems to reduce the likelihood of future depression.

Longitudinal studies will sort out whether minimal interventions can be successful in the long run. Some researchers have suggested that more minimal interventions will be successful for people who have less serious gambling problems, while more intensive ones are for those who have more substantial problems (Robson, Edwards, Smith, & Colman, 2002).

> **IMAGINE THAT!**
> The colorful convicted felon and former governor of Louisiana, Edwin Edwards, held high-stakes poker games at the governor's mansion and gambled frequently in Las Vegas and Europe. To avoid detection, he purportedly used such pseudonyms as E. Nuff, T. Wong, and Muff Alotta, the latter being the name of a popular Cajun sandwich.

Develop a Gambling Intervention Tool Box

Getting a client moving on any action is a step in the right direction. The more the professional works with people with gambling disorders, the more tools and strategies he or she will collect. We encourage professionals to build not only their networks, assessment packages, and treatment strategies, but also an intervention toolbox of actions a client can easily and quickly take that lead in the right direction. We have included an example of 30 small actions a client may take from a toolbox.

Thirty strategies to stay away from gambling:

1. Cut up credit cards.
2. Bar yourself from gambling establishments.
3. Only carry cash.
4. Have a trusted friend/person manage your money.
5. Direct deposit of money.
6. Internet block.
7. Build a budget.
8. Risk training.
9. Go to GA meeting.
10. Have an emergency "to-do list."
11. Follow a journal program.
12. Plan activities in advance to remove the urge to gamble.
13. Avoid "free time" through time management.
14. Try new and stimulating activities.
15. Spend money on other leisure activities.
16. Phone someone first.
17. Have a cap on withdrawal amount.
18. Fun—do something you enjoy.
19. Exercise.
20. Go on a date with a husband/wife/partner.
21. Work the 12-steps.
22. Develop a new hobby.
23. Take a course such as "Building on Self-Esteem."
24. Practice healthy nutrition.
25. Make a plan to repay your gambling debts.
26. Go see a counselor.
27. Attend pressure-relief group meetings to aid with financial problems.
28. Learn to play an instrument.
29. Go stay with friends or family for a while
30. Make a plan and ensure that you don't put yourself in a situation in which there will be the temptation for gambling.

Workbook and Journaling Programs

Some clinicians and researchers have suggested workbook-based therapy. L'Abate and his associates (L'Abate, 2004; L'Abate & Kern, 2002) have been among the most vocal in suggesting structured, manual-driven treatments,

Dylan, Rosemary, and the Jack of Hearts

Dylan, age 22, came in to see a counselor with his fiancée, Rosemary, also 22. Rosemary stated that Dylan was depressed and preoccupied with playing video games. Whenever they went out, he rushed home to play whatever new version of his favorite game was available on their computer. Their communication had broken down and he was becoming sullen, avoidant, and spent more and more hours alone. Based on what she had learned in an abnormal psychology class, Rosemary believed that he might be experiencing major depression. The counselor conducted a normal interview for detecting evidence of major depression. Dylan had none of the core symptoms, though he did report some problems with sleeping and paying attention. His appearance was of an anxious, almost volatile young man, looking as if he were about to be caught at something.

After several sessions, counseling was proceeding without goals or success. The counselor thought that Dylan was having second thoughts about the upcoming marriage and asked him.

Dylan stated that he was comfortable with his future marriage. However, "What I'm not comfortable with is telling her about my debt. I'm not playing video games, you see. Since last year, I'm $30,000 in debt from online poker.

"Give me enough time and I'll make it back, probably before the wedding. What ever you do, don't tell Rosemary."

---

tailored for specific addictions. These types of interventions have proven effective in substance-abusing clients and more recently may be promising for people with problem gambling. They have the advantage of being minimally invasive and inexpensive. They are convenient and do not stigmatize the client.

However, in the study by Pallesen and colleagues (2005), the statistical-effect size was the smallest for treatments associated with workbooks, compared to other techniques, such as cognitive-behavioral interventions. Combined workbook and motivational interviews may work better than either alone, though the literature is not clear here (Hodgins, 2004). One tool we recommend is Howatt's (2000) Journal 45—a program that provides the client with an opportunity to learn about internal locus of control. Rational Emotive Behavioral Therapy (REBT) irrational thinking as well provides a template for daily goal setting and processing of emotions.

Cultural Pathways of Recovery

As discussed Chapter 1, although many gamblers will spontaneously recover from gambling problems, it is not clear what cultural pathways influence this process. Social support is important and may determine whether a person matures out of addiction. When social support is positive, it may be a source of restraint and socialization. Social networks that model negative behavior, on the other hand, can lead to higher base rates of aberrant gambling and may serve as a stimulus for relapse.

The use of cultural resources is dependent upon appropriate models within the culture to emulate. In some communities, these are not present. For example, in middle-class neighborhoods there are few role models for people who spontaneously overcome gambling problems. The prevalent belief is that expensive, formal treatment and on-going involvement in therapy are necessary for any *real progress*. In minority communities it may be more common to find people who stop gambling without treatment because of the idea that formal treatment is an expensive luxury.

Some communities may be more tolerant of rehabilitation. In middle-class and largely white communities, there are few role models for recovery from pathological gambling. When a person goes to jail for a gambling offense, he or she has problems reintegrating into an unforgiving community. In minority communities, there is often more likelihood that a person will find hope and forgiveness.

African-American communities may have strong traditional religious institutions. White practitioners often feel uncomfortable discussing the contributions that the church can make with African Americans and their recovery. When in doubt, it is okay to ask how the church can be of assistance. Latino and Hispanic groups are so heterogeneous that generalizations regarding cultural pathways cannot be made.

Rural poor, including black and white people, often have strong traditional community or religious ties that may seem old fashioned. Community status is frequently related to church attendance and participation. This offers the possibility of redemption, despite past wrongdoings. Often the theology of these churches encourages public confession and making amends.

Sometimes people will recover as a result of general lifestyle changes associated with increased self-efficacy. In our society, this occurs when people take on certain roles. These may include marriage, becoming a parent, entering the workforce, and job promotions. Sometimes a life-threatening experience also will cause a person to stop gambling completely.

Summing Up

From other addictions, we know that there is rarely one treatment that works for all clients. Many clients require multiple treatment episodes and require a variety of services. Addiction, including gambling addiction, impairs motivation. Therefore, traditional approaches that cajole, threaten, or shame people into change are not likely to be effective.

Many forms of psychotherapy can be classified by their similarities. Curative aspects are generally those that empower clients, rather than denigrate, as has been traditionally done in addiction treatment. Among schools of therapy, behavioral and cognitive-behavioral treatments have received the most empirical support.

Theories of recovery determine which direction we proceed with our interventions. Traditional Disease Model theorists believe that compulsive gambling is a progressive disease and can be treated only with total abstinence; treatment must continue for life. Alternative Model theorists believe that addiction is multicausal and diverse treatments are often appropriate. Stage theories, such as those of Prochaska, help conceptualize change as a process, rather than as a state. This approach is often most helpful in determining the timing of interventions.

Key Terms

Levels of care (not to be confused with levels of severity; e.g., Level 2: problem gambler):

Level 0.5. Early intervention for clients who do not meet the criteria of a gambling-related disorder, but who are at high risk.

Level 1. Outpatient treatment. One-on-one interaction, traditionally face-to-face, but now may include telephone or Internet.

Level 2 Intensive outpatient. Structured program of 9+ hours per week.

Level 2 Partial hospitalization. Highly structured program of 20+ hours per week.

Level 3. Hospitalization, either brief or extended.

Alternative model. A model of recovery that is anything other than the Disease Model, and assumes that many factors can cause disordered gambling (not just biological ones). Advocates believe that treatment should be individualized and that, for some, gambling abstinence may not be the best or only desired outcome.

Disease model. A model of recovery whereby disordered gambling is believed to be largely determined by biological factors. It is assumed to be progressive, chronic, and often fatal, requiring intense treatment for the duration of the client's life. This model usually is supported by Gamblers Anonymous.

Motivational toxicity. A loss of ability to be motivated about anything other than the addicting experience.

Personal attributions. The act of attributing success to our personal levels of motivation; consequently, failure at a task means we must have been unmotivated or did not try hard enough. Some counselors make the mistake of reasoning this way, and pass blame to the client.

Pressure-relief groups. A feature of GA, composed of people who have a longer history of recovery and who volunteer to assist newcomers with legal and financial problems.

Recommended Reading

Four levels of care are described, purportedly applicable to every physically addicted person. Available at www.health.org/govpubs/bkd157/101.as0x.

Addiction Counseling Review: Preparing for Comprehensive, Certification and Licensing Exams by Coombs (2005).

Addiction Recovery Tools edited by R. H. Coombs, W. A. Howatt, and K. Coombs (Thousand Oaks, CA: Sage Productions).

Becoming an Addictions Counselor: A Comprehensive Text by Peter L. Myers and Norman R. Salt (2000). A text that comprehensively reviews addictive disorder case management.

Encyclopedia of Behavior Modification and Cognitive Behavior Therapy, Vols. 1–3 by Hersen and colleagues (2005). This is a massive, but magnificent collection that will be your ultimate resource on everything behavioral and only slightly less on everything cognitive behavioral.

Encyclopedia of Cognitive Behavior Therapy by Freeman and colleagues (2005). This is more focused than the previously mentioned volume, and is extremely useful. Every clinic that works with gamblers should have both of these books.

How Do Slot Machines and Other Electronic Gambling Machines Actually Work? by Nigel Turner and Roger Horbay (2004). Available at http://www.camh.net/egambling/issue11/jgi_11_turner_horbay.html.

Integrating the 12-Steps into Addiction Therapy: A Resource Collection and Guide for Promoting Recovery by Finley (2004). The intent of this book is to provide clear explanations and practical tools for clinicians who are considering integrating 12-step participation into their work with their clients or patients and who want to learn more. While primarily appropriate for pharmacological addictions, much of the material transfers to use in gambling. Material is available on a CD-rom and can easily be customized.

Motivational Interviewing: Preparing People to Change Addictive Behavior (2nd ed.) by Miller and Rollnick (2002). One of the best reads for a professional interested in digging into this recovery tool in more detail.

Questions to Consider When Selecting a Treatment Program by The National Council on Problem Gambling.

Transtheoretical Therapy Toward a More Integrative Model of Change by Prochaska and DiClemente (1982). An effective resource that provides an overview of the Transtheoretical/Stages of Change model.

A discussion on the varieties of bipolar cycling can be found at http://www.psycheducation.org.

Association of Family and Conciliation Courts (AFCC; http://www.afccnet.org/) focuses on CHILDREN.

"The Bettor Choice," Problem Gambling and the Family (http://www.dmhas.state.ct.us/gambling/family.htm). Speaks directly to the issue of children affected by disorded gambling family members.

GamAnon (http://www.gam-anon.org/gamanon). All clinicians should become familiar with this web site.

New York University Medical Center Department of Psychiatry (http://www.med.nyu.edu/psych/assets/adult_adhd_1_1.pdf). Additional information regarding the need for screening for ADHD and the previous instrument can be found at this web site.

Responsible Gaming Counsel (http://www.rgco.org). This Ontario group works with individuals and organizations to encourage healthy and responsible gaming and avoid problem and compulsive gambling. The site provides an abundance of new research, often from clinics at the grass-roots level, boldly attempting more novel solutions to gambling than you may find in the more polished university-based studies.

World Health Organization's Adult Self Report Screen (ASRS) by Kessler et al. (2005). A good screening instrument for adult ADHD.

To learn more about the interworking of how a slot machine really works we recommend the Safe@play Slot Machine tutorial at http://www.gameplanit.com.

A current resource providing an overview of many of the recovery tools that addiction professionals are using is William Howatt's Journal series that includes: *Journal 45*—45-days journal program; *Sparkle Kitty*—principle base life lessons: *My Personal Success Coach* and *My Personal Success Coach Journal*—self-help tools for self-discovery and life management that are being currently used to treat persons with addiction disorders. Each product is a workbook or journal e-book. For more information contact A Way With Words at words@ns.aliantzinc.ca.

TESTING YOUR KNOWLEDGE

ANSWERS

1. Enhanced self-efficacy   2. Endorphins   3. Different schools of psychotherapy   4. Is not   5. Think

---

TRUTH OR FICTION

QUIZ ANSWERS

1. False   2. False   3. False   4. True   5. True   6. True   7. True

CHAPTER 6

Continuing Care: When and How Should Clients Be Discharged?

TRUTH OR FICTION QUIZ

After reading this chapter, you should be able to answer the following questions:

1. There is little consensus on what the goals of recovery should be. True or False?

2. Optimally, clients leave treatment when it is programmatically convenient. True or False?

3. Gambling can be conceptualized as a potentially chronic disorder. True or False?

4. *Therapeutic discharge* is a synonym for *step-down* services. True or False?

5. If a client is not making progress, it is not necessary to refer the client for any additional treatment. True or False?

6. Clients are required to give notification if they wish to terminate from treatment in the intensive stage. True or False?

7. Counselors are required to make *equivalent referrals* when clients are terminated or administratively discharged. True or False?

Answers on p. 205.

Highlights of this chapter include how to identify recovery goals. It also provides criteria for exiting a client from treatment and the legal, moral, and ethical issues surrounding it. There are answers and information regarding continuing-care plan procedures and guidelines, and how to assess community resources during the recovery process.

Recovery—What Are the Goals?

The more immediate phases of intervention often are referred to as treatment, while the entire process is usually referred to as recovery. Clinicians concur that the goals of treatment involve cessation or reduction in gambling. However, there is little consensus on what the goals of recovery should be.

Furthermore, we know little about when clients should be discharged or to what types of care. Even if these gaps in our knowledge were filled, we often lack sufficient resources to meet the needs of our clients. This often results in a stilted form of treatment, in which clients are intensely engaged in powerful therapies and then suddenly find there is nothing more available for them. Nor is there much available in the community to help them transition into a more normal life. Unlike alcohol treatment, few communities have sufficient natural resources to help recovering gamblers once they have made it past the initial first steps.

As stated in Chapter 5, there is controversy regarding whether a lifetime commitment to total gambling abstinence is the best way to achieve a satisfactory life for the problem or pathological gambler. The question of a possibility of eventual return to moderated gambling is emotionally laden and outcome data are not clear. At this point, many researchers believe that a reduction in gambling is an appropriate outcome for some gamblers. They cite data showing that many formerly highly pathological gamblers now wager, following therapeutic intervention, apparently at a more reduced and *reasonable* pace. Others disagree and strongly believe that any type of return to gambling is doomed to failure. Some suggest that recovering gamblers may be able to socially gamble by buying a lottery ticket, but must stay away from their games of chance (e.g., VLT) for life.

Regardless of how clinicians feel on the abstinence-restraint gambling controversy, most everyone agrees that gambling is best conceptualized as a *potentially* chronic disease. Presently, we do not know how to *cure* any addiction. We do know ways of managing addictions, including gambling disorders. Often, we can do so very successfully.

According to the addictionologist Thomas McClellan and his associates (2000), addiction treatment should be administered and delivered similarly to the way treatment is delivered in other unremitting or chronic conditions. Sometimes, lifetime treatment may be necessary, as it is for diabetes, many forms of heart disease, or hypertension. Relapses, unfortunately, are characteristic of all addictions and are often endemic. Limiting our clients to only a few treatment sessions, as some providers do, may produce poor results.

Arbitrarily drawing a line between when a gambling client has *recovered* and when he or she might need additional care often fails to address the complex and vicious nature of gambling addiction. The current cost-containment fad in behavioral health care is to provide a very limited number of sessions and then to pronounce a disorder as *cured*. People who relapse are then considered *untreatable* and do not receive additional help. This is logically outlandish. Services should be available to anyone who needs them, regardless of whether they have *completed treatment* in the past or not. Ideally, recovery from addictive gambling is the cessation of all gambling problems throughout the client's lifetime *and* the substitution with more positive, more gratifying, and healthy behaviors. This is a process that may demand ongoing intervention at various times in life.

Criteria for Exiting Clients from Supervised Treatment

Too often, a criterion for exiting a program is that clients have exhausted insurance. It is also common to administer a fixed number of treatment sessions, whether four or twelve or thirty. Clients then are considered to have reached *maximum therapeutic benefit* and are discharged from treatment.

A more preferable way of determining exiting criteria is whether the client has sufficient resources for recovery. In this scenario, clients would no longer be permanently discharged any more than patients with chronic illnesses are discharged. We dispose of the idea of cure that has been leftover from early twentieth century psychoanalysis. We also avoid the clumsy term *remission* and its biomedical fatalism. Acceptance of the concept of remission implies an inevitability to relapse that might become a self-fulfilling prophecy.

Optimally, *clients leave treatment when they have the self-efficacy to cope with their own gambling problems.* This may involve mastery of skills in a discrete time frame. Clients may receive additional interventions as necessary, such as medication, stress reduction, or behavioral therapy. As previously mentioned, using the term *reversion* implies that a person has strived for and reached a higher stage, though the person may also slip back periodically, occasionally, even routinely.

These distinctions are not merely semantic. They indicate that people can and do get better over the long term. Their setbacks and temporary negative situations are not necessarily predictable in advance. They may require diverse services, including more comprehensive treatment, at various times in their recovery trajectories. We expect progress, but understand that addiction is chronic and some deviation from the linear pathway is realistic.

Different services can be provided during periods of reversion, depending on what is necessary. If clients revert, they may be monitored more frequently with checkups. At checkup times, the counselor can check recovery-based behaviors (self-help participation, avoidance of relapse triggers), health-promoting behaviors (exercise, healthy eating, sleeping patterns), and the client's mental health (stress, depression, mood instability, and anxiety).

However, the responsibility of detecting evidence of reversion is shared with the client. This shift in responsibility makes clients critical partners in the process of managing their own addictions. In fact, aggressive *help-seeking* by clients, following a detection of a problem, is viewed encouragingly. Eventually, the stigma associated with reversion and early detection will disappear as *addiction self-management* becomes more accepted. Imagine how different our behavioral health care system would be if clients could call their counselors following a reversion and be greeted in an optimistic and hopeful spirit, rather than shamed!

Discharge Criteria for Different Problem Intensities

Almost everyone accepts that treatment should be tailored to meet each client's needs. Unfortunately, a uniform *one-size-fits-all* approach is often used for discharge. Not surprisingly, it does not work well, and many clients complete treatment and then are lost to rapid reversions without appropriate follow-up intervention.

Traditionally, discharge often occurred when a counselor determined that a client was *well*, whatever that means. For example, in 12-step programs, a client might have had to work through a certain number of GA-related steps, as judged by a counselor or a therapeutic community. Theoretically, this provides a degree of flexibility to better meet the needs of the client. Too often, however, a number of factors combine to produce discharge criteria without any validity or reliability. Clients with insurance, or who were therapeutically congenial to work with, often are kept longer in treatment. Sometimes, those with the greatest need seem to be discharged first. Effective treatment programs specify at the beginning what behavioral criteria are required for discharge.

Operational definitions of discharge, or step-down criteria, offer some improvement on subjectivity. These delineate the length of treatment or participation in a specific number of treatment modules. Many of the popular cognitive-behavioral treatment programs are time-limited and structured to include a particular number of content modules. Clients are ready for discharge when they complete the treatment or a certain number of these modules.

Evidence-based discharge, or step-down, occurs when clients fulfill a number of criteria to show that they are ready for the next phase of treatment. This evidence may be behavioral (e.g., when a client shows that he can avoid gambling for a specific period of time and can find alternative leisure activities). This evidence may be a change in the score of a particular instrument, such as the SOGS (South Oaks Gambling Screen). Evidence may also be more subjective, based on the client's mastery of addiction concepts that are thought to be necessary for successful treatment.

Client-centered discharge, or step-down, stresses the notion that discharge should be based on behavioral criteria obtained from individually negotiated treatment plans. These treatment plans should be constructed with the client at the first session and should clarify how success will be measured. If done correctly, this helps motivate the client further by personalizing goals and tying them to progress involving behavioral changes associated with gambling.

Too often, practitioners view treatment plans as interruptions in service, rather than as opportunities for enhanced motivation. By using the treatment plan as a roadmap for how the client can reasonably expect to change, the client is empowered to continue in treatment and to make the necessary transformation.

Level 2 Gambling Problems and Mastery-Based Discharge: Using Cognitive Corrections

Mastery-based discharge can be structured around whether clients have successfully mastered common cognitive themes that are often misunderstood by gamblers. Some common examples are as follows:

1. Gambling is an inexpensive pastime or cheap entertainment for me.
2. The longer I play, the more likely I am *due* to hit (a lack of realization about the separation of events in gambling).
3. I have to gamble to have a good time.
4. Gambling relaxes me or is good for my physical or mental health.
5. I am more fun to be around when I gamble.
6. Machines or gambling venues are *due* to pay off at specific times.
7. Gambling is a skill-based game.
8. Smart people have an advantage in gambling.
9. Other idiosyncratic distortions, such as "My wife likes me better when I gamble," or "I can relate to my boss better when I gamble."

Since there is no paper-and-pencil test to determine whether the client believes these or not, it is usually necessary for the clinician to ask the client why the statement is not true and evaluate the client's answer in the same way as if scoring an intelligence test. This is an inexact method, but one that is better than subjective assessment without tapping the client's cognitive beliefs.

For Level 2 gamblers, we do not address cognitions specific to the loss of control. Once people feel that they have lost control in the presence of the casino, bookie, or other gambling stimulus, they almost always meet criteria for Level 3 gamblers and require more stringent treatment for discharge or step-down of services.

Level 3 Gambler Discharge or Step-Down Criteria

Mastery discharge also can occur for Level 3 gamblers, although it is more complex to measure. For Level 3 gamblers, the first concern is that these clients have basic psychiatric stabilization. This level of treatment must continue until there is substantially less psychiatric distress than was present when they entered treatment.

Table 6.1 illustrates some other concerns that should be addressed and resolved before discharging someone into a less intense treatment modality. These are in addition to those in Level 2 discharge. Some of these can be documented as having been mastered through clinical judgment. Some of these can be documented by a clinical interview. Some of these criteria are services that are received without any indication of specific success.

Table 6.1: Criteria for Level 3 Gamblers to be Discharged

- Understanding of the dynamics of the chase

- Mastery of concepts of partial rewards and other relevant schedules of reinforcement

- Obtaining financial counseling

- Obtained help and support for other co-exisitng addictive disorders, if appropriate

- Introduction to GA and related groups

- Introduction to family therapy, if appropriate

- Vocational evaluation, if appropriate

- Psychiatric, psychological evaluations, if appropriate

- Reduction in acute stressors, which may lead to gambling

- Leisure counseling, if appropriate

- Addressing physical, instrumental needs, such as housing, shelter

---

Discharging clients merely because they are free of the immediate urge to gamble has never received empirical support. It is unlikely that self-reports regarding treatment success are accurate at this stage, as they are likely to be inflated and overly optimistic.

Discharge Criteria and Concerns during Various Stages of Recovery

Discharge during treatment may occur for a variety of reasons. Clients may want treatment to end, or the service provider may become unavailable, with no one to fulfill the need. Clients may realize that they are not ready for change and may decide, in conjunction with the therapist, to continue treatment at a later date.

Often, clients will seek discharge at the very beginning of treatment. The benefits of gambling suddenly outweigh the costs, and they are no longer interested in wagering reduction or cessation. Or, clients may reconsider and no longer see major consequences to their gambling. On the basis of Prochaska's model, a client may be in an earlier stage than he or she initially appeared on intake. The best you can do is provide the client additional information and avoid stigma. Stay away from adding to the client's sense of failure that therapy is something that "I've already tried and failed."

The first stage of recovery is often labeled as intensive *treatment*. At this time, the client usually receives the maximum therapeutic *dosage* of whatever is to be administered. During this period, clients are usually supervised more than they will be at a later period and often a counselor is available for contact via phone or other mechanism whenever there is an emergency.

Abrupt discharge during intensive treatment usually is based on several indications that the client is not responding well to services. Discharge may be to a more appropriate, higher level of services, or to a lower level, in the case in which problem severity has been misidentified. A client may have been diagnosed as having a gambling problem when, in reality, the client was experiencing a bipolar disorder.

IMAGINE THAT!

For the 2006 NCAA Men's Tournament, there were over 1,200 types of bets that could be made on the Internet. These included the obvious, such as who would win or be in the Final Four; they also included *real-time* wagering on which player would score the next foul shot or score two baskets in a row. The extreme rapid action and frequent changing of betting odds may make this year's version of Internet wagering more attractive—and addictive.

Typically, once clients have completed some type of intense treatment, they receive *step-down* services. This is a technique common in cognitive-behavioral and behavioral service delivery and involves either decreasing sessions or providing booster sessions at a later date. This is often the highest risk period for most clients, apart from those people who simply terminate treatment at unpredictable times.

The goal of a controlled discharge during this period is to reduce relapse by fostering the structure that promotes ongoing recovery. Ideally, a person uses this time to be *faded* from the intense level of services provided in the acute treatment phase. Some clients are not able to manage a step-down transition. Care providers need to recognize this and plan accordingly. If gambling and other addictions are assumed to truly be chronic, then it is appropriate to treat people for prolonged periods, as in the case of hypertension or diabetes. Treatment may need to be open ended and periodic, as needed.

Optimally, there is contact with a counselor during this early period of recovery. In this stage, clients are learning how to replace gambling-related addictive thoughts, feelings, and behaviors with alternative thoughts, feelings, and behaviors. Practitioners planning a discharge during this phase need to be very mindful of the client's capacity to find alternative addictive experiences. One risk to manage is other addictive disorders (e.g., a person quits gambling and starts drinking). It is important to manage risk and discharge when the odds are stacked in favor of risk mitigation as much as possible.

Some clinicians have noted that people in this phase are apt to discover other problems that may be *more primary* to them. For example, they may believe they have a bipolar disorder requiring treatment or an ongoing developmentally related problem with particular authority figures. They may be forced to decide between gambling treatment, which they believe is essentially completed, and additional treatment aimed at a broader domain. At this time, there seem to be many client transfers from one practitioner to another. There is an open-door policy that, should gambling become a more primary concern, the client should return immediately.

A mutual and optimal discharge is most commonly planned during the Maintenance Phase of treatment. This phase occurs when clients avoid the harmful effects of gambling but also find their own pace for recovery. Clients are able to weave their life narratives into a coherent story in which the addiction saga of gambling is but one area of their journey, one stop on their quest. Clients almost always are able to terminate successfully, though they may do so with the door wide open if they have future problems.

Discharge and the Developmental Recovery Processes

One finding from numerous AOD studies is that a long-term recovery process often requires multiple episodes of treatment. As with other chronic illnesses, relapses in gambling addiction may occur even after successful treatment. As reiterated in the Principles of Effective Treatment in Chapter 5, addicted people may need prolonged and multiple treatment episodes to meet their goals and progress through life. With this in mind, we do not prescribe a single pathway that applies to all clients. However, Figure 6.1 identifies common themes in recovery that often change as a person begins to move away from the immediacy of addiction and into other aspects of the life of recovery.

In early recovery there is a preoccupation with the addictive stimulus as excessively powerful. This occurs for good reason. A person has very recently been under very substantial *stimulus control.* The 12-step expression of avoiding people, places, and things summarizes the need to avoid stimuli that can exert this control.

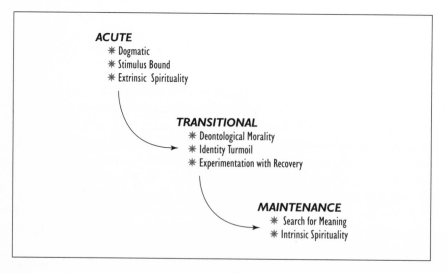

Figure 6.1: Common phases of gambling recovery.

The recovering clients in early stages also tend to redefine their life histories into a period before and after recovery. At times, to outsiders, this dichotomy seems forced and even arbitrary; however, it often is necessary in order to change the strong associations with the addictive experience. By redefining who we are, we change our associative networks around our addictions, allowing our new selves to be less influenced by addictive stimuli.

In the middle recovery periods, clients often attempt to repair the lifestyle damages caused by their gambling addictions and develop a more balanced and healthy way of living. They may begin the process of experimenting with alternative modes of recovery. For example, they may reduce formal treatment but become more involved in activities that assist personal or social growth. As abstinence solidifies or *crystallizes*, more routine aspects of life become less problematic. For example, the gambler can attend church without thinking of stealing the collection plate and running off to visit a casino.

Therapists often note that clients can *burn out* during this period. There is no empirical research that this is true or even a good definition of what this means. However, teach clients to pay attention to their own mental health needs to avoid entering into classic codependent relationships with self-help groups and people that they sponsor. Teach them to manage their time commitments conservatively. Some changes in client motivation and attitude during this period may be the results of affect or mood instability, and this may be addressed in other areas of treatment.

During the Maintenance phase, clients continue a program of growth and development and maintain an active-recovery program to assure that they don't slip back into old addictive patterns. Some clients affiliate with 12-step groups for life. Others transition to alternative activities such as church or civic groups. Still others look for additional sources of meaning in their lives. Some simply put the nightmare of addiction behind them and want to bury the experience.

There is no empirical evidence that one way or path is the best or even which is likely to be the safest. Clients who relapse during the Maintenance phase are often quick to ascribe this to failure to *work a program* during recovery. On the other hand, there are many anecdotal accounts of clients who work programs but experience relapses. The counselor or therapist needs to be honest with clients. We do not know whether affiliation with GA and ongoing counseling will reduce relapses, though we suspect that, for many people, it will. For others, the advantage may be minimal and outweighed by other factors.

Continuing Care Plan Procedures and Guidelines

Continuing care needs to ensure that clients have access to services when they need them again. Procedures should be in place to set up ongoing mental health and other services prior to their need (Wiger, 2005). As mentioned often, aberrant gambling (like other addictions), is a chronic disease necessitating treatment for life. This may place a burden on record keeping and it may be helpful to invest in some form of automated system that reduces paperwork.

Statutory requirements and ethical standards mandate that all clients must have some written and realistic plan for continuing care. Even those who are discharged for *therapeutic reasons* must have access to appropriate services. Otherwise, clinicians risk ethical problems and charges of *abandonment,* which can have serious ethical implications. Counselors may not stop providing services for those with high probabilities of treatment failure; nor may they stop out of anger or the belief that the client is at high risk for future relapse. If other appropriate services are not immediately available for clients, then counselors may not cease treatment. This includes withholding of treatment for nonpayment (Nagy, 2005).

Discharge plans have to be realistic, with a genuine likelihood that the client can complete them in a reasonable fashion. For example, having the client take three or four different forms of public transportation to get to one appointment following a hard day's work is not a realistic goal for a discharge plan. Above all, document discharge plans (Luepker, 2003) and discuss them with the client.

Remember, you may be asked in litigation or by your ethics board why your discharge plans were structured as they were. Each aspect must be defensible, for your own good as well as for the client's (Knapp & VandeCreek, 2006). When in doubt, seek peer review, keeping the name of the client confidential in the process.

CASE STUDY

Sam—Shuffled Around

Sam is 34 and has been in treatment in four outpatient facilities. He has relapsed severely three times. He notes the following:

"I do okay as long as I am seeing a counselor a couple of times a week. But when they try to cut me back to once a month or so, that's when I [screw] up. I just don't do well unless I can get counseling every week. I go to GA, but that doesn't seem to do it.

"I just feel like the counselors have this idea that I'm cured at the end of their program. You know, if the program has 20 sessions, then all my problems are supposed to be gone by then. If the program lasts 3 months and has three sessions a week, I'm cured at the end of 90 days.

"It would be nice if I was. But I just feel that every time I go through one of these programs, I just shut another door behind me, if you know what I mean?

"I'll probably always need some kind of help to stay off the bet. I just hope I can find it."

In some clinics, many clients are discharged involuntarily for any number of reasons. Attorneys advise special care for these so-called *therapeutic discharges* that practitioners have chosen without full cooperation from the client. (Exceptions are made when the client threatens the therapist.) For a general discussion on these issues, see the excellent books by Handelsman, Gottlieb, and Knapp (2005), which, although not specific to addictions or gambling, are good sources of information concerning ethical issues.

The consensus is that when these clients are terminated, the practitioner must provide them with alternative referrals. However, practitioners must be careful with the types of referrals and cannot be cavalier. Relevant to clients in the United States, where clients may pay privately, practitioners must provide *referrals that have a similar fee as the original treating provider. Standards of care dictate that you cannot refer to someone who is more expensive, if this would place an undue burden on the client.* This is a potential problem for those providers who discount their fees and the client cannot afford to pay the discounted charge. (Often, these providers may be *done in* by their best intentions; be careful not to assume too many obligations.)

If the client was making progress, you must give referrals that have a similar "theoretical orientation." For example, a provider cannot simply refer a client to GA.

If the client was not making progress, practitioners *can refer the client to another option, such as a different modality.* In fact, in many cases, practitioners are ethically required to at least evaluate their treatment and consider whether other methodologies might be more appropriate.

The referral option cannot be *transparent.* An example: One counselor worked in an outpatient clinic. She noted that clients who were therapeutically discharged were given the address of the county general hospital in case of a crisis. It would have been apparent to anyone that this was simply an administrative ruse, destined to *turf* clients elsewhere.

Counselors may fulfill the legalities of statutory requirements by performing only minimal standards of continuing care. Quality clinical interventions go beyond this and address concerns proactively, through monitoring of continuing care plans, procedures, and guidelines. Avoid problems with transitioning clients by addressing these and other similar concerns:

1. Clients need to receive advance notice of termination or transition dates. Remind them frequently and loudly.
2. Clients need to have an advanced understanding of the rationale for transitioning or termination. Explain this in a non-punitive manner that clients can understand, and phrase it in the most therapeutic language possible. This means that if the client has an eighth-grade education, use eighth grade language. Do not use legal speak to protect your self. To our knowledge, no court has sided with therapists who have confused clients with complicated treatment plans.

3. Prior to any transition to less intensive services, clients need to have an opportunity to ask any questions and solve any of their misunderstandings. This is especially important in a very structured program, such as a workbook-administered program. Sometimes clients will complete these programs and then ask "Why haven't I seen a counselor?" Or "When will I see a counselor?" At that point the practitioner suddenly realizes that the whole intervention has been somewhat unsuccessful. The client never grasped many points of the essential intervention! It's good that the counselor knows this; it's too bad the counselor did not know it earlier.

4. There is also a growing sentiment that clients need to be provided with additional referrals at the time of transition, in case they believe that the continuity of care is inadequate or insufficient. Clients may find that levels of treatment provided are not congruent with their needs. Ethics boards have suggested that these may represent subtle but serious issues that counselors and therapists need to consider.

5. Anticipate problems in the transitioning and discuss them with clients. Document that you have discussed them.

6. Remember, clients can terminate any time that they want. They do not have to give a reason, nor do they have to terminate in the manner in which the counselor chooses. The counselor does not have the option to pressure clients to return for a termination session or to complete paperwork, once they make it clear that they wish to end services. Do not call up a client to get a signature on a termination document, despite what your supervisor requires.

7. Although there are no specified number of sessions required prior to termination, community standards and ethics boards are taking an increasingly serious view of cases where clients are discharged with insufficient treatment and discharge plans. For questions about this, consult with peers.

8. Begin thinking of client discharging before the details of treatment. This means, have an idea of what the discharge services should involve (e.g., What changes would you like to make in clients' lives? What will they be like when they leave, compared to when they came?).

This list is not exhaustive. There are many more concerns that the skillful and caring therapist constantly considers prior to discharge. By anticipating problems, transition into appropriate levels of treatment can be accomplished more smoothly.

Legal, Moral, and Ethical Issues

Addictions counselors, along with other mental health professionals, are ethically and morally bound to provide appropriate pre-termination counseling regarding available options prior to ending any therapeutic relationship. This includes a discussion of options if terminated, whether or not the client wants intensive treatment, or if the client cannot afford the fees associated with treatment. Clients who are discharged or denied services because of therapeutic issues (e.g., their own behaviors of missing sessions, continuing gambling, use of alcohol or other drugs, etc.) cannot be summarily denied additional treatment options (Nagy, 2005). Otherwise, counselors risk ethical charges of abandonment or improper termination, which may be a serious concern.

Proper and Improper Methods of Termination

To begin the termination process with a client who has not suggested termination is a trickier issue than many practitioners assume. Policies and procedures should be in place. Furthermore, these should include behavioral criteria that highlight frequency and reduce necessity to rely on clinical judgment and subjective assessment of clients' motivations and intentions.

These policies should be subject to peer and outside review and should be in place before termination issues arise. Clients should be aware of them, optimally having them explained and noting through written consent that they have participated in this process. For clients who may be litigious or a danger to themselves or others, peer consultation is important. It is recommended that procedures following termination be presented to the client in writing and that, if possible, clients sign for these. If no signature is available, for example if the client has missed many appointments, it should be noted why the client did not sign.

CASE STUDY

Cincinnati Simon: Gambling Munchausen's?

Cincinnati Simon was actually from Oregon, but chose the moniker to honor the famous gambler, Pittsburg Phil, the first professional horse player. Simon had once been an absolutely audacious gambler who would bet on anything at anytime. However, he had not gambled in years, with the help of therapy—lots of therapy.

Simon's pattern in life involved lots of moves to pursue jobs in the defense industry. When he would find a new town, he also would find a new counselor or, in some cases, two or three. He would run up hundreds and thousands of dollars of therapy bills and then suddenly vanish. He repeated this pattern for ten years, until apparently he tired of it.

Between the requirements for confidentiality, the occasional pseudonyms he may have used, and the numerous addresses that he had, no one was the wiser. Besides, what would anyone do? Simon seemed so appreciative of therapy and seemed to be making such progress. He was so convincing! He just never paid a single bill.

By accident, several counselors found that they had been part of Simon's common pattern. There was nothing to do but live and learn.

Your supervisor may be concerned that the client signs multiple copies of each form. You, on the other hand, are more concerned that the client *understands* one copy. Guess what? You are correct. If serious repercussions arise from issues concerning transfer of services, you will be the one grilled, not your boss. Frankly, the regulatory agencies concerned, will not stand behind you when it comes to whether clients understand the documents imposed on the health-care population. If you have doubts, find a lawyer *before* you have trouble or make a legal or ethical error (Pope & Vasquez, 2005). Do not rely on malpractice insurance to "bail you out" of these situations. They may fall short of expectations.

If you have heard this 1000 times but believe it will not happen to you, since you are a well-meaning person—wrong!

Invest in an attorney as a new form of catastrophic insurance coverage. Aggressively reduce your risk by following the advice of a legal expert in detail. Make sure this individual understands mental health concerns. The chapter by Pope and Vasquez (2005) will orient you to the process of how to find a mental health attorney before you have problems.

We cannot stress enough that unscrupulous clients and litigation agents may make your life as a gambling therapist occasionally challenging and complex. Please do not let this get in the way of quality treatment. However, be aware that any of your activities could involve court or judicial review. Act as if all of your documents and interventions will be reviewed by a hostile attorney. You might be subpoenaed. Your records could be encumbered. Be prepared to know what your next step will be before you are in a crisis.

Abandonment

Abandonment is often used by clients as grounds for legal or ethical complaints. Abandonment may be claimed when counselors do not make themselves available when the client needs services. It may involve counselors failing to establish appropriate after-hours contact procedures for clients who are experiencing an emergency. It also may involve clients who have been suddenly terminated for therapeutic reasons, which often means the client is not paying his bills or is still gambling.

IMAGINE THAT!
One online gambling site in 2005 featured an ad from an attorney offering to take the cases of gamblers who were "mistreated by counselors and therapists."

The slick brochures for an attorney placed on cars at an East Coast race track in 2004 promised to represent anyone on contingency who had been "unfairly accused of being a pathological gambler."

Gamblers in trouble often are desperate for cash and may be tempted to take unscrupulous legal action against you. We have seen more than one case where an attorney solicited clients for exaggerated claims that have almost been settled. There is a great deal of desperation. You can minimize these problems by following procedures that reduce transitional friction.

Assessing Community Resources

As mentioned, *community resources are important to consider when discharging a client.* The process is much easier if practitioners discharge clients to a town that supports recovery by providing many services that the recovering gambler needs. However, there are no formal ways of measuring the potential resources that a community has and how they can be used for recovery.

Since there are no scales or numbers that can be attached to this assessment, the following questions may be helpful

1. Are there other recovering people in town?
2. Are these people willing to assist others in recovery? Reasonably, many people prefer to maintain anonymity regarding their gambling problem.
3. Are there any GA meetings? If so, the downside is that there are likely more stimuli associated with relapse as well, such as casinos and lotteries.
4. If the client is involved in other 12-step groups, do these groups comprehend the dynamics of gambling disorders? Some 12-step groups insist that gambling cannot fit into the Disease Model, because it does not have a substance that is toxic. The counselor may have to educate other 12-step groups about gambling and differences between this disorder and chemical addictions.
5. Is there a community-based or accessible psychiatrist who understands gambling (preferably) or addictions? Pharmacological intervention with gamblers may be vastly different from other addictions. As many as three quarters of people in GA may be on some form of psychotropic medication. This antimedication bias that is common in 12-step groups is not common in GA.
6. If a psychiatrist is not available, is there someone else in the medical community that fits this description?
7. Does the community have formal leisure resources besides gambling? In many towns that are experiencing the growth that comes from placement of a casino, there may be few other leisure options besides gambling. People often erroneously believe that there is always something to do for the creative person who chooses to find it. This is not necessarily so. In many small towns, life may revolve around the casino.
8. Are there a range of options for the client's spiritual quest? If clients find that they cannot manage their recovery within the confines of their previous religious involvement, are they able to find a different *spiritual home*? In many areas, spirituality may be rigidly tied to one approach or denomination. As people recover, their views of God and religion may become broader, and unless communities are able to support that, it could serve as a serious impediment to recovery.

IMAGINE THAT!

Strange Odds and Wagers Found at Internet Wagering Sites

The world will end by 2010	10,000/1
President Bush is a space alien	5,000/1
A nuclear war will break out somewhere in the world by 2010	4/1
A vaccine for HIV will be discovered by 2010	18/1
The Chicago Cubs will win the World Series	Various odds, all high

9. Are there employment opportunities? Often, some of the better opportunities come from networking through other pathological gamblers who are at a more advanced stage of recovery.

10. Are there mental health and counseling services for family members? As many as three quarters of families will need individual, group, or family therapy if they have a member who has a gambling disorder. This is easier to access in some towns than others.

11. Is the town or community open and *prorecovery*? This may be harder to ascertain. However, some towns and cities seem much more willing to give people the needed additional chance. Others refuse to adopt anything but an extraordinarily rigid, moralistic model regarding addictions.

12. Is health care available for the gambler and family during the fragile early stages of recovery? In many cases, previously proud, high-functioning people will be on some form of public assistance. The administrative structures involved in delivering these services vary state by state in the United States. Levels of services also differ.

Organizing Recovery Supports Where Lacking

There are some things professionals can do when discharging people into communities that have few recovery supports. Encourage the pathological gambler, along with others in recovery, to organize a GA meeting. Often, this is more of a commitment than organizing an AA meeting, because the emotional demands of GA usually are more intense than those associated with AA.

Professionals can encourage the client to have a liaison with Alcoholics Anonymous. As stated earlier, AA is agreeable in most situations regarding the inclusion of pathological gambling. In some locations there are a few *old-timers* who resist the notion that AA should be open to anyone except those with a drinking problem. However, during the past 15 years, most towns have adopted a more *California variety* eclectic AA that is more open to multiple addictions. Care needs to be taken here. Some people with gambling disorders are active participants in AA and other 12-step groups but, in one case, an AA group met weekly in the lounge of a newly opened casino.

Professionals also can encourage clients to attempt alternative forms of recovery such as Rational Recovery. These alternatives are discussed in the volume by Coombs and Howatt (2005).

Styles of Recovery: Methods of Disease Management

Styles of recovery refer to patterns in which people acquire wager-free or wager-controlled life directions. Often, people develop a style of recovery as a way of disease management. These may or may not involve traditional services and traditional conceptualizations of addiction. Usually, people develop these styles after having engaged in some formal treatment, though not always. With the advent of the Internet, many people are approaching treatment with their own style already defined, based on what they have read.

The therapeutic community has tended to endorse only one style of recovery: complete abstinence and *working a program* with professional intervention and 12-step involvement. This is based on the AA model, in which recovery is often promoted as a lifestyle. There are options for recovery other than total lifestyle immersion, and there is no evidence that one style of recovery is best for any particular person.

As explained in Chapter 1, people may mature out of problem or pathological gambling. This is less likely for people who have extreme problems, other psychiatric difficulties, or more complex social situations. For these people, formal treatment is recommended as a style of recovery.

Attendance at GA alone without other treatment is often pursued by many people as an appropriate recovery. Most clinicians believe that GA, when used alone, is not very effective. This belief may be due to the fact that people who attend GA as the sole treatment often are the most impaired and have the most social and financial problems. We need more data on these high-risk people before we can recommend GA as the sole method of recovery. If it works for some, that is good. However, clients probably will need to supplement it with something else.

Some people have criticized recovering gamblers who identify strongly with GA as tending to substitute one addiction for another. This seems like a superfluous criticism, because problem or pathological gambling is psychiatrically devastating and may be fatal. A more appropriate concern might be that family and other obligations are neglected because of over involvement with GA. Take care not to superimpose personal values on the client and the client's family. The enthusiastic pursuit of recovery is often an appropriate goal, provided that other obligations and instrumental goals are not neglected.

For others, contact with GA may be helpful, but transitory. These clients want to take what they can from 12-step treatment and then move on. The key variables involve whether GA meets the client's unique needs. GA may be particularly suited for the early days of gambling abstinence. Members have concrete strategies for coping and for financial restitution. As abstinence is maintained through time, there may be less need for this basic treatment and the client may search for other areas of support or interest.

As mentioned, many people recover through spiritual renewal that is independent of professional interventions. For example, they may discover or rediscover a faith and, through a personal transformation, cease gambling. Unfortunately, for each person who experiences this genuine spiritual recovery, there are probably several pretenders. These people find that their addiction exists as a life apart from their faith and soon find that good people can be pathological gamblers and do bad things. If they are unable to resolve this paradox, they often will oscillate between extremes of religion and frenetic periods of wagering.

Another style of recovery discussed in Chapter 1 is gambling reduction. The gambler gradually slows down wagering. This may occur over a period of months or even years. The sudden emotional outbursts and frenzied elation that accompanies winnings are replaced with the doldrums of the grinding and almost monotonous wagering patterns. While there may be peaks and valleys of enjoyment, the end tedium is the same. Why gambling becomes boring to some people and not to others is unknown.

This type of extinction typically shows a *spontaneous recovery*, which occurs when there is a brief return to some degree of the previous behavior. Usually these *extinction bursts*, as psychologists like to call them, are short-lived and, if not directly reinforced, are soon extinguished.

Yet another style of recovery is change that accompanies therapy for other problems. This is common in cognitive therapy, as the following case demonstrates.

Chris, a 36-year-old business executive, entered cognitive therapy for depression and for a number of relationship failures. During the sixth session of therapy, Chris mentioned to her therapist that she could not pay her therapy bill because she had spent too much money on Internet wagering. The therapist inquired further and determined that Chris had a problem, not only with Internet wagering, but also with wild speculation regarding penny stocks, television bingo, television horse racing, and Internet poker. However, all of these gambling ventures follow rejections in relationships. The therapist decided to concentrate on depression and obtained a promise from Chris that she would not gamble until treatment was over. Chris was able to keep her promise. Treatment was successful, and she did not gamble excessively again.

Many people who recover from AOD find recovery in alternative lifestyles, such as pursuing art, music, aesthetics, Eastern spirituality, and perhaps a simplified life. There is no empirical data regarding this, but our clinical impression is that few gamblers in recovery take these paths, at least initially. The *satori* that accompanies alcoholics' moments of clarity may be less common in gambling.

A style of recovery that has recently emerged that has been rooted in GA involves a radical abandonment of finances. In GA, pressure-relief groups encourage gamblers who are in financial trouble to turn over finances to someone else, such as another group member. Some people take this further and have chosen to abandon money completely, as much as possible. After repaying whatever debts they owe, they live life as a volunteer, perhaps working for a nonprofit agency, basically without money, which they see as an unnecessary temptation. They dedicate their lives to making amends by doing whatever they can to help humanity through radical volunteering and communitarianism. While this type of recovery is not for everyone, it is an intriguing extreme for some people.

Spheres of Recovery

This topic refers to the question concerning which areas are altered during a recovery. Reasonably, clients and their families want to know "What will change?" Often, this question should be rephrased as "What can change?" or "What is reasonable to expect if I cease pathological gambling?" These questions often are not so subtle requests for additional information so that clients can weigh the costs of change and the benefits associated with new behaviors.

It is important that the counselor, therapist, or referring agent not overplay the immediate advantages of gambling treatment. Often, gambling cessation provides few immediate benefits. The smoker, excessive drinker, or drug user feels better in days or weeks. The gambler may feel only tension and anxiety, compounded by financial frustration and despair that is no longer escapable through fantasy and distraction. Full disclosure of the courage to recover is required for long-term success.

However, counselors often overlook that gamblers improve physically. Sexual health also improves. No research presently has been undertaken to suggest whether sexual satisfaction increases following gambling cessation. Our hunch is that it does. Usually couples, in which one or both have gambling problems, do not have the time for good, or even passable, sex.

Mental health is another sphere of recovery. Problem and pathological gambling cause anxiety, depression, aberrant thinking, avoidance, and low self-esteem. Although symptom reduction does not occur immediately, there will be an improvement in these areas.

Uncle John's John

An online gambling site recently purchased the toilet of Jerry Garcia, late guitarist and cofounder of the legendary rock group, the Grateful Dead. Perhaps they intended to display this salmon colored, otherwise nondescript item to fans, possibly at traveling exhibitions. However, the toilet was stolen and its whereabouts remain unknown. This only added to the media hype.

The same gambling venue bought a number of other items sure to generate immediate interest. These included a 10-year-old, half-eaten grilled cheese sandwich, with an apparent likeness of the Virgin Mary, purchased for $28,000 on ebay. Another "popular" item is Pope Benedict's VW Golf, purchased for an astounding $244,590.83.

Family and Concerned Others Involvement and Spheres of Recovery

Unlike drugs or alcohol, we do not know much about recovery processes of families of problem and pathological gamblers. Earlier accounts suggested that once a gambler stopped, the system would return to a degree of normal behavior and all would be well. Obviously, this does not fit the experience of most clinicians. Based on the theory of McCown and Johnson (1993), we hypothesize that routine family recovery may not be possible in some situations. These are the conditions under which the psychological identity of other family members is involved in maintaining the gambling. For example, a husband who has gained a positive community reputation of *long suffering* will have problems when his wife stops gambling, compared to someone with less of a public emotional investment. Examples of this occur in classic family therapy where systems are enmeshed, but they can occur in more subtle contexts.

Family recovery also may be more difficult where there has been an emotional or physical cut off. Recovery for families may involve either reconnecting emotions or deciding to cut themselves off from the destructive gambler. The specific pattern that a family follows depends on family dynamics and the personality of the family members. For families where members cannot have a sense of self while a member is gambling, then it may be necessary for family members to disengage from the imminent hope of a reunion and recovery. For other families, where the sense of self may have existed but has been shattered, then a recovery that allows for reintegration into a functioning unit may be possible.

Clinicians need to be able to offer families a variety of services. At any point in the recovery process, families may change their minds regarding whether they wish to continue with the gambler. At this time, we may need to be able to refer client families to services that help them separate amiably and with minimal pain, despite the fact that this runs against our values and training.

Alton—"Just Lucky"

Alton is a 40-something counselor in the Midwest. He saw Stan for six sessions of therapy concerning Stan's Internet wagering. Stan stated that he was not interested in working with his wife and refused to allow Alton permission to contact her "under any circumstances."

Following the six sessions, Stan returned to his previous pattern of staying up all night and running up his and his wife's credit cards. His wife left him and began divorce proceedings.

Several months later, Alton received a letter saying that he was going to be sued, basically on the grounds that he had not notified the wife that Stan had slipped. The wife claimed that her credit and reputation had suffered, due to Alton's negligence.

Alton discussed this with his insurance carrier who stated that the suit was "probably meritless," although Alton was depressed that he could be sued for trying to abide by routine clinical practice.

Fortunately for Alton, the wife dropped the suit, since she reconciled with Stan. Alton considers himself "just lucky" to have missed painful and infuriating litigation. He is still uncertain what to do when faced with clients who refuse to sign releases of information to contact spouses.

Presently, there are no standards for whether the duty to warn extends to the property rights of family members at high risk for separating. The best protection for yourself, your clients, and their families is to find out what the law is in your jurisdiction and work out procedures before you need them. Have them approved by a competent attorney who specializes in mental health law (Pope & Vasquez, 2005a). Then, follow them and make sure that you document having done so.

Rates of Recovery and Failure

Data regarding this key point are unclear. Data are often collected only for weeks or months, not the necessary years required to demonstrate the success of longitudinal changes. This is starting to change, but knowledge is far from complete.

Gamblers Anonymous maintains the most pessimistic view. Anecdotal accounts of members claim that less than 5 percent of gamblers maintain abstinence. Critics point to the low numbers as evidence of the ineffectiveness of this program. However, it may also attest to the fact that the most problematic gamblers with multiple problems and risks are the ones treated by GA.

Some private programs report claims that 20 to 50 percent of people are abstinent following treatment. Hodgins, Wynne, and Makarchuk (1999) have shown that about 40 percent of disordered gamblers will experience a degree of recovery on their own. Other studies suggest between 29 and 60 percent will experience some form of recovery, whether through maturing out, spontaneous recovery, or through one of the forms of formal treatment.

Assessing the number of treatment successes and failures is difficult. This is true because people who enter treatment are usually more severe. Furthermore, they may tend to have many more comorbid psychiatric disorders. They have fewer social supports, often have legal problems, and may be unemployed. Regardless of whether there are low rates or high rates of recovery, these overall data tell us little about specific individuals. If you are counseling a person who has a gambling problem, it usually does no good to remind yourself and the client of the occasionally dismal rates of recovery. Instead, it is more helpful to remain optimistic about the person as an individual and to realize that sometimes change occurs *despite the odds*.

However, the best studies to date have shown that *formal treatment* is very effective. A recent meta-analysis indicates that treatment is effective and the results are robust (Pallesen et al., 2005). Meta-analysis is a statistical procedure that allows researchers and clinicians to combine studies and therefore compare treatments in a greater way than is possible from the conclusions generated from single studies alone. Developed primarily in response to research questions in psychotherapy, it has proven helpful in medicine and in other areas where studies often produce uneven or contradictory results.

In their review, Pallesen and colleagues (2005) found 37 studies in the literature that had been conducted comparing some aspect of gambling treatment to some form of comparison or control measure. Of these studies, several were excluded because they did not focus on eliminating gambling per se or did not have adequate information to compute a meta-analysis. *All 22 studies that remained showed a beneficial effect of gambling treatment.* This is quite remarkable for any type of therapy intervention, but the news gets better. The treatment effects were typically impressive.

Subjects included represented *pooled data* from 1,434 people. The mean age of this group was approximately 40 and about 72 percent of the participants were males. The overall effect size at posttreatment was 2.01 ($p < 0.01$, 95 percent confidence interval [CI] of effect size = 1.90–2.13), which translates into approximately 97 percent minimum effectiveness range. Although, Pallesen and colleagues (2005) downplay the results, this is a very strong statistical effect size. In other words, gambling treatment, as we now practice it, works. It also provides the argument of the need to continue to look for gambling treatment prevention and treatment best practices to offset the potential psychosocial negative impacts of pathological gambling.

POINTS TO REMEMBER

- Optimally, clients leave treatment when they have the self-efficacy to cope with their own gambling problems.

- The responsibility of detecting evidence of reversion is shared with the client; clients are seen as critical partners in managing their own addictions.

- After intense treatment, clients typically receive step-down services in which service delivery decreases or booster sessions are provided at a later date. This is often the highest risk period for most clients.

- A long-term recovery process often requires multiple episodes of treatment.

- Clients can *burn out* during the middle recovery period as they attempt to repair their lifestyle damages. Encourage them to manage their time commitments conservatively.

- If other appropriate services are not immediately available for clients, then counselors may not cease treatment.

- For clients who pay privately in the United States, practitioners must provide *referrals that have a similar fee as the original treating provider.*

TESTING YOUR KNOWLEDGE

1. Counselors must provide appropriate *pretermination counseling* regarding available options prior to ending any therapeutic relationship. True or False?

2. Gamblers Anonymous is an effective sole method of recovery. True or False?

3. It's important that counselors overplay the immediate benefits of gambling cessation to heighten the client's motivation. True or False?

4. Studies suggest between _____ percent will experience some form of recovery, whether through maturing out, spontaneous recovery, or through one of the forms of formal treatment.

Answers on page 205.

Summing Up

Despite the fact that everyone uses the term, there is little consensus on what the goals of *recovery* should be. This is even more problematic because in many cases recovery from gambling may involve a life-long process. In the present climate, treatment services often are too limited through a particular period of time. The philosophy presented in this chapter is that this runs against the realities of addiction. Optimally, clients leave treatment when they have the self-efficacy to cope with their own gambling problems. Not every client recovers the same way. People use their experiences and resources in different ways to manage their recoveries. Therefore, personal, family, community, and other resources are important to consider when you discharge a client.

There are many ethical problems that may occur when you discharge problem or pathological gamblers. Discharges need to be carefully planned and under no circumstances can be designed in a punitive fashion. There are *no rain dates* for discharge. You have to get them right the first time, since the client may have only one chance. To protect yourself and your clients, consult with a mental-health attorney prior to any problems occurring.

Key Terms

Client-centered discharge. Occurs based on behavioral criteria obtained from individually negotiated treatment plans constructed with the client at the first session, and clarifies how success will be measured.

Evidence-based discharge. Occurs when clients fulfill a number of criteria to show they are ready for the next phase of treatment.

Mastery-based discharge. Is structured around whether clients have successfully mastered common cognitive themes often misunderstood by gamblers (e.g., gambling is a skill-based game).

Operational-based discharge. A structured discharge based on completion of a certain number of treatment modules.

Recovery. The entire life-changing process.

Treatment. The more immediate phases of intervention.

Recommended Reading

How to Survive and Thrive as a Therapist: Information, Ideas, and Resources for Psychologists by Pope and Vasquez (2005b). To navigate concepts that graduate school may not have taught about being a helping professional, this book is an outstanding resource and worthy investment as it will assist in defining questions and situations that we sometimes like to gloss over. We recommend this tool to be on your shelf as it is an excellent resource.

Issues and Ethics in the Helping Professions by Corey, Corey, and Callahan (2006). The challenges of termination, balancing ethics, and customer satisfaction with running a business can be trying. This is an excellent tool for professionals for assisting in defining core consideration in caring for clients.

Illinois Institute for Addiction Recovery (http://www.addictionrecov.org/counsgam.htm).

Mental Health Addiction (MHA) Services (http://www.mha.sjcg.net/as/ gambling/older_adults/). Information on problem gambling resources, life changes, family and friends, and regional resources is available at this web site.

TESTING YOUR KNOWLEDGE

ANSWERS

1. True   2. False   3. False   4. 29 and 60

TRUTH OR FICTION

QUIZ ANSWERS

1. True   2. False   3. True   4. False   5. False   6. False   7. True

CHAPTER 7

Posttreatment Recovery Management: Models and Protocols of Relapse Prevention

TRUTH OR FICTION

QUIZ

After reading this chapter, you should be able to answer the following questions:

1. Relapse prevention models are all uniformly the same. True or False?

2. Cognitive-behavioral theorists believe that the lack of self-efficacy can trigger relapse. True or False?

3. Psychoanalytic literature suggests that the dysphoria that accompanies gambling cessation relates to internal conflict from punishment. True or False?

4. The social network of the pathological gambler is usually broad. True or False?

5. Severe anxiety and depression following gambling cessation are therapeutic and should not be treated. True or False?

6. Mindfulness is related to Buddhist teachings. True or False?

7. Mindfulness is recommended as an exclusive, stand-alone form of treatment for severe gamblers. True or False?

Answers on p. 237.

Highlights of this chapter include a view of relapse prevention models including behavioral, cognitive, and cognitive-behavioral examples. This chapter also identifies potential determinants for relapse and proactive strategies for dealing with the triggers of relapse. It answers questions about monitoring recovery and how to build community links that will help prevent relapse.

Relapse Prevention

This chapter is mostly speculative. We know much too little about what we should do for gamblers following treatment. Most of what we discuss is extrapolated from findings in AOD or is based on clinical experience.

Relapse prevention is the combination of psychosocial and other interventions aimed at helping maintain abstinence or control in gambling or other addictive behaviors. Relapse prevention models work by attempting to override addictive behaviors with other choices or mental processes. An observation that similar rates of relapse often exist across addictions prompted the development of relapse prevention models (Orford, 2001). These models are as pharmacologically diverse as alcohol, nicotine, heroin, and cocaine. This suggests that common mechanisms, not common addictions, may contribute to these very high relapse rates. Proponents of relapse prevention models strive to understand these common mechanisms and thereby reduce future problems of slips and lapses.

A tenet of relapse prevention is that the counselor can use relapse possibilities or occurrences therapeutically and instructively, which allows clients to continue progress despite periodic setbacks. When educating about relapse risk, the gambling counselor can infer that relapse happens sometimes, but it is not inevitable. At no time, as some ill-informed critics have mistakenly charged, does the counselor dismiss the seriousness of a return to uncontrolled gambling. However, if these deviations from therapeutic goals occur, they may provide an opportunity for clients to learn from mistakes. The counselor and client work together to make sure that brief slips, or *lapses*, do not develop into a major problem of uncontrolled gambling, called *relapses*.

In relapse prevention, the counselor and client seek to identify the factors associated with a return to addictive behaviors. Often, 12-step groups have identified these same factors. They may include emotional states, physiological variables such as anger or hunger, and self-statements, including self-fulfilling prophecies.

Models of Relapse Prevention

Relapse prevention models have different emphases. Models draw heavily from one another and the *cross pollination* has produced useful hybrids. Common relapse prevention models are rooted in behavioral, cognitive, and cognitive-behavioral therapies.

In the framework of relapse prevention, we understand that lapses are discrete episodes that involve partial or complete return to behavior *associated* with a return to pathological gambling. For example, a client who withdraws money out of an ATM machine while anticipating a gambling junket may be experiencing a lapse. Withdrawing money from the ATM machine is the behavior associated with a return to gambling.

Discrete episodes of isolated gambling may or may not qualify with this milder designation, depending on the goals of the treatment plan.

A relapse often is more serious. It represents a return to a previous addictive behavior. When a person in gambling treatment handles a stressful situation by checking into a rundown casino motel and gambling crazily on penny slots, the person is experiencing a relapse. Similarly, when someone has gambled with restraint for several years, then begins wagering extravagantly and beyond reason, the person is experiencing a relapse.

The distinction between a lapse and a relapse may depend on treatment goals. With total abstinence as a treatment goal (as defined by the Disease Model), any type of gambling may be viewed as a relapse. Many people believe that the classic Disease Model is not congruent with relapse prevention and the concepts of lapses and slips. On the other hand, when therapeutic goals are different, the client's experience of starting to gamble and then showing restraint may be a therapeutic triumph.

Behavioral Models of Relapse Prevention

Behavioral models emphasize the importance of classical and operant conditioning in fostering relapse. From the AOD literature it is clear that people, places, and items associated with past use can trigger relapse. Although research regarding gambling is less conclusive, evidence suggests that exposure to items previously paired with pathological gambling may produce craving or a return to wagering.

More than in any other addiction, money is commonly associated with gambling. Exposure to currency or coins may provoke a relapse. Certain locations are likely to be extremely high risk for the gambler attempting control or abstinence. These include anything that resembles the location where he or she previously wagered. One pathological gambler stated he felt he was at high risk for relapse when he saw a picture of the domed stadium where he won a $19,000 wager 10 years ago.

Behavioral models of relapse prevention frequently emphasize the following:

- Minimizing stress (which is a nonspecific activator of a variety of problems, including relapse)—some clinicians believe that *uncontrollable* stress may be particularly disruptive
- Reducing proximity to gambling venues, which serve as a cue
- Avoiding association with gambling friends or those still involved in the lifestyle, who may serve as a cue
- Moderating conversation about gambling, since conversation can serve as a cue for craving or for relapses
- Relaxation, because it is difficult to be aroused about gambling when you are relaxed
- Exercise, for the reasons previously stated

- Increasing structured activity, because structure is antithetical to the cue of boredom
- Substitution of pleasant events or rewards, contingent on avoiding gambling—this is what is known as *contingency management* or self-rewarding

Remember that behaviorists consider relapse a natural part of the extinction of responses. If responses are not rewarded, when in the presence of a cue, they gradually reduce in intensity until they go away. This follows a lawful pattern that most people can remember from their introductory psychology courses. However, these responses usually exhibit spontaneous recovery—they may recur without the presence of overt reinforcement or obvious cues. If the therapist misinterprets spontaneous recovery as failure of therapy, it undermines treatment. Instead, the client may need education about spontaneous recovery and possibly some booster therapy sessions.

Some behavior therapy approaches use *cue extinction,* in which exposure is flooded, so that it no longer is associated with signals of appetitive behavior. A psychologist who specializes in behavior therapy should oversee this approach. If performed inappropriately, it may intensify craving and facilitate relapse.

Cognitive Models of Relapse Prevention

Cognitive models advocate to correct the misunderstandings that make gambling seem more worthwhile than it really is (Ladouceur et al., 2001). Cognitive models of relapse assume that this knowledge has been *unlearned* somehow, often by subsequent associations.

Booster sessions often are required, because many things act to overwrite memory, prompting the necessity of *reminding* with additional sessions. A cognitive model reteaches these facts and reestablishes the truth that gambling is an expensive and usually foolish pastime. Relearning forgotten material happens more quickly each time; therefore, subsequent relapse prevention sessions tend to be quicker and more effective.

A practical problem associated with cognitive therapy and relapse prevention is that clients can conceal whether they have returned to their faulty ideas. The practitioner does not know what to monitor. Few overt behavioral indicators suggest a person is experiencing cognitive distortions that might be leading to a relapse. Self-reports are very unreliable. People will likely say they are simply fine and that they believe gambling doesn't pay. At the same time, they may be reading silly books on how to beat the slots, roulette, or keno.

Cognitive-Behavioral Models

Cognitive-behavioral models integrate behavioral and cognitive aspects of relapse theory (Marlatt & VandenBos, 1997). Relapse is a multicausal process related to an ongoing failure to regulate behaviors through cognitive feedbacks. Deficits that place a client at very high risk for slipping include poor coping skills, especially those relevant to negotiating with others to reduce the stimuli for relapse.

Specific events may trigger discrete episodes, but two other variables bring on a tendency to relapse. The first is a lack of *self-efficacy* to avoid the addicting substance or experience. If people believe gambling is irresistible, naturally, they will give in to the first bookie who asks them to place a $20 bet on their home team.

The second is that a client returns to a *positive view of his or her addiction*. In AOD, a favorable assessment of the benefits of use often will prompt a relapse. This is more likely when people minimize the costs of past addictive behaviors. In gambling, this can occur when people feel that it is necessary to wager on a sporting event to enjoy being with friends. They may forget that bankruptcy and mortgage foreclosures also were involved when they gambled before.

Cognitive-behavioral relapse prevention is concerned with techniques to address these smaller *lapses* and to keep them from becoming full-blown relapses. Examinations of relapses indicate that small and apparently minor decisions often contribute to the probability that the client will experience a relapse. Often, these involve denial of risk factors, or seemingly innocent actions that place the client in greater likelihood of longer-term relapsing.

One determinant of whether a lapse becomes a relapse is the self-fulfilling attributes that follow lapses. Marlatt & Gordon (1985) call this the *abstinence violation effect*. This is the belief that once an addiction-related slip occurs, a catastrophic relapse is inevitable. Translated into gambling treatment, this means "Once I gamble only once, I am completely done for." Marlatt & Gordon (1985) argue that slips can be isolated events, unless we believe otherwise. Once we believe we are going to relapse, we behave in a self-fulfilling manner. Some advocates of the Disease Model believe that relapse prevention encourages slips by discounting their seriousness. This is not true, as practitioners usually realize.

Other determinants of relapse may be particular thoughts or beliefs that may have devastating consequences. Some of these follow.

Belief that relapses are inevitable.

The inevitability of relapse makes resistance to gambling a futile effort. Therefore, the gambler has no reason to try to resist the cravings.

Belief that relapses are impossible.

Twelve-step groups have been quick to point out that relapse can occur to anyone, regardless of the person's previous abstinence history. Believing that "It won't happen to me" makes people overly confident; this may result in people ignoring relapse cues.

Belief that God intervenes to allow chance to favor people in need.

Many gamblers have prayed to get out of a jam and it has appeared to work. Therefore, they develop an odd theology, based on the idea that God will always pull them out when they really need it. They continue to gamble, believing that when they are truly in dire straights, they will benefit from divine intervention.

Belief that all problems (finance, stress, etc.) need immediate solutions.

Anxiety associated with this belief may prompt a person to begin gambling again. Financial pressures may be a major cue.

Belief that "What did not work in the past will suddenly start to work."

An example is a system or method of wagering that led the gambler to bankruptcy. Now, for some reasons, the gambler believes the method is more viable or it will suddenly bring on the money that it failed to win in the past. The gambler may elaborate with a sudden bit of *insight* to assist the erroneous thinking. Of particular concern is when clients fixate on sudden ideas that they feel will correct previous patterns of erroneous wagering. They never do and, inevitably, lead to more financial ruin.

An Integrated Model of Relapse Prevention

An integrative model by the Ontario Counsel presents relapse prevention as a two-factor process. Relapse risks involve both cognitions and behaviors. High-risk cognitions are associated with beliefs that a person can control the results of an uncontrollable event. For example, cognitions that are associated with relapse may involve beliefs that sports events can be predictable enough to beat the odds in a consistent fashion.

Behavioral relapse factors place the person near gambling opportunities. These include driving near a casino or racetrack, being near a lottery terminal, or using the Internet in an unsupervised manner.

Baumeister's Model of Self-Regulation

An alternative to the orthodox relapse prevention models has been developed by the well-known social psychologist Roy Baumeister and his associates (e.g., Baumeister & Vohs, 2004). It incorporates theories that are congruent with contemporary cognitive ideas about the self, yet its techniques are often behavioral. The ideas from this model are very useful for relapse prevention because clients can make sense of them and learn them.

The model stresses three aspects of psychological impulses that lead to relapse. First concerns latent motivation, or a person's wants and needs, both conscious and unconscious. Second concerns the concept of an activating stimulus. Third, the model specifies how these two combine. The specific impulse to return to addictive behavior often seems to emerge out of *nowhere*. Actually, it may emerge from the interaction between motivation factors and the activating stimuli that are present. Given the propensity and the stimulus, people naturally tend to believe that ideas *just pop into their heads*.

Relapse prevention derived from this model involves understanding the concepts of latent motivations and decreasing the activating stimuli. By realizing that urges result from an interaction between sentiments and stimuli, the latter can be altered or avoided. When clients are able to sense the emergence of an impulse, they can use behavioral approaches such as relaxation or distraction.

Proactive Strategies for Preventing and Dealing with "Triggers" for Relapse

Triggers, or flashpoints, often prompt rapid relapses. Researchers have known since the middle of the previous century that environmental stimuli and thoughts may prompt a sudden and unexpected relapse. Although there is less empirical research regarding the role of triggers in gambling relapses, there are many anecdotal accounts.

Common behavioral triggers are shown in Table 7.1. These were obtained from accounts of people who have slipped and are not *empirical* in the usual sense. However, they are useful and clients often can agree with them and see their relevance.

Many of these are specific stressors. Some of these stressors seem to push people in opposite directions. For example, vacation or added work stress probably indicates that any change in work status is associated with a tendency toward relapse. Similarly, an increase or decrease in family responsibilities may be associated with return to problem or pathological gambling.

Often, these triggers act in a way delineated by Baumeister's model. They put a person in a position where he or she suddenly has an unexpected urge to gamble and cannot understand the source for this obsession. Triggers act in this manner by increasing the stimuli for relapse, increasing stress, or by allowing more opportunity for relapsing. A counselor usually can spot these triggers before the client does and reduce their dangerousness.

Cognitive Triggers

A cognitive account emphasizes that the triggers involve erroneous and dangerous relearning about the probability of gambling success. These triggers tend to grow slowly but produce quick results. Some of these triggers are in Table 7.2.

Table 7.1: Behavioral Risk Factors Associated with Relapse.

- Being around people who gamble
- Failing to disclose a problem to a spouse or significant other
- A sudden influx of money in the gambler's life
- Excessive and unsupervised time off from work
- Solitary periods on the Internet
- Watching sports for prolonged periods of time
- Sports "high points," such as the Super Bowl or Breeder's Crown
- Use of alcohol or other drug
- General tendencies toward immoderation
- Indulging in reminiscing about the "good ole days" or "near misses"
- Boredom
- Stress
- Sad periods
- Happy periods
- Bad news
- Change in family or marital status
- Geographical location
- Transitioning into a "step-down" or less supervised program of services
- Transfer, retirement, or death of a therapist
- Reduction or elimination of GA meetings in a person's schedule
- Increase or reduction in family responsibilities
- Vacation
- Change of season
- Running out of psychotropic medications
- Change in health status
- Change in local gaming laws
- Greater access to computerized wagering
- Restoration of credit (for Internet wagering)

Table 7.2: Cognitive Triggers.

- "Insight" or other feeling that gambling can "be beaten"

- Feeling that you are "due," either because of previous bad luck or because of the good things you have done in kind to others

- Feeling that you have special talents in gambling

- Feeling that God has made you lucky

- Feeling that this is your lucky day, as evidenced by observing a number, hearing a lucky song, seeing a lucky person

- Feeling that God or fate "owes you one" to make up for past injustices or recent good works

---

CASE STUDY

Lou—Who Was Impatient

Pathological gamblers often are plagued by a difficulty with deferred gratification. Put it simply, many people think they want immediate change. Consider Lou, a recovering gambler, treated for depression. He began a routine dosage of antidepressants. Realizing it might take 3 to 4 weeks at minimum to achieve therapeutic effect, Lou asked his psychiatrist to administer electroconvulsive therapy "Because it's faster.... I just don't like to wait on anything, ever."

This was the first time in the psychiatrist's 32 years of practice that a patient had requested electroconvulsive therapy as a first approach to treatment. The psychiatrist, naturally, refused.

Often, cognitive triggers strengthen internal drives. When they interact with salient cues or new opportunities, they can produce dramatic changes of behavior. The good news is that, since evidence shows a person often has these thoughts for a while, the therapist can work with the client to help modify them and avoid a serious slip or relapse.

Triggers in Cognitive Behavioral Therapy

Table 7.3 highlights various triggers that may be associated with relapse in the cognitive-behavioral model.

The difference with these triggers is that they emerge without much warning. Usually, they are suddenly occurring thoughts that magnify a person's drive and gambling opportunities. They affect both parts of the cognitive-behavioral equation. Since they emerge so suddenly, they are particularly dangerous. The best strategy is to look for these seemingly innocuous beliefs and confront the client before they get out of hand.

Table 7.3: Extreme Beliefs Associated with Relapses

- I am genetically destined to have a drug and alcohol problem or some type of addiction.

- It's hopeless because my "disease has worsened."

- I am a person of extremes.

- What doesn't kill me makes me stronger.

- I need to test myself, just once, just to see.

- I don't have any other way of dealing with the stresses I am facing.

- I am afraid I am developing another addiction.

- I am just not myself anymore.

- I am bored, so it is justified.

- It is just my circumstances.

- It's just a phase I am going through.

- I'm just not having any fun in life without gambling.

Developing Relapse Prevention Plans

Relapse prevention plans include specifics of how clients will both receive further treatment and avoid future perils with the goal of minimizing relapse. Usually, it is the task of step-down providers to develop relapse prevention plans, although these plans may be included as part of the termination of regular treatment (Ghodse, 2002).

Design relapse prevention plans along the major areas identified as problematic, where people are likely to slip. Relapse prevention is not separate from other aspects of therapy; rather, it is integrated from the beginning of the intake interview. The counselor begins assessing what the client's trigger points are and are likely to be. The client learns to think this way and begins to anticipate future problems, within the model of treatment.

The counselor and client explore the client's tendencies toward relapse and attempt to turn them into a new therapeutic tool. Talk about potential triggers sooner than later; it is not necessary to wait for the client to slip. The specifics of an ongoing relapse prevention plan may involve proactive suggestions by the counselor.

Table 7.4 illustrates a customized and very short-term relapse prevention plan established during the transition to a less intense treatment level. There is no elaborate explanation for the plan's suggestions, as the client may not understand the necessary concepts behind them nor understand them when experiencing the desire to gamble. The relapse prevention plan supports a client who experienced extra trouble when he encountered triggers in everyday language. For example, someone might say "I'll bet that" and the client would believe that this undermined his abstinence. Then, he would stop and try to analyze the source of his temptations and why they really weren't indicative of his present urges. By that time, he might be at risk to return to gambling. At this point in his recovery, he needed to avoid this mental spiral of obsessive-compulsive symptoms and concentrate on his immediate requirements.

Table 7.4: Avoiding Cues for Relapse

Relapse Prevention Plan for _____

Week of   _____

1. Avoid gambling-related thoughts, situations, people, and even words that remind you of gambling. (For some people, even phrases like "I'll bet on that" or "you bet I will" are a problem.) If you find yourself "suddenly" in front of a casino or other gambling venue, do not go in. Do not try to figure out how you got there or why. Avoid these situations or GET AWAY ASAP.

2. Carry only as much money as you will likely need in the immediate future. Excessive money equals more chances to find gambling opportunities.

3. Remove all but one credit card. Make sure your partner gets the bill in his/her name.

4. This week in particular: Do not feel bad about things that "might have been." Try to live for the present. When you feel excessively bad about the past, you may be tempted to try to make it up by gambling again.

5. ATTEND YOUR NEXT APPOINTMENT—THE TIME IS WEDNESDAY _____ at _____.

6. The clinic number, if you run into trouble, is XXXXXXXXXXXX.

7. Even if you slip and start gambling again, COME TO YOUR NEXT APPOINTMENT.

8. GIVE ME A CALL IF YOU HAVE PROBLEMS.

The following handout for clients is more generic (see Table 7.5). It focuses on the process of questioning and rejecting automatic thoughts. It is primarily informational, though it does provide some *action orientation,* telling the client what to do in an emergency. This type of generic handout is great for people who need to affiliate and see that they have a disorder that other people have also. It is better for people to feel this way, rather than believing their disorder is unique or that they are different from everyone else. This latter group tends to look at generic accounts and find fault in them, drawing distinctions instead of similarities.

Relapse prevention plans also can address specific behavioral traits that place clients at high risk for relapse. A recovering gambler wrote the next handout, shown in Table 7.6, concerning moderation. It reiterates a common theme of some gamblers in recovery: "My life has involved nothing in moderation!"

Immoderation may lead to relapse. Someone who begins thinking immoderately should be careful, and ask friends and family to point out these traits. The person can ask a GA sponsor to point out better ways of coping, or talk to a counselor or therapist about learning new skills for avoiding the *me-focused* life.

Table 7.5: Handout on Questioning Automatic Thoughts

Gamblers in recovery find it helpful to reject acting on automatic thoughts. These are thoughts that seem to pop into our heads.

Many gamblers pride themselves on being impulsive by nature. Researchers have found differences between healthy and unhealthy impulsivity. Healthy impulsivity involves ideas that are enjoyable, fun, spontaneous, supportive, and show creativity. Negative or unhealthy impulsivity involves thoughts that demand an undesirable action. Unhealthy impulsivity is destructive. Sometimes gamblers in recovery confuse the two and may need extra time to sort through their thoughts. Therefore, they may want to avoid acting on any impulses and get in the habit of thinking first. Following is good advice for the recovering gambler.

The 1-minute rule is a good rule for handling impulses—if an idea pops into your head, think about it for a minute before doing anything about it. If you have a thought about gambling or other risky behavior and cannot get rid of the thought in about a minute, then the thought may have hold on you! Talk to someone—right away. This can be a friend, a GA sponsor, a family member, a counselor. This thought may just keep recurring. Be with someone until the thought goes away.

Table 7.6: Moderation by Phil M. (please pass this on if it has been useful)

Sometimes you can tell people are going to slip because they get into "big thinking." They forget about being moderate. Some examples are:

- They talk loud and out of turn.

- They always focus the conversation on themselves.

- They want the best in material possessions, when they can't really afford them.

- They overdo work or stress themselves about things that aren't as important as they might think.

- They eat too much, sleep too much, argue too much, and criticize too much.

- They take on more responsibility at work, without learning from their past mistakes.

- They strive to meet impossible deadlines, to please others.

- They may try to bite off "more than they can chew."

- They pay off too much of their debt.

- They show off their new good fortune.

Common Themes in Relapse Prevention

Regardless of the type of treatment, it is common for new problems to arise during the follow-up stages. The competent counselor is aware of this and prepares a relapse prevention plan with these concerns in mind.

Emergence of Sadness and Subclinical Depression

Clients who cease gambling often report feelings of sadness. Others have a pervasive sense of disagreeableness, lack of motivation, antagonism, and general unpleasantness. Few things seem to motivate them, except memories of past gambling winnings. If clients fulfill the criteria of a formal psychiatric diagnosis, they need treatment for this disorder. Usually, these disorders are subclinical, meaning they do not meet criteria for a formal diagnosis, but usually are notable and affect the client's life.

Psychoanalytic literature has suggested that dysphoria that accompanies cessation of gambling relates to inability to express emotions. Many pathological gamblers experience *alexithymia*, where they cannot describe how they feel. This also may be a risk factor for relapse, since the gambler feels the only time he or she can release his or her feelings is while gambling. Be aware and realize that gamblers may express emotional situations *through* relapses. We recommend including cognitive-behavioral treatment for depression if the client shows these symptoms. The volume by Burns (1999) listed in the Recommended Reading Section is very helpful.

Sleep

If a client is not adhering to a regular sleep schedule, he or she may need to consult with a physician regarding the presence of a possible sleep disorder. In a pilot study conducted by our research team, sleep disturbances predict relapses. This is not necessarily a causal relationship because anxiety, depression, emerging bipolar symptoms, and general stress, as well as substance abuse, may interfere with sleep. On the other hand, the *cognitive fuzziness* that comes from not sleeping causes poor judgment. Poor judgment causes relapse.

Clients should sleep when the rest of the world sleeps. Strikingly few pathological gamblers are able to do this, even when they are obtaining sufficient sleep. They may sleep the required 7 to 9 hours, but in odd, frenzied periods. Some of this may be due to underlying bipolar problems. The majority of the problem may relate to habit and misinformation. Adhering to a sleep schedule at night and working, going to school, and doing what most of the rest of the world does during the day reduces opportunities for unsupervised wagering.

As one pathological gambler stated, "Gamblers are creatures of the night. Most of the action that we get, the real action, comes when everyone else is sleeping." A normal sleep cycle at normal hours reduces this risk.

Excessive caffeine intake is a common problem of recovering people who cannot sleep, as is smoking. Education regarding caffeine may produce dramatic results in a short period, though with accompanying rebound expected from caffeine withdrawal. When in doubt, consult a health care professional.

Modification of Social Networks

An important part of recovery is association with those who do not gamble. The gambler attempting to avoid a relapse needs to be with people who have other interests. The social network of the pathological gambler is usually *insular*. Usually, any extended contacts with nongamblers are fairly superficial and trivial. Acquaintances and, if any, friends, tend to be people who normalize excessive, problem, or pathological gambling, often because they do it themselves. The reference group for gamblers is other aberrant gamblers. No wonder insight is so difficult! When clients start associating with people who have different values, they want more from themselves and begin to believe they can meet these goals.

Associating with people who gamble excessively may cause reemergence of cue dependent symptoms, as many relapse theorists have noted. One reason is that gamblers talk positively about gambling. This may prime clients to crave former experiences and forget the painful aspects of their pasts. The best strategy to prevent these risk factors is for the client to begin redesigning his or her social network to emphasize people who do not gamble too much. Often, GA is very helpful here, because GA members support change and can help the client find other acquaintances who do not gamble abusively. We are likely to maintain change when we associate with people who support our changes (Kottler, 2001).

Reduction in Other Addictive Substances

For successful recovery, the gambler needs to stay away from other addictive substances and behaviors. Other addictions make thinking clearly that much harder, which makes relapses more likely. Clinical experience suggests that many people may drift from gambling to another addictive experience, such as drugs or addictive sexuality. Many with disordered gambling have histories of other addictions (Kausch, 2003), and these addictions may become more of a problem when a person stops gambling. The clinician needs to monitor this carefully, especially during the early stages of a relapse prevention program.

We also know that many gamblers smoke (Grant & Potenza, 2005). Daily tobacco use is associated with stronger urges to gamble. Whether smoking is causally related to gambling is not known. What seems common is that gamblers in the early phases of relapse prevention often increase smoking. This can occur even when the previous history of smoking was minimal. The client will have to decide the timetable for giving up this *crossover* addiction.

Exercise

In general, most heavy gamblers do not exercise. There are plenty of exceptions, including some athletes, yet most people with disordered gambling prefer to watch sports rather than participate.

This sedentary lifestyle may contribute to boredom and much more. Everyone knows that exercise is good for the body and mind. The more we know about exercise, the more it appears to be useful for a variety of psychological disorders, including depression and anxiety (Anshel, 2006). Some convincing evidence suggests that exercise helps stabilize people with bipolar disorders who are otherwise medication resistant. The nonspecific aspects are an increase in self-esteem and self-efficacy. Exercise may even temporarily raise our intelligence levels. Not bad for something that is free!

A number of books are available to assist the practitioner in helping the client start an exercise program, and the benefits are listed in Table 7.7. The volume by Anshel (2006) is very useful for developing a program during the relapse prevention phase of treatment. Importantly, it does not go beyond the expertise of counselors and therapists by prescribing exercises that require more intense supervision.

Remember: Health care professionals should evaluate clients prior to beginning an exercise program. Document that you have suggested this to your client.

Table 7.7: Regarding Exercise

Exercise seems to be a no-brainer. Its benefits include:

- Weight control

- Reduction in risk of developing colon cancer

- Help in blood pressure management

- Prevention of heart disease

- Management or prevention of diabetes

- Maintenance of muscle and bone strength and tone

- Gains in psychological well being that may be as effective as antidepressants or anti-anxiety drugs

With all of these benefits, it is clearly one of the best deals going! Then why don't more people do it? One reason is that many people believe *exercise myths*, such as:

- "I have to be strenuously active to receive a benefit." This is simply not true.

- "I will never stick to it." You don't know unless you try.

- "It's too hard for me." It's not, when you start gradually.

- "I'm too old." People exercise under medical supervision at any age.

The bottom line: Inactive people improve their physical and mental health by becoming even moderately active on a regular basis. Clients should talk to their doctors about how much exercise is right for them. Upon doctor approval, here are some tips that other gamblers in recovery have found helpful:

- Start gradually, so you avoid burning out and being injured.

- Pick an exercise you like. When you gambled, you had games or bets you preferred. Find an exercise you prefer and you will be more likely to stick with it.

- For most people, a little variety is important. You did not make the same bet every time. It would have gotten boring.

- Many people benefit from exercising with a partner. The mutual commitment makes it tougher to get out of on the days when you just don't feel like it.

Monitoring and Negotiating Follow Up in Recovery

The ongoing monitoring of recovery is an important aspect of most addiction treatment; however, monitoring of gambling recovery is unlike that of AOD clients, because there are no relevant physiological markers. Your duties are also different because there are fewer court-ordered clients, though this may change as judges and prosecutors become aware of the usefulness of treatment. Therefore, recovery monitoring has to be *more voluntary* than it often is in AOD. The counselor has to negotiate a reasonable follow up that appeals to the client. The hard-handed techniques that occasionally work for AOD clients do not work for people in these situations. They will walk away, and you will not see them again, until they have failed and are in crisis.

To keep clients in follow-up, appeal to their interests—plain and simple. If treatment was not particularly successful, clients will not participate in any monitoring and will be lost to follow up. Do not force them into a model that works for AOD.

At the onset of treatment, do not specify that a provision for therapy is that they commit to follow up. In fact, you cannot ethically demand that they complete any follow-up sessions whatsoever. They are free to withdraw at any time. On the other hand, be sure to provide follow-up services if you promised to do so.

During follow up and monitoring, a *carrot* might be the opportunity to talk with the counselor about something *other than gambling*. The following vignette is an example of a counselor who has earned the client's respect through building trust in the early phases of therapy.

CASE STUDY

Benji: The Therapeutic Relationship As the Reward

"I kept going to my counselor after I completed my sessions because I liked her. She's honest and a good person. I knew that after we worked on my gambling problems, we could work on other stuff. I have a lot of issues from my childhood, you know, I was raised with a kind of twisted family.... What kept me in follow up was getting to see her, to work through some of this other [problems].

"She gained my trust. When she helped me work through some of the problems from gambling, I knew that she could help me with some other things that I've locked away ...

"I'll keep coming back as long as she wants me to; and hopefully, we can work on other stuff, too. I'm sick of talking about gambling. I think that's in the past. But if she wants me to come back, I'll do it."

In this case, the counselor's relationship with the client is what keeps the client in a monitoring program. If the counselor had failed to apply principles of effective and nonspecific counseling, the client would be lost to any type of follow up. Because the relationship emphasizes trust, Benji will continue to see the counselor despite some reservations that he is tired of gambling treatment. By discussing other concerns with him, the counselor keeps Benji attending every session, even though Benji is tired of discussing his treatment progress in his cognitive-behavioral gambling therapy.

A counselor cannot deny opportunities for the client to receive other necessary mental health services simply because the client has not participated in the follow up the counselor wanted. If the client needs services, the counselor has an ethical obligation to provide them or refer the individual to someone who can.

Reversions are common, though usually temporary deviations from the goal of a life without gambling problems, as are lapses. As explained in Chapter 1, the word *relapse* implies more helplessness than we wish to impart; the term *reversion* better indicates that a setback is temporary. This sets the stage for prevention through ongoing monitoring, often in a way that the concept of relapses does not. Figure 7.1 illustrates some of the connotations of these two definitions.

When clients feel they have a major role in determining whether they revert, they are more likely to participate in follow up. Their active participation is more likely when they reject the medical determinism that may be associated with the concept of relapse.

Emergency Plans

In other areas of addiction treatment, it often is helpful for the client and counselor to construct an emergency plan for situations in which the client feels relapse may be imminent. This usually includes instructions that the client agrees to follow if urges feel beyond control.

"RELAPSE"
- Older Term
- Weakness-Oriented
- Implies Possibility of Permanence
- Medical Connotations
- Fatalistic
- Implies Helplessness

"REVERSION"
- A Temporary Setback
- Strength-Oriented
- Less Medical Connotations
- Less Notion of Inevitability
- Implies Future Progress and Hope
- Implies Striving Towards Higher State

Figure 7.1: Connotations of two terms for departure from treatment plan.

There is no literature regarding the use of emergency plans for clients with gambling problems. Our experience is limited to clients at highest risk, who have relapsed previously, and who are now having difficulty in maintaining their goals regarding gambling. We believe that emergency plans need to include the expectation that the client will succeed. Communicate that reversions are common but not assured. Early intervention can halt long-term relapse.

Some other suggestions may include the following:

1. Emergency plans need to include the telephone numbers and names of people to call. Make a list with several choices in case availability is a factor.
2. Emergency plans need to have the number of GA, a sponsor, or gambling help line, if relevant.
3. Emergency plans need to include concrete instructions for distraction, such as deep breathing, thought stopping, or simply removing oneself from bad situations. Discuss and practice these techniques with the client in advance.
4. Emergency plans often benefit from including something emotional, such as a saying, quotation from a family member, or a picture of a person or place that the client associates with abstinence.
5. Keep emergency plans short. Avoid lengthy rationale for actions. Remember, the client is in a crisis when reading this plan and may not be thinking well.
6. Emergency plans also include an emphasis on increasing accountability to others during a crisis period.

Obstacles in Relapse Prevention: Emerging Difficulties

Recovery from an addiction involves a change in attitude, values, goals, and lifestyle. There are many mistakes and miscues along the way. Other problems appear to arise out of nowhere. We refer to these as *emerging problems*, because they seem to develop over time and usually are unpredictable in advance. They may appear gradually or suddenly, disrupting well-planned relapse prevention protocols.

Emergence of Psychiatric Disorders

People in the early and even middle phases of recovery may develop a mood disorder, anxiety disorder, or even show signs of a thought disorder. It is impossible to know whether these emerging disorders predated the disordered gambling. We do not know the direction of causality. At this point in recovery, these questions are irrelevant. Unless treated, the probability of relapse is high.

Throughout the volume, we have stated to treat bipolar disorder aggressively. Many counselors and therapists have outdated knowledge about the treatment of bipolar disorder. Psychiatry has made substantial advancements in the diagnosis and effective control of bipolar disorder that many nonmedical mental health personnel are slow to incorporate. Antiseizure medications, either as monotherapy or in combination with other agents, sometimes offer an alternative to lithium. The atypical antipsychotics have a more effective therapeutic goal than sedating a patient. Advances are occurring rapidly in establishing optimum guidelines based on patients' symptoms and histories. This is why a psychiatrist is essential for your team.

Some clinicians believe that depression following cessation of gambling is part of normal mourning of losses and should not be treated. A process of intense mourning may often occur. However, if the mourning becomes more powerful, the client may meet the criteria for a mood disorder. It is unethical to fail to treat a client who has depression. Some counselors still believe that the depression is therapeutic because it keeps people from relapsing. There is absolutely no evidence for this and it exposes clients to real dangers, as well as possibly contributing to relapse.

We reiterate that therapy for the depressed gambler does *not automatically mean medications.* For unipolar depression, psychosocial therapies are unquestionably as effective as medications. In the long run they are less expensive, because there is less likelihood of relapse. Furthermore, due to the risk associated with induction of bipolar disorders, physicians should probably be careful in using typical antidepressant drugs.

Clinicians often may overlook the emergence of anxiety and its potential seriousness. Anecdotal accounts suggest that when people stop gambling, they may be more likely to develop a number of anxiety disorders, including panic attacks and generalized anxiety. Any of these conditions may prompt people to begin wagering again or seek anything that will quickly reduce anxiety, such as alcohol or benzodiazepines. Address anxiety disorders, as they can be very disruptive if they become problematic. Effective cognitive and behavioral treatments are available as an alternative to the classic antianxiety drugs, such as the benzodiazepines.

Other problems to look for are excessive hoarding behaviors, *compulsive shopping* (in people who are financially solvent), and somatic complaints. Clinical experience suggests that these *Obsessive Compulsive Spectrum Disorder* problems may emerge following gambling cessation or reduction.

Emergence of Physical Problems

The counselor should note the client's general physical appearance. Has there been an excessive and unintended weight change? Does the client look tired? Within the domain of your professional licensure and competence, ask the client how he or she is feeling. Have there been any changes? Ask about any burning, chest pains, change in bowel or bladder habits, change in sleep habits, change in appetite, shortness of breath, or cough. If problems are noted, relate them to the treatment plan and make sure that the client follows through with seeking appropriate care. People in recovery often tend to minimize physical difficulties, because of so many other things going on in their lives. Here, take care to prod them along, if necessary; advocate for them; but mostly, be there to support them.

Also within your professional capabilities and licensure, ask the client about the side effects of medications. Sometimes clients report a different account to you than to a medical provider. Often, they feel that the medical provider does not have enough time to see them or talk with them. They might be unassertive and forget their questions. On the other hand, they might be aggressive and uncompromising, exaggerating their medication reactions. The extra time you give in the follow up may mean the difference whether they stay on needed medications.

One thing is certain—do not take a passive stance during this period of recovery, expecting to keep the treatment *clean* by only discussing gambling-related matters. The client will have a variety of concerns, ranging from information about practical knowledge ("Say, how do you get a car registered in this state anyhow?") to emotionally charged issues ("Since I quit gambling, I've been going to porn sites every day.") Remain an active listener and supporter, helping the client to problem solve, without inflicting your agenda. This is what makes the art of counseling so hard.

Emergence of Couples and Family Problems

Often, these are the most significant emerging issues and the most apt to serve as cues for relapses. Partly, this is based on the client's expectation that, once he or she gains some control over wagering, any damage done to his or her family will magically disappear.

Family therapy literature has highlighted how problems will emerge following cessation of an addiction, since the addiction had previously diverted attention away from the problems. Expect an increase in family tension following the improvement of a disordered gambling family member. Naturally, this is disheartening to the gambler and occasionally may prompt a relapse.

A vulnerable area is sexual intimacy. Sexuality is often absent when one partner is gambling. To restore satisfactory sexual interactions, partners may need to relearn many roles and change their expectations. This situation is uncomfortable and can serve as an impetus for a relapse or, in some cases, may spark a depressive episode. If you are embarrassed with this aspect of counseling or lack appropriate experience, seek supervision and training. Refer clients to people who can be more helpful.

Problems with children also are important and difficult to predict. Often, a family system will act to work around a dysfunctional member. When the member returns, the disequilibrium changes the dynamics regarding discipline and other routine tasks. This may result in a situation in which parental rules are not consistently enforced, encouraging children to test limits. This in turn acts to prompt a frustration, added tension, and the endpoint of relapse.

Regardless of emerging problems, half of recovered gamblers say that family involvement was an important part of their recovery. Often, the best structure for incorporating the sentiments and concerns of families is GamAnon. As previously mentioned, GamAnon is similar to AlAnon, though—like with GA and AA—there are differences. A common feeling among many clinicians is that gambling has a much more serious downward spiral than other addictions producing more complex and often more negative problems and reactions for families. Consequently, there may be more anger, frustration, hostility, and emotional walls in GamAnon.

Community Linkage as Relapse Reversion Prevention

Community resources can help prevent relapse. Following are some useful ones.

Community-Based Vocational Counseling

In our experience, over half of the time, problem or pathological gamblers cannot return to their previous employment. Combined with erratic work histories, gamblers often need redirection regarding vocational choices. This knowledge and skill is usually outside of the primary counselor's expertise. Remember, the counselor cannot be an expert in everything and does not help the client when skills are beyond his or her training.

It is useful to form a referral network with vocational counselors. State agencies have taken severe cuts in recent years but still may be helpful in providing these services. Also, look at universities that have counseling programs, since they may provide this service at a reduced or waived fee.

Proprietary career counseling is usually too expensive and irrelevant for the needs of people with severe gambling problems.

Academic Counseling

Clients without a high school degree should make a high school equivalency degree an immediate goal. Fortunately, many state agencies promote this goal and usually there are some available community resources. Help also may be available at local offices associated with community colleges.

In our experience, unless people with gambling problems receive appropriate academic services from university and college counseling centers, they have almost no chance of completing higher education. This is probably due to difficulties in attention and concentration, as well as chronic procrastination. However, these people are often independent and resistant of further intervention from yet another counselor. Many believe that seeking academic help is an indication of weakness or stupidity. Be honest with the client and model cooperative behavior.

Academic counselors can work exceptionally well with a variety of people, including those in recovery. Often, they have expertise in working with people who have common comorbid difficulties, including ADHD and depression. Once clients understand their part in the recovery process, there is usually much less resistance.

Financial Counseling

Many proprietary and nonprofit financial counseling firms are available in the United States. On any night, there may be half a dozen advertising on television. Usually, these firms boast of a national presence with many offices, and that they have helped thousands of people. Be careful! A client's creditors usually pay these companies. Just because a financial counseling service describes itself as a nonprofit organization, it does not guarantee that their services are legitimate or in a client's best interests. There are good financial services available, but proceed with caution.

Many universities, military bases, credit unions, and similar groups operate nonprofit credit counseling programs. Financial institutions, local consumer protection agencies, and GA are good sources of information and referrals. Usually, these are safer because they do not have a conflict of interest. Most offer a sliding scale for their services.

Reputable credit counseling organizations can advise clients on managing money and debts and meaningfully help a person reduce financial stressors. Counselors are certified and trained in the areas of consumer credit, money and debt management, and budgeting. Counselors usually discuss a person's entire financial situation and help the person develop an individualized plan. An initial counseling session typically lasts an hour, with an offer of follow-up sessions. Frequently, the finances of recovering gamblers are more complex and require several sessions.

Debt Management Programs (DMPs) are services for which a person agrees to make payments to an agency, which in turn, has negotiated a reduction in credit card fees from the person's creditors. Often, this duplicates some of the activities that GA performs. Some GA members believe that a compulsive gambler should pay creditors at whatever rate he or she agreed to pay, as part of appropriate restitution. Take special care when referring someone to one of these programs, as many are frankly unscrupulous.

The Federal Trade Commission states that consumers should be wary of credit counseling organizations that:

- Charge high up-front or monthly fees for enrolling in credit counseling
- Pressure clients to make voluntary contributions

- Won't give out promised free information without a credit card number
- Try to enroll clients in a DMP without reviewing individual financial situations
- Offer to enroll clients in a DMP without teaching budgeting and money management skills
- Offer to enroll clients in a DMP over the telephone
- Demand that clients make payments into a DMP before creditors have accepted them into a legitimate repayment program

Pastoral Counseling

A pastoral counselor can address psychological and spiritual concerns. Pastoral counselors are in most major Protestant denominations, as well as the Roman Catholic Church and the Jewish faith. In most cases, they work with people of faiths different from their own. Typically, pastoral counselors go beyond science and into the realm of religious belief, where many practitioners of other mental health fields are not generally comfortable.

Pastoral counseling has an extensive history, though only now is it becoming fully professionalized. Some organizations credential people with minimal formal education. Others, such as the American Association of Pastoral Counselors, require that practitioners be trained in psychology, theology, and receive personal psychotherapy.

Pastoral counseling often is most helpful for existential distress that formal mental health treatment cannot answer. An example often posed by the gambler in recovery is the question of "Why does a good God allow people to get into this much trouble?" This is not usually a question for any science-based helping profession, since it involves theology.

Leisure Counseling

A consultation with a leisure counselor can help the gambler answer the question of "What can I do besides recover?" Currently, most practitioners do not see the value of providing separate leisure counseling, perhaps because they lack exposure to these helpful practitioners. Leisure counselors are very helpful, but hard to find. Most leisure counselors work primarily with the elderly, because of the demand for services in this population. Usually, they are not familiar with the needs of people across the lifespan. Occasionally, university programs provide leisure counseling that may be applicable for our population. Ask around and add it to your resource list.

Health Counseling

The counselor or therapist should not assume expertise in this area. Be a coach, but not a source of knowledge. Urge people to seek treatment and monitor their efforts. Encourage, but do not cajole.

Common physical problems include:

- Hypertension
- Cholesterol problems
- Diabetes
- Dental problems
- Obesity
- Neurological difficulties
- Bronchial problems
- Untreated infections

These involve physician treatment and ongoing monitoring by a qualified health professional. Encourage collaboration between the client and these providers.

Telephone and Internet Follow Up

Impressive results for AOD clients have been found by one research team using telephone contacts, rather than face-to-face follow up (McKay, Lynch, Shepard, & Pettinati, 2005). However, highest-risk clients continued to show a benefit if telephone contacts accompanied face-to-face contact. Perhaps for our highest-risk gambling clients, a combination of the two procedures may be warranted.

Some practitioners use the Internet as a follow up. One method is to encourage clients to email you at regular intervals. You respond and assess their progress. Be prepared that this is more work than it seems, and you will be spending a great deal of time, perhaps with dubious returns. Emailing about complex, emotional issues is difficult for both counselor and client. Often, you will spend many more hours following up on email contacts than you would on the telephone. Clients may not understand that email does not guarantee instant access to you, as it might if you were simply online chatting. This is more of a problem with young people, who are used to multitasking with an open messaging system on their computers.

Another strategy involves Internet relapse prevention groups. Open discussion groups may be run by GA members or others and vary in quality. Visit these sites for several weeks before recommending them. Some may quickly turn away from their topics or threads and become forums for all kinds of concerns. The best way to find them is to enter your requests into search engines or to ask around, since they change, disappear, and consolidate frequently.

Restricted or closed forums are limited to specific clients who have gone through certain types of treatments or treatment with a particular counselor or group of counselors. Participation at restricted sites may be combined with structured workbook exercises to provide additional follow-up activity.

There are no data as to whether Internet discussions are helpful; but at the very least, they give clients some structure and something positive to do with their time. However, difficulties regarding Internet access may compromise the integrity of these treatment goals for some people. Also, remember that the gambler in debt may not have a computer or Internet access, especially following a step down from treatment that is more intensive.

Computer and workbook interventions can be used as secondary prevention for other addictions (L'Abate, 2004). In a persuasive article, Prochaska (2004) summarizes the necessity for population-based treatment prevention and advocates a broader approach. He argues that individual treatment, advocated by many professionals, has been ineffective in recruiting addicted clients and retaining them into treatment. He believes that computers and computer-delivered therapy may now provide the link from a clinic to a home-based treatment-delivery system. Furthermore, computer methodologies may allow targeting for multiple problem behaviors, such as clients who have several addictive disorders simultaneously or who have several health risks that would require diverse treatment counselors.

Take care that your client can handle the computer. Is there a history of gambling on the Internet? Is your client likely to become addicted to something else by using the Internet, such as shopping, Internet sex, gaming, or excessive chatting? Be careful and use best judgment; standards of care and warning flags are unknown for people using this tool in recovery.

Family and Concerned Others Involvement during Posttreatment Recovery

In AOD, there are many models of *co-recovery*, in which a pathological family enters treatment together (Brown & Lewis, 1999). At the time, we do not know enough about gambling recovery in the context of family processes to know how to treat it effectively within the family (McCown & Chamberlain, 2000). Sometimes, techniques borrowed from AOD may produce outstanding results. However, we suspect that some of the dramatic cases reported in early studies are not typical. Often, families are too severely damaged by gambling to expect healing.

A useful model for working with families is presented by (Federman, Drebing, & Krebs, 2000). The authors' approach offers supportive guidance and counseling to the family and friends of the problem gambler regarding limit setting, without being judgmental. The authors believe that family members must first cope with their own emotional responses to disruption. Only then can they choose to rebuild bridges to repair family relations, as much as possible. This approach teaches new skills that allow the family to recognize what it can and cannot control. It empowers the family to seek reconciliation, if desired. It salvages what can be preserved, while not sacrificing the health or integrity of other family members for the sake of a previously dysfunctional system.

Find other hands-on techniques regarding the family in the AOD volume by McCollum and Trepper (2001). This is a practical book that offers realistic solutions to many frequent problems regarding families or significant others.

Preventing Chronic Relapses

One way the practitioner can prevent chronic relapse is to remain open to the client's needs and timetable for recovery. Too often, we insist on providing a single protocol for everyone, administering treatment on a schedule that is convenient for us. If treatment fails to work the first time, we claim that the client is treatment resistant and a therapeutic failure. Often, these people are in Prochaska's Precontemplation phase, in which treatment is administered prematurely. By closing the door to future treatment because of our programmatic concerns, we guarantee relapse.

Also, reduce chronic relapse by letting clients know that you are there for them, pulling for them. During treatment, affirm that they are people first and *cases* second. You are there for their good and as their partners in recovery. In this manner, if they slip or relapse for a substantial period, they will not feel so stigmatized and embarrassed to ask for your help again.

Chronic relapse is probably most likely to occur when people lose hope. If a client appears to be shutting off therapist support, it is often helpful to assist the client in marshalling potential resources, such as family and church. Often, it is helpful to be less of a therapist and more of a consultant and advocate. Sometimes successful counselors have to act as personal coaches, providing skilled context-specific advice about areas that have nothing to do with gambling. Some therapists are not comfortable in aspects of treatment that deviate from the strict protocol of a treatment manual. These people work well in demonstration projects, but not necessarily in the real world.

Mindfulness

Some clinicians are emphasizing a *new* approach to chronic relapse prevention: *mindfulness*. The beliefs surrounding mindfulness stem from Buddhism and are popular in many Eastern cultures. A major component of mindfulness is being aware of the present moment and not overcome by fears and apprehensions. Mindfulness, as a philosophy, involves ongoing *learning to live in the moment, but not be ruled by the negative thoughts of the moment*. This is congruent with the AA and GA statements, "This, too, shall pass."

The development of mindfulness may involve many techniques that help a person rise above momentary thoughts of anxiety, depression, and despair. These can include meditation, exercise, emphasis on breathing, and becoming more aware of stress. Techniques may be incorporated into traditional

Vince P.—When Mindfulness Backfired

"I'm 54. I'm an alcoholic and I've been sober for 21 years. But, I never quit gambling and my problem just got worse through the years. I started seeing a gambling counselor because I came to realize I 'might' have a problem in that area, too. Like I didn't know! I guess it was the last part of denial. Now, if I could only quit smoking....

"For me, the meditation crap and all of that is useless.... I stopped going to counseling when they started pushing that [strategy] on me. I wanted to quit [counseling] as a winner. I don't like to give up on anything. But when they started telling me about mindfulness, it just lost my interest.

"Part of quitting is learning to be logical. When they tell you to do that Eastern [stuff], it is the opposite of logical. I just don't see any need for it. To me, it is the opposite of what I learned in the first part of counseling.

"I'll admit that I'm gambling again. I don't want to go back to the way I was, but I'll just have to see how it goes, I guess."

cognitive-behavioral treatment or may be taught independently (Breslin, Zack, & McMain, 2002). See the Recommended Reading section for further information about this promising approach.

Currently, we do not recommend mindfulness methods as the *exclusive* treatment during recovery. This is why we did not present them in earlier chapters. They are still untested for gambling and, although they may perform well for alcohol and some other addictions (Marlatt, 2002), gamblers may simply be too cynical and disagreeable in the initial stages of treatment to "buy into this Eastern (stuff)," as one client said. However, once clients have some success working with you, you have some credibility. Use this advantage to suggest something that they never considered before, perhaps capitalizing on their desire for novelty.

Any time you recommend an intervention reminiscent of Eastern philosophies, be culturally aware. Many people consider Eastern religions religiously offensive. Even secular uses of meditation may be highly problematic for some clients, such as conservative Christians or Islamic clients. Do not interpret this as resistance. Instead, find a different name for your techniques or find new techniques. Other clients find these approaches *too soft* or *California-ish*, and will not accept them.

POINTS TO REMEMBER

- Lapses are discrete episodes that involve partial or complete return to behavior *associated* with a return to pathological gambling; whereas, relapses are more serious and represent a return to a previous addictive behavior.

- Evidence suggests that exposure to items previously paired with pathological gambling may produce craving or a return to wagering.

- Be careful not to misinterpret spontaneous recovery as failure of therapy; it may undermine treatment.

- One determinant of whether a lapse becomes a relapse is the self-fulfilling attributes that follow lapses. Marlatt & Gordon (1985) call this the "abstinence violation effect." It is the belief that once an addiction-related slip occurs, a catastrophic relapse is inevitable.

- Environmental stimuli and thoughts may prompt a sudden and unexpected relapse.

- Relapse prevention is not separate from other aspects of therapy; rather, it is integrated from the beginning of the intake interview.

TESTING YOUR KNOWLEDGE

1. If responses are not _____, when in the presence of a cue, they gradually reduce in intensity until they go away.

2. _____ is where behavioral responses may recur without the presence of overt reinforcement or obvious cues.

3. Self-reports are very unreliable. True or False?

4. Sleep disturbances predict relapses. True or False?

5. To keep clients in follow-up, appeal to their _____.

Answers on page 237.

Summing Up

This chapter emphasized the multifaceted nature of problems that clients can have when they are beyond the acute stages of recovery. Counselors must be vigilant but also empowering, aiming toward the eventual goal of shifting responsibility of prevention onto the client.

Relapse prevention can occur from a number of theoretical orientations or perspectives. Its aims are often the same: to teach clients to feel empowered to monitor their own thoughts and behaviors and to respond appropriately. Clients have to learn which cues in their environment are problematic. Counselors can be helpful by reducing the *learning curve* that otherwise would only come through years of trial-and-error experience on the part of the clients.

A competent counselor helps the client by rehearsing relapse prevention strategies and having emergency instructions in place.

Other events may cause long-term relapse. These include family, vocational, leisure, and financial problems.

Key Terms

Contingency management. Part of a Behavioral Model of relapse prevention that emphasizes a substitution of pleasant events or rewards contingent on avoiding gambling.

Co-recovery. When a pathological family enters treatment together.

Cross-over addiction. A drift from gambling to another addictive experience, such as drugs or addictive sexuality.

Emerging problems. Other problems that seem to arise out of nowhere during recovery. They seem to develop over time and usually are unpredictable.

Lapse. Discreet episode that involves partial or complete return to behavior *associated with* a return to pathological gambling (e.g., withdraws money from an ATM while anticipating a gambling junket).

Mindfulness. A strategy for relapse prevention, stemming from Buddhism. Its main component is being aware of the present moment and not overcome by fears and apprehensions.

Relapse. A return to a previous addictive behavior (e.g., gambling crazily on penny slots).

Reversion. An alternate, and perhaps preferred, term for relapse, which better indicates that a setback is temporary.

Recommended Reading

Additional information about bipolar disorders and gambling can be found at http://www.mooddisorderscanada.ca/findinghelp/gambling/report/index.htm.

Federal Trade Commission (http://www.ftc.gov/bcp/conline/pubs/credit/kneedeep.htm). For more current and comprehensive information on credit counseling, counselors and clients should see this web site.

The National Sleep Foundation (http://www.sleepfoundation.org). This web site is good for basic information regarding sleep.

The Ontario Counsel (http://www.gamblingresearch.org). An integrative model that presents relapse prevention as a two-factor process.

The Feeling Good Handbook (Rev. ed.) by David Burns (New York: Plume, 1999). Dr. David Burns is one of the prime developers of cognitive therapy and has developed a fast-acting, drug-free treatment designed to help the clinically depressed. In *The Feeling Good Handbook,* he adapts cognitive therapy to deal with the wide range of everyday problems that plague so many (e.g., chronic nervousness, panic attacks, phobias, and feelings of stress, guilt, or inferiority). *The Feeling Good Handbook* teaches how to remove the mental obstacles that bar you from success—from test anxiety and fear of public speaking to procrastination and self-doubt.

Mindful Recovery: A Spiritual Path to Healing from Addition by T. Bien and B. Bien (2002). This is a book for clients (and therapists) that shows how to use simple Buddhist practices to manage anxiety, cravings, and emotional swings.

Gorski and CENPS (http://www.relapse.org/) provides detailed resources on relapse prevention. This web site will link you to a resource for relapse prevention education materials as well as professional development. Relapse prevention, as in AOD, is an entire skills set. As mentioned earlier, the field of gambling relapse prevention is green pastures. While research looks for new insights, some lessons learned in the AOD world may assist in developing effective relapse prevention plans for people who want to stay away from gambling.

When looking at relapse prevention strategies, there is value in considering the global theme of prevention. Two excellent resources are the Institute of Medicine at http://www.iom.edu/ and Substance Abuse and Mental Health Services Administration (SAMHSA) at http://www.samhsa.gov/. Also, visit the Alberta Alcohol and Drug Abuse Commission (AADAC) at http://corp.aadac.com/alcohol/the_basics_about_alcohol/alcohol_brochures_relapse_prevention.asp, and Dual Recovery Anonymous (DRA) at http://www.draonline.org/relapse.html.

TESTING YOUR KNOWLEDGE

ANSWERS

1. Rewarded   2. Spontaneous Recovery   3. True   4. True   5. Interests

---

TRUTH OR FICTION

QUIZ ANSWERS

1. False   2. True   3. False   4. False   5. True   6. True   7. False

CHAPTER 8

New Beginnings: Moving Beyond the Addiction

TRUTH OR FICTION

QUIZ

After reading this chapter, you should be able to answer the following questions:

1. Behavioral toxicity is intensified because normal rewards often are difficult for the recovered gambler to attain. True or False?

2. Emerging symptoms include problems that occurred following cessation or reduction of gambling; for example, alcoholism as a symptom substitute or excessive weight gain. True or False?

3. Broad traits are another term for lower-ordered traits. True or False?

4. Positive emotions may block negative emotions and may also act independently to contribute to physical and mental health. True or False?

5. The benefits of belonging and contributing are primarily due to a reduction in anxiety. True or False?

6. Metaregulation refers to an ideal that is never met. True or False?

7. Most families are able to successfully reconcile in this final stage of recovery. True or False?

Answers on p. 260.

Highlights of this chapter focus on how a person might move beyond mere prevention of relapse, discussed at length in Chapter 7, and into how to broaden—even enjoy—life. There are variables affecting a person's life changes including personality, family, and emotional stability to name a few. The chapter presents various therapy options depending upon the client's needs. Community support also is discussed and strategies that can help support a person through this final stage of recovery.

Moving Beyond

A goal for the final stage of recovery is that clients move beyond focusing on the daily struggles of avoiding wagering and develop a broader perspective on life. Under some circumstances, clients can use their experiences to develop deeper, more satisfying qualities to their lives. They can learn and benefit from their addictive experiences, despite all of their horrors. Not every client wants to or can reach this goal. However, for those with drive and motivation, this potential achievement can be an important motivational force during the earlier and more turbulent periods of recovery.

Clients and counselors often ask whether recovery is ever completed. The answer is dependent upon the theoretical model that the counselor and client endorse. For some models, such as many cognitive-behavioral models, the end stage of recovery is operationally defined by a limited period. For other, more open-ended forms of treatment, such as GA, it is usually believed that active involvement in the recovery community should be life long. For people advocating both extremes, and those in between, it is often helpful to work toward establishing long-term, alternative sources of rewards. These involve helping the disordered gambler find enduring mechanisms to pursue a more satisfying life that replaces the motivator and reward of gambling with something safer, more enduring, and less destructive.

Despite achieving abstinence, the disordered gambler may still find it hard to experience good feelings. Too often, nothing is as intense or as pleasurable as the feeling from unrestrained and crazy wagering. Usually, the gambler finds that the most powerful human rewards the rest of us encounter are boring, dull, and devoid of previous passion. The intensity of betting has robbed the gambler of responses to the things that most of us appreciate. This is known as *behavior toxicity*, a process by which other rewards lose attractiveness. It is usually reversible, but it may take time, perhaps months or even years to undo.

Behavioral toxicity is intensified because normal rewards often are difficult for the recovered gambler to attain. Social relationships may be tattered and fragmented. Families have been tested and the strains are often beyond repair. The gambler does not have any money and cannot afford to take days off for vacation or to be with friends. One recovering gambler with this problem described his situation this way: "I've traded in the hell of gambling for the purgatory of a progressive tedium. The gambling was worse, sure thing, but the purgatory is pretty miserable, in its own damn way."

To feel positive, the recovered gambler may engage in various forms of *self-medication*. As previously described, the gambler may smoke, drink excessively, and often may eat unhealthily in the quest for sensation. Despite these extremes, life is often experienced as episodes of empty moments, "of disconnected sequences of excessivenesses" as a literary-oriented client expressed it.

Clients may often *behave* extremely, rather than partake of substances. For example, on the socially acceptable side, a client may become a *workaholic* or a *churchaholic*, while more destructive behaviors include excessive shopping, extraordinary sexual behavior, or family instability. One person at this stage of recovery, a lawyer, could only derive satisfaction from life from directing law suits against corporations that he believed had hurt the public. He performed this behavior tirelessly, fanatically, and entirely for free. However, though others admired his dedication, they thought that he needed *balance.*

The recovering gambler may have to learn ways of experiencing the world that do not involve the thrill of the wager. Instead, the gambler may learn to find other comparable rewards that strike a healthy balance. The quest typically extends beyond abstaining from wagering and preventing relapse. It often involves learning to enjoy and experience life. This is the phase of new beginnings that some gamblers eventually reach. Others choose more pedestrian paths, staying content to achieve abstinence in the here-and-now of daily life. There is no correct path or one way.

We have talked about some ways of reconnecting through exercise, meditation, mindfulness, and other methods as aspects of relapse prevention. For some people, though, it is not enough. This final stage involves the slow process of gradual healing that does not occur overnight. Perhaps it is a phase that is almost beyond empirical investigation, because for so many people it seems to be an individual journey. Consequently, this chapter is not prescriptive. It simply suggests some paths that clients have taken at different times.

Recovery in Psychological and Mental Health Domains

As discussed in Chapter 7, mental health concerns typically involve removal of preexisting symptoms and monitoring of emerging symptoms. Preexisting symptoms may include those caused by the gambling disorder, as well as those that came after a person developed aberrant wagering. At this point, the direction of causation does not matter. Emerging symptoms include problems that occur following cessation or reduction of gambling; for example, alcoholism as a symptom substitute or excessive weight gain.

In our research of long-term abstinent gamblers, who obtained help through distance treatment, about half report problems with low-grade depression. In some cases, these symptoms are so severe that they meet the criteria of formal psychiatric diagnoses. Some people may use psychotropic medications monitored by appropriately trained physicians. Others may need cognitive-behavioral therapy or other appropriate treatment for depression. Some disordered gamblers, in this final stage of recovery, will meet the criteria of dysthymia, reporting symptoms of gloominess, low drive and depleted energy, chronically low self-esteem, and a pessimistic outlook. This condition may be more common when there is a family history of panic disorder, social phobia, and alcohol use disorders or major depressive episodes, as well as bipolar disorder. Physicians should be aware that in some cases psychotherapy is a preferable treatment, because medication may induce bipolar symptoms. This is probably rare, though it is a serious concern.

Some clients may be at risk to drift into a pattern of serial addictions. While these people successfully manage to avoid developing classic pharmacological addictions, they may tend to become workaholics, *shopaholics*, sexual addicts, religious addicts, Internet addicts, video gaming addicts, and so on. It helps to think of them as basically good people who tend to overdo and consequently abuse any single source of reward. They tend to have lives that are *moderate in almost nothing*. An example is Helen, a 47-year-old associate professor of nursing at a major university, who, despite the absence of any psychiatric symptoms, experienced seven passionate religious conversions to different faiths within 4 years of cessation of gambling. Medically-oriented practitioners sometimes need to be reminded of the behavioral similarities between addictions and how addictions can drift or abruptly change from one to another. A review of the "Three Cs of Addiction" from Chapter 1 may be helpful.

Other psychological problems during this final recovery stage may be idiosyncratic to the particular person. This means that a person may run the gamut from just about anything conceivable and defy generalizations.

Previously, we have suggested the volume by Corcoran and Fischer (2000), *Measures for Clinical Practice: A Sourcebook,* third edition. This resource allows the clinician to measure over 400 specific problems as they emerge. The volume becomes very useful again during this period, when unpredictable problems arise at a higher-than-expected base rate.

**IMAGINE THAT!
EXTREME SPORTS—
HARMFUL OR HELPFUL?**

As stated in Chapter 4, some gamblers and other addicted people try to find substitution thrills in activities like snowboarding, parachuting, parasailing, windsurfing, white water rafting, and other *edgy* sports. In particular, younger recovering gamblers often become fanatical about these pursuits.

However, extreme sports may not be a panacea. We do not know how much is healthy and how much is excessive. Moreover, no one knows whether intense thrills from these sports may prime relapse, perhaps in the way that certain experiences prime epileptics to have seizures. We need more research to know for whom extreme sports are desirable and for whom they are likely to be substitutions of one addiction for another.

Personality Changes

Many people in this stage of recovery want to change their personalities. This is often a motivating force throughout earlier phases of treatment, especially when people promise to spouses and family members to change once their gambling addiction is more under control. But what does personality change actually imply? Is it really possible?

Here, we need to distinguish between various levels of personality. Many heorists believe that personality may be categorized by *broad traits,* such as neuroticism, extraversion, and conscientiousness. In some accounts, these are called *super traits* or second-order traits. Since traits are not something that we can directly see, there is disagreement about how many traits exist. Arguments are complex and revolve around mathematical and experimental discussions. Regardless, many psychologists agree that at least two super traits are fundamental. These are partly due to genetic factors and partly due to environmental factors:

- **Emotional stability** (also called neuroticism)
- **Extraversion-introversion** (also called sociability and surgency)

There is increasingly strong evidence for three more super traits, also with genetic components and also modifiable by environmental influences:

- **Conscientiousness** (also called *anality* [by Freudians], judging-perceiving [by Jungians])
- **Agreeableness** (also called tender-mindedness, warmth, feeling-thinking)
- **Openness** (also called experience, culture, intuiting-sensing)

These broad traits are not dichotomous, meaning that we are not one extreme or another. Instead, we are more or less extraverted, or more or less agreeable, compared to someone else. Psychologists note that they are normally distributed, which means that most of us are in the middle.

Furthermore, we usually have flexibility throughout life. Scores sometimes change through maturation, learning, life circumstances, and for reasons that we do not understand. Unless we have extreme traits, we can usually be adaptable. For example, most of us can be emotional when it is appropriate and stable when it is called for.

However, people at the extreme ends may have problems regulating their behavior. Traits are often hard to permanently change in therapy. A more reasonable goal is to use therapy to learn to work around them. An example is that a very introverted person may learn social skills for specific situations. This person may even decide to find a career that he or she can feel comfortable in, using skills associated with an introverted personality. It usually is not helpful to try to enter therapy to change a trait. Too often, we do not know how to do it very well.

More relevant to the discussion of what can change in personality may be the conceptualization by the psychologist Gordon Allport. He focuses on *cardinal traits,* which are overriding characteristics that practically define a person's entire life. For the disordered gambler who is active in addiction, the cardinal trait is a tendency to gamble excessively. This is how everyone knows and responds to the gambler. It is what immediately stands out about the person. Allport believes that every personality characteristic has a function, even exaggerated ones. Allport does not believe that it is necessary to look to the past to understand the significance of personality characteristics and values as they function *today.*

Allport believes that cardinal traits can change. Some ways may include the passage of time, sudden insight, various types of psychotherapies, maturation, and sometimes through what others have labeled *corrective emotional experiences.*

Also, Allport believes people could be described by a lower level of description. This includes five to ten central traits. Not everyone is described by a cardinal trait; however, everyone is describable by five to ten characteristics that really stand out. Because they are so subjective, these characteristics often are impossible to quantify. For example, your idea of being a mean-spirited person may be entirely different than mine. Allport labeled these as *central traits.* Gamblers in this stage of recovery have identified the following central traits as targets for change.

Rudeness	Hopelessness
Sexism	Cynicism
Hostility	Humorlessness
Time urgency	Denial of feelings
Authoritarianism	Egotism
Racism	Bitterness
Catastrophizing daily events	Impracticality
Projecting responsibility	Grandiosity
for failure onto others	Thoughtlessness
Aloofness	Impulsiveness
Avoidance	Dependency
Coldness	Attention seeking
Detachment	Vulnerability
Disorderliness	

All of these personality traits can be changed through counseling or therapy. Once clients are motivated, change seems to occur rapidly.

Psychotherapies

A surprising number of people in this recovery stage decide to pursue psychotherapy. Usually, motives are for personal growth or to treat problems they see as important, though not necessarily critical. An example of the latter might be someone who consistently has trouble with family members and wants to change this pattern or understand why this pattern repeats itself. Often, these current problems are indirectly related, or perhaps even unrelated, to the earlier gambling dysfunction. Popular options include behavioral or cognitive-behavioral therapies, discussed earlier. At this stage, people also become interested in other forms of therapy that are less commonly applied in earlier phases.

Psychodynamic Therapy

Psychodynamic therapies include a variety of methods that involve interpretation of symptoms, often thought to be due to unconscious causes. Client insight

Jorge: A Personality that Found Himself

Jorge is a 28-year-old lawyer. He quit gambling 3 years ago after accumulating $500 in gambling debts while in graduate school. This is his account:

"I've heard other stories about how people are thousands of dollars in debt when they quit. But to me, $500 was a great deal of money at the time," he said.

Jorge wanted to reduce his tendencies toward excessive perfectionism and obsessiveness. These were major problems that he had identified as obstacles in securing stabilities with families and friends.

"I used to think of myself as ambitious and simply someone who was thorough. Now I realize that I was overly methodical and too analytical in almost everything that I did. At one point in my life, I numbered all of the pieces of paper that I used during the year! There was no reason. I was just afraid that someone might take something that belonged to me. I started a type of therapy aimed at working with my negative thoughts. I had a lot of what my therapist called 'disagreeable conscientiousness.' I controlled things simply because I could, I guess so that other people couldn't.

"I was stingy. That is a good word from childhood to use.

"I'm getting over this, but very slowly. It does not occur as fast as I would like, naturally, and some days I feel like I will never get there. I don't know that I'll ever change completely, but I'll learn to work around ... most of these issues. That will be good enough for me, really."

is usually the endpoint of successful treatment. Once clients have achieved a prolonged period of abstinence, some find it helpful to shift from a problem-centered approach to this modality. AOD literature, however, suggests that this is not a good choice for the first year of abstinence.

The counselor who assisted the client in obtaining gambling stability is typically not the appropriate therapist for this type of clinical work. This is normally true regardless of the counselor's other training and talents. Psychodynamic theorists usually believe that previous roles, such as being available on a more crisis-oriented basis, disqualify a person from conducting effective psychodynamic therapy with clients.

Narrative Psychotherapy

Proponents of narrative psychotherapy believe that many forms of successful therapy involve a process akin to personal story-telling. Healing often means rewriting one's personal story so that the story involves a coherent account that involves enhanced personal meaning (Leiblich, McAdams, & Joselson, 2004). Usually this meaning tries to make sense of the suffering or struggle that the story-teller encountered along the way. The narrative may have a moral or lesson, and may be of value to others. Patterns may emerge that were not observable, except through hindsight.

Narrative therapy may be of special importance because the memories of gamblers may be so imbued with gambling-related events that the gambler has little else in his or her past. For example, one may not recall much about his or her wedding, but may remember in great detail when he or she bet the filly Applause, at Bowie Race Track, at 10 to 1 in the Eighth Race, winning wire to wire. On the other hand, as mentioned earlier, there is evidence that disordered gamblers probably do not remember their losses very well. Often, disordered gamblers may need the guidance of an experienced therapist to help them through this reconstructive process of reclaiming their own memories.

Unlike psychodynamic approaches, narrative psychotherapy does not customarily look for clues or meanings in behaviors. Instead, it allows rebuilding, based on reinterpretations. Rather than Freud, it is rooted in the theories of Alfred Adler and psychologists such as George Kelly, who believed that our perceptions of events were the things of most importance to us. It is less archeological than architectural. It seeks to build rather than to uncover.

In dynamic forms of psychotherapy, a client aims at getting toward an approximation of the truth. In narrative psychotherapy, the therapist and client might strive for a lower goal. They realize that memory is always fallible and memories always are being revised. Therefore a purpose of therapy is to give us experiences we can live with and learn by. Neither psychodynamic nor narrative therapy is necessarily superior or correct for the aberrant gambler at this phase of treatment. Each has a particular use, perhaps with dynamical approaches being favored by clients who want a more intellectual orientation to treatment, while narrative psychotherapy is more natural for people whose lives seem to need completion or emotional fulfillment.

Humanistic Psychotherapies

Eventually, it is possible for clients to move beyond symptoms and into a more positive and permanent mental health. Numerous theorists believe that there is more to life than "Experiencing no harm." Humanistic psychotherapy may be one way some clients can obtain this goal.

The Humanistic Tradition in psychology believes that a primary motive is to *self-actualize*. The characteristics of the self-actualized person include spontaneity, problem-centeredness, affinity-for-solitude, democratic values, and creativity. In addition:

- Emphasis is on the conscious awareness of personal responsibility
- Focus is on the need for growth and realizing full potential
- Belief that human nature is potentially positive and life-affirming
- Focus is on growth, instead of deficiency
- A philosophy of tolerance and forgiveness, rather than fairness and reciprocity

- Striving beyond minimal requirements and always demanding more of the social and moral selves, particularly in the area of personal accountability

Self-actualization is probably an impossible goal in the early stages of gambling abstinence. Clients must almost always think about *lower* tasks. They cannot see their behavior globally but are forced to see it in a narrow perspective. Recall Action Identification theory that postulates that, until we master a skill, we have to give attention to it at a lower level; and we are forced to define it by lower descriptive terms. Gamblers struggling with the early stages of recovery define their behavior as "Avoiding betting" or "Staying out of jail." Later on, after they have some control, they may use concepts that illustrate that they are defining their behavior on a higher level. The gambler may use terms such as "I'm living the way I should" or "I'm doing what I need to find real happiness."

Abraham Maslow, an American psychologist that you may remember from introductory courses in psychology, postulated a hierarchy of needs that many counselors see relevant to this stage of recovery.

- Lower needs must be satisfied before we can proceed to higher needs.
- A need hierarchy emerges during development, with lower needs emerging earlier in life than higher needs.
- There are five levels of needs: Physiological, safety, belongingness, esteem, and self-actualization.

Other theorists have suggested that we may become fixated on an earlier level of need and try to *overmeet* the need in an unhealthy manner. This is likely to occur when we have been deprived. When this occurs, even when we have met the need, we never seem to get enough of it. An example is the recovering gambler who builds a grandiose house, despite the fact that he or she lives alone and clearly does not need the space.

Figure 8.1 shows a hypothesized fixation on a single level of the hierarchy, in which a person revisits the level repeatedly. With each revisit, the person's perception of the fulfillment that he or she requires for the need varies and may increase. People who are moving toward self-actualization show fewer of these signs. Humanistically-oriented psychotherapy can help this process for clients who are stuck.

Carl Rogers's theory focuses on the way to foster and attain self-actualization. He provides an empirically tested methodology that has received substantial support. Rogers believes all of us can reach actualization, if given unconditional positive regard by parental figures. Despite the fact that all children need this, most parents place substantial conditions of worth on children. As a result, we often develop anxiety and other problems. Rogers's approach to therapy, entitled Client-Centered Therapy, is designed to get a person back on a path toward self-actualization. Rogers believes that the client must feel accepted and understood in a positive and unconditional manner.

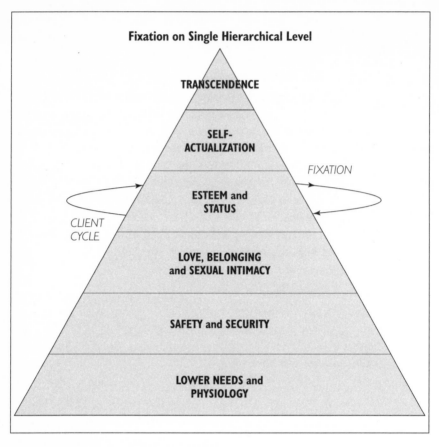

Figure 8.1: Example of fixation on single hierarchical level. Person cannot rise to address higher needs because of "over meeting" lower ones.

Increasing Positive Emotions and Happiness

Most people benefit from increased positive emotions. Clients and practically everyone else can profit from a lifelong habit of developing ways to make themselves smile, laugh, and love. Positive emotions may block negative emotions and may also act independently to contribute to physical and mental health. The influential psychologist Barbara Fredrickson (2003) believes that experiencing a positive emotion leads to states of mind that indirectly prepare an individual for later hard times. Feeling good is good for you, and gamblers especially need to do it more. The emerging science developing around applied practical emotions is beginning to generate many hands-on strategies for clients interested in pursuing this option.

However, clients who are preoccupied with their identities as fractured and damaged recovering addicts may not be able to learn to experience positive emotions. These people are often dreadfully serious, sad, and solemn. While they may be effective in some spheres of their lives, they do not seem to have much

Is Jeff a Good Candidate for Humanistic Psychotherapy?

"I'm 63 years old. I started gambling when I was, I don't know, maybe 14. I started at an East Coast harness track. I played cards at school. By the time I went to college, which was at an Ivy League school, I had poker games running every night in my dorm. I thought I was a pretty good player.

"After college, I obtained an MBA. It wasn't hard and I had a lot of time to play cards and go to the track. After my first job, I found a bookie that I could contact at work and that opened up the world of football betting. Eventually, I was fired for performing poorly at work, but I found another job the next week.

"The same thing happened for the next few jobs. I don't really remember, because the economy was performing poorly and it was easy to confuse my job performance with the general economic climate. The real culprit was my gambling.

"I saw my real talent during that time—management. I was very good at leading people. When I wasn't gambling, I was a great boss, a natural leader.

"I've been off the bet for 9 years. I've bought three small companies. I guess I am what you might call a natural manager. I have a hard, but productive leadership style that pushes people to their maximum. For the most part, they thank me for it later.

"The power I get from management is more of a thrill than gambling ever was. It is very hard to explain it to people, unless they have experienced it."

---

happiness. Perhaps it is useful to help them find some aspect of life to celebrate, perhaps even seemingly mundane areas, like clouds, television, children's books, or daily comic strips. People need to find even small things that make them smile.

Sometimes, random acts of kindness can help spread happiness. This idea seems absurd when you first consider it. However, the more you think about it, the more profound it becomes! You pick out someone that you don't really know and you do something nice for them, for no reason except that it is good and right. If you do it routinely, it is likely to make you much happier.

Another approach to a deeper level of contentment is incorporated in the concept of *reflective happiness*. This is a scientifically-based approach, based in part on theories that happiness is related to specific skills. These skills can be taught, which is important, since they are often not learned in other settings.

In their past, many gamblers found that, in order to experience happiness, they had to live on the edge. They thrived on excitement. As they recovered, they ceased this emotional rollercoaster and stopped living on the precipice. However, often this seemed to occur with a pervasive sense of boredom. Not only did they become depressed, but also joyless and bland.

Jason: "The World Looks Nicer"

"It took about 3 years into my recovery, but I gradually began to experience feelings the way I think everyone else feels them. I can't explain it. It's not like I had an eternal case of depression, but I know that things changed. It's more like a veil being lifted over the world so that I could gradually see things in color. Funny thing is that it took months for life to get this way. When I quit gambling, day after day, things just had this bland, what's the word, façade and then suddenly—cool!

"Gradually, I began to see beautiful things where I saw nothing before. And let me tell you. Nice."

Jason, 24, graduate student in the Midwest

As recovery continues, there is a tendency to separate these extreme behavioral excesses from happiness. The gambler may find that he or she no longer has to live life with extraordinary excessiveness in order to experience what he or she once defined as *happiness*. Instead, happiness can come from self-regulation or moderation. During this postrecovery phase, the gambler may need to discover that it is rewarding to regulate desires. As one gambler recently said, "I feel more peaceful inside. Therefore, I don't need that carnival outside all of the time."

The process of down regulation and reward through moderation is quite normal. It is part of the process of *metaregulation* that all of us experience. This is when we adjust our thoughts, behaviors, moods, and feelings to expected and unexpected situations. Disordered gamblers often learn to do this with a variety of tools, including various psychotherapies, GA, even medication. Metaregulation is an ideal. No one obtains it for very long! There is a wide range of variations in human behavior for any situation. All of us, even the most *normal* people, show many exceptions to ideal behavior every day. None of us ever *gets it right* all of the time. Even the healthiest among us is never *completely normal*. People who are in this stage of recovery realize that to be human means to make emotional and social errors.

Moral Development

During this phase, the recovering gambler has the opportunity to strive for a deep level of moral growth. This concept is not a new one. The philosopher Socrates discussed the legendary *Ring of Gyges,* which reappeared in a bit different form in the popular *Lord of the Rings,* 2,400 years later. Socrates' advisory talked about a secret ring that, when worn, would make the wearer invisible.

With such a ring, what was the purpose for morality and justice? Many people have asked a similar question throughout the years.

Socrates, on the other hand, believed in universal moral truths that were self-evident, but only through the process of a virtuous life. People unwilling to pursue this struggle do not and cannot comprehend moral truth. For Socrates, once you have struggled to obtain wisdom, you are more likely to realize that morality is part of the nature of the harmonious soul. You no longer ask "Why?" and it becomes part of your nature to understand the reason for moral action.

In more contemporary discussions, Lawrence Kohlberg's theory of Moral Development reached a similar conclusion, using different language. Kohlberg notes six stages of moral development, which are collapsible into broader categories. People progress from one category to another through interacting with each other, thinking about moral problems, and discussing them.

People with problem and pathological gambling are almost always in the Preconventional Level of development, characterized by the following traits:

- Action out of fear of being caught
- Blind obedience to rules and authority, "Just because it says so"
- Unquestioned loyalty to superiors
- Actions primarily out of operant rewards and punishments

The next broad level, the Conventional Level, categorizes many people in most stages of early and middle recovery.

- The client is capable of generating mutual interpersonal expectations.
- However, relationships are categorized by conformity, with expectations of uniform reciprocity.
- Mutual trust, rather than suspicion, is a characteristic of relationships.
- Roles are characterized as "nice" and "pleasant."
- Emphasis is on doing one's duty and fulfilling obligations.
- Emphasis is on maintaining the social order.

Postconventional and Principled Levels involve ethical principles based on moral abstractions. In these stages, people emphasize basic rights and the democratic processes that give everyone a say, progressively defining principles by which agreement will be most just. Few people in recovery get to this level. It is arguable that few people in most societies achieve this type of moral development at all.

Beyond Selfhood

Since the time of Socrates, philosophers have focused on a distinction between happiness as pleasure and happiness as a balance between fulfilling oneself and one's obligations. Increasing empirical research suggests that there are benefits from people having commitments to others, on a more specific level to individuals and family, and on a broader level to their communities. This is perhaps what the well-known psychiatrist Alfred Adler labeled as *social interest,* or a desire to contribute to the well-being of the whole. This transcends the narrow interests of the self or even the family.

Contemporary psychological research now suggests that people benefit both from *belonging* and *contributing.* This benefit is beyond that measured by a cessation of negative symptoms, such as anxiety or depression, or positive symptoms, such as exuberance or joy. Belonging and feeling exert a life affirming attachment that appears to cause us, in some situations, to live healthier and longer.

In our society, we often have to make an effort to contribute to the well being of others. Increasingly, social institutions are structured so that we can isolate ourselves conveniently from the concerns of our neighbors. While we don't really want to help, we want more gossip, more dirt. By giving, rather than taking, we find that we can passively acquire a gift of health.

This is not a new concept. The ancient Greek philosophers referred to it as *eudemonia*, which roughly translates as *happiness*, and they hotly debated how to obtain it. Aristotle, perhaps the most famous of the moral philosophers, popularized the idea that we do not gain happiness by pursuing pleasure. Instead, we gain it by leading productive and balanced lives. Happiness is a product of other productive activities of living and not a goal that is obtained by pursuing it on its own.

There is no single source or list of activities that the disordered gambler in recovery can automatically pursue to guarantee finding this kind of happiness. Some continue to stay involved in working with the recovery process of other gamblers. Some find it in, what many of us might consider, more routine volunteer work, at least by the standards of the colorful pasts of many gamblers. It is still amazing to see a disordered gambler find joy in teaching children to read or caring for stray animals. Others find connection and meaning in broader forms of social or even political activism. Oddly, it does not matter whether the activism is associated with the left or the right, liberal or conservative causes. Involvement seems to be the key variable.

The psychologists Deci and Ryan (2000) present another useful framework for the development of a normal self that may be relevant following an addiction. In their work on *Self Determination Theory*, they state that people are motivated by two classes of rewards. *Intrinsic aspirations* come from within a person. Some examples are the desire for meaningful relationships, personal growth, and community contributions. These compare with *extrinsic aspirations*, such as for the rewards of money or fame. An overwhelming body of research shows that intrinsic aspiration is more beneficial for physical and mental health.

Deci and Ryan's research has focused on an important question: Is it what we strive for that makes us happy? Alternatively, is it the reasons that we pursue goals that are important? In many cases, the answer is happiness lies in both areas. Goals are important. The *whys* of attaining them also are important. This has significant implications for addiction and the growth and recovery that can follow.

In the early stages of treatment, a person avoids relapse to escape the pain of returning to gambling or for some other more extrinsic reward or motivation. In later treatment, when a person is more intrinsically motivated, he or she avoids excessive gambling simply because it is the right thing to do. The person in the early stages of gambling treatment cannot understand this argument. The intrinsically motivated person can understand this and can seek reward from knowing that he or she is motivated by an intrinsic need that is now second nature.

A way to avoid chronic relapse is for clients to become more intrinsically motivated. The counselor does this by encouraging clients to develop interests, thinking, and a way of living that are motivated by values that are different from the ones that drove them previously. The counselor constantly challenges clients to reflect on why they find a particular goal worthy and challenges them to think beyond their stereotyped ways of responding.

Beyond this, a way to move into their own final phase of recovery is to explore their own interests, now with the confidence to develop them on their own. They no longer need guidance or direction to find meaningful challenges and rewards in life. They have learned to pursue a course of moderation of selfhood, without the constant assistance of a counselor for restraint or reassurance. If they choose to remain in therapy, it will be in a deeper capacity than they previously imagined, with much different benefits.

Family Recovery

If the disordered gambler's family is intact, there may be serious problems that may exist for a lifetime. As stated throughout this volume, the gambler often expects the family to celebrate and accept his or her immediate changes. The family, on the other hand, is justifiably wary. Family members have heard the gambler say that he or she will change, perhaps time after time. They have built up expectations, only to have them cruelly dashed. Perhaps through extensive counseling, they have stopped enabling behaviors and now set reasonable limits.

Usually, it is the disordered gambler that feels he or she wants more from his or her family than he or she is afforded. On the other hand, the family may have made a series of decisions to permanently set limits that conflict with the gambler's expectations. Often, these decisions are irrevocable and it does not help anyone to pursue false and fantastic goals of reconciliation when it is impossible. If a full family recovery is possible, any reconciliation may be extraordinarily slow, perhaps taking years.

Family systems theorists often argue that disorders such as gambling are metaphors for deeper, *structural* problems within the family system. This theory has been difficult to test because there are few experiments that anyone has been able to construct to test it. What the family theorists are probably more clearly accurate about is that, when the gambler returns to the system, the system has changed. It is not the same system that he or she believes he or she left. The system has moved on, and what the gambler is responding to is a memory, probably a faulty one at that.

Family therapists were also quite accurate when they noted that some new problems may emerge when people stop addictive behaviors. There is little evidence that symptoms are *passed on,* meaning that if the gambler gets better, someone else in the family soon becomes symptomatic. (On the other hand, one has found a way of directly testing this hard-to-measure theory). There is, however, evidence that the family dynamics, or method of operation, change when someone in the family becomes addicted. For example, a family may have adapted to the mother's frequent absences from the house by developing extended support networks outside of the home. When the mother tries to regain her previous roles after a period of normal life, she may be met with what seems like resistance. Grandparents, aunts and uncles, and mutually nurturing siblings may be seen by an outsider as sabotaging treatment when all they are doing is continuing the patterns that kept them a functional family for so long.

Often, families are *excessively sensitized* to the presence of the troubled gambler, even when the gambler is in long-term recovery. They do not want anything reminiscent of gambling back in their lives, partly because they do not trust the person and partly because they have been conditioned to feel this way. They may cut the person off physically or emotionally, as is often done when they attempt to end codependency. They may exaggerate problems as means of defensively avoiding any difficulties before they arise. While this may help the remaining family members, it may demoralize the disordered gambler who craves for the lost family contact and roles.

Very often, dysfunctional gambling obscures problems of physical and sexual intimacy. These problems may have been preexisting, though they may also be intensified when the gambler ceases gambling. However, partners may be slow to realize that they no longer feel intimate about each other and that, while the gambling was the focus of marital interaction, these problems were not addressed. Depression and financial stress may also cause a lack of physical and sexual intimacy. At this stage of recovery, intimacy problems are a legitimate focus of treatment and can be pursued without threatening the outcome of gambling treatment.

When disorders of intimacy primarily involve sexuality, it may warrant the psychiatric diagnosis of Inhibited Sexual Desire (ISD). This disorder is occasionally due to physiological problems, but usually is thought to be due to a lack of communications, problems with power struggles, resentment, anger, hurt, and disappointment. In other words, it is common with many of the negative feelings that accompany living with a person with gambling problems.

At this point we don't know whether marital therapy can be substantially helpful for the disordered gambler and his or her partner. It is sad for everyone involved when one member of a couple wants to respark closeness, while the other does not. The divorce rate for people with disordered gambling is extremely high, probably higher than for other addictions. This is an area where we hope that further research can help us design more useful clinical interventions.

Vocational Recovery

The impact that dysfunctional gambling has on vocation is usually more devastating than that of AOD. Often, the gambler has felonious behavior directed toward the workplace or coworkers. He or she may, for example, have forged checks or even extorted other workers. Illegal gambling convictions, as well as legal convictions involving schemes to finance gambling, are common. As noted before, often gamblers cannot return to their previous job, unless the employer is a team member in the rehabilitation effort from the beginning.

> **IMAGINE THAT!**
> During the period between 2001 and 2006, at least 10 former professional athletes admitted to having gambling problems. However, none stated that they gambled on their own sports while they were playing. Some treatment providers estimate that the number of professional athletes with gambling problems is much higher and that some gamble on their sports while they actively play. Regardless, the combination of very competitive natures, seemingly endless cash at hand, and substantial spare time, may place these athletes at particular risk when they retire.

As much as possible, employers need to be involved in rehabilitation. Often, this is simply not realistic and the tarnished reputation from performance of a previous job forces a person to change careers. Apart from criminal records, employers increasingly use credit checks as employment screens. This may produce a poor outcome for prospective employees who are recovering gamblers.

Another vocational-related impairment may be uneven academic performance. Often, impaired gamblers make several attempts to begin higher education. These attempts are ineffective, due to a multiplicity of problems. It is common to see these people having started college on numerous attempts, only to fail each time. Usually they have varied excuses, which boil down to the facts that they gambled too much and studied too little.

Many gamblers in the final stage of recovery want to complete college, or more. It is important to nurture and sustain these dreams. Yet it is also important to nurture them realistically. Some gamblers, even in this stage of recovery, still tend to be grandiose about education. A person's abilities and interests must match reality. For example, a 53-year-old without a high school degree may realistically think she has the ability to pursue a doctorate in mathematics. She might well. However, given her life situation, which may include caring for her elderly parents and her children, this pursuit would be ill-advised at the moment.

On an optimistic ending to this section, some destructive gamblers develop gambling problems because they do things to excess. They may have had tremendous successes in business and may have believed that by pursuing gambling with the same zealousness, they eventually would be successful. These people are usually less of a vocational or employment challenge, although these folks often need to learn to moderate themselves and reign in their occasional narcissism and tendencies toward workaholism.

Following rehabilitation, some people seek employment as a counselor in an addiction-related field. The motivation for helping others is admirable, though should be pursued with caution. The belief that an addictive experience per se makes someone an expert in recovery is incorrect. Many times clients can be harmed when untrained *experts* claim special privileges to be abusive or sadistic in the name of *therapy*. All counselors, recovered or otherwise, need to have basic clinical skills, which include an understanding of human motivation. They also need to be able to control their own impulses and motivational processes and not subject clients to the unpleasant and disagreeable aspects of their own personalities, if this is a problem for them.

If a client wants to change careers and become an addictions counselor, someone needs to examine his or her motives. Clearly, it is not for vast economic rewards, unless the client has been given incorrect information! Sometimes, clients may be motivated by feelings of narcissism, that they are more competent than those that helped them. Occasionally, clients and others are motivated by sadistic impulses to punish people with whom they identify. These counselors are truly dangerous and sometimes we do not screen well for them.

Simply, the rationale that recovery is necessary to becoming a counselor makes no sense. No one expects dermatologists to have skin disorders or urologists to have prostate problems. Often, experiences of people are very helpful, though sometimes they are not and sometimes they may actually interfere. The addictions profession has an obligation to carefully screen people who want to become addiction counselors. We need to be careful about automatically referring the gambler who has achieved some abstinence into human services professions.

CASE STUDY

Point of Controversy

Nancy Petry and her associates have found that addictions professionals have a ten times higher rate of gambling problems than the base rate of the normal population. Clinical accounts have shown incidences in which addictions counselors gambled on all kinds of events, including the HIV status of patients, the number of days until patients would be discharged, and the number of drugs that would be found in patients' drug screenings.

It appears that many people who work in addiction settings are "addiction prone" and this may be a risk factor for the recovering gambler. Do you think that this might influence your advice to people who, in recovery, want to become addictions counselors?

Physical Health and Spirituality

An excellent discussion and hand out about the desirability of pursuing physical health during postrecovery is available in the volume by Blume (2005). As clients reach the final stages of recovery, they begin to see health as something more than the absence of disease. Some clients vigorously pursue this new definition of health; others choose not to do so. Clients may become fastidious about diet, exercise, stress, and lifestyle issues that contribute to health in a way that others find peculiar, given their past indifferences. An example is Stu, a former denizen of smoky backroom craps games, who now drinks bottled water and eats organic vegetables. There is no way to predict who will follow which particular course.

Not everyone is this far-reaching in their concerns, naturally. However, many people have a heightened degree of health awareness and counselors often wish to encourage this. Refer clients to practitioners who can help them meet these goals. Information is available on the Internet for people interested in New Age and other health issues. Counselors may feel reluctant because they are encouraging referral to untested or occasionally unscientifically warranted treatments. This is a valid concern. Clients can benefit from discussions that help evaluate claims of various practitioners and place health information in a proper context.

Many people who reach this stage of abstinence report a profound sense of spirituality. This is hard to discuss with people and is hard to describe. Faith can be a liberating source of strength and renewal. It can also be stifling and oppressive. Faith can help preserve the body and mind but similarly it can be divisive and corrosive. While most people believe that true faith creates compassion and love, more toxic aspects of religion often create hostility, anger, pettiness, and attention to superfluous areas of life.

When people develop a sense of spirituality, it is often tied to unconventional thinking about God not limited to doctrinal adherence. The literature of self-help groups includes reference to "God of our understanding." This may be baffling and even infuriating to people from traditional religious groups. "How can a person claim to have belief, if the person believes in *nothing*?" is something that is frequently asked. On the other hand, conventional religious affiliation is sometimes, though not always, restrictive to people who see themselves as more spiritual.

Spirituality is impossible to successfully define. For many people, the concept of some type of harmony is one of the components. Nearly everyone who writes about spiritual life discusses not only the harmony, but the progressive stages. The therapist needs to take particular care with clients who are in this phase of the journey. Many of us consciously or unconsciously may try to influence our clients' beliefs. This is especially true if spirituality is an important aspect in our own lives. We often believe that the choices we made—even the choices not to make certain choices—are the choices that clients must make. We have to watch ourselves carefully and may need to seek supervision if we suspect that our beliefs are an undue source of influence.

Sometimes, disordered gamblers who reach this stage simply want to be left alone. They do not want a spiritual commitment or want to seek a moratorium on this process to avoid a premature foreclosure. Counselors who make statements about their long-term outcome because of their spiritual status make great errors. Spiritual commitment or religious affiliation is neither necessary nor sufficient for recovery. Neither is *working a program*.

The more we understand about addictions, the more we are beginning to understand that recovery, especially in its latter stages, is individualized and idiosyncratic. Insisting that what works for one person must work for others is both inhumane and bad science. Eventually, we can do better. It starts by listening to our clients and their needs.

Summing Up

Many people who have achieved some stability in their lives following cessation of gambling seek various paths to enhance their mental health. Many people want to change their personality. Often, these paths are not the same as those that helped them achieve initial control over their destructive gambling and can include depth psychologies or mindfulness. Often, there is an increasing emphasis on returning to the community or to others and a discovery of a deeper sense of self than was previously possible. Occasionally, gamblers in recovery will experience insightful moral development and a profound sense of spirituality.

POINTS TO REMEMBER

- Cardinal traits are overriding characteristics that practically define a person's entire life, and they can change through what some have called *corrective emotional experiences*.

- Psychodynamic therapies include a variety of methods that involve interpretation of symptoms, often thought to be due to unconscious causes. Client insight is usually the endpoint of successful treatment.

- Narrative psychotherapy proposes that many forms of successful therapy involve a process akin to personal story-telling. Healing often means rewriting one's personal story so that the story involves a coherent account that involves enhanced personal meaning (Leiblich, McAdams, & Joselson, 2004).

- The Humanistic Tradition in psychology believes that a primary motive is to *self-actualize*.

- Some new problems may emerge when people stop addictive behaviors.

TESTING YOUR KNOWLEDGE

1. _____ is a desire to contribute to the well-being of the whole.

2. A way to avoid chronic relapse is for clients to become more intrinsically _____.

3. People benefit both from *belonging* and _____.

4. Goals are important; so are the _____ for attaining them.

5. According to family theorists, when the gambler returns to the family system, the system has _____.

Answers on page 260.

Unfortunately, despite all of these possibilities, sometimes the miracles stop. Family relations may be shattered beyond repair. Job prospects become dismal. An arrest record continues to haunt a person throughout life. For some clients, the possibility of a completely new beginning may be a dream. For these people, it may be necessary to decide whether they wish to remain identified in the role of recovering gambler. This socially sanctioned position affords them some forgiveness, but at a price of reduced freedom. Usually, there are no clear answers.

Key Terms

Behavior toxicity. A process by which other rewards (besides gambling) lose attractiveness, are boring, dull, and devoid of previous passion.

Reflective happiness. An approach to a deeper level of contentment based in part on theories that happiness is related to specific skills that can be *learned*.

Metaregulation. When we adjust our thoughts, behaviors, moods, and feelings to expected and unexpected situations.

Social interest. Psychiatrist Alfred Adler's term describing the desire to contribute to the well-being of the whole, transcending the narrow interests of the self, or even the family. People benefit from a sense of *belonging* and *contributing*.

Recommended Reading

Random Acts of Kindness Foundation (http://www.actsofkindness.org/). For more information about this simple, yet fascinating idea of random acts of kindness, check out this web site.

We strongly recommend checking out Martin Seligman's link at http://www.reflectivehappiness.com. It is one part cheerleading, one part self-help, and two parts sheer fun. You can spend hours here learning to be happier through real exercises that you practice daily. Go for it!

Additional information about Self-Determination Theory can be found at http://www.psych.rochester.edu/SDT.

Following are two outstanding books about being a human being in this stage of recovery: *Choice Theory* by W. Glasser (New York: Harper Collins, 2000) and *Emotional Intelligence* by D. Goleman (New York: Bantam, 1995).

Treatment and Recovery Resources (http://www.asam.org/web/treatrec.htm) contains a variety of resources.

Bella Online (http://www.bellaonline.com/articles/art41234.asp) is a voice for women recovering after addictions.

Addiction and Change: How Addictions Develop and Addicted People Recover by C. C. Clemente (2003) is a good read.

Aftercare: Chemical Dependency Recovery by Dennis L. Siluk (2004) at http://www.iUniverse.com provides a discussion on continuing the care continuum that has insights and relevance for recovering gamblers.

Journal 45: A 45-Day Program to Create a New Beginning by Howatt (2001).

My Personal Success Coach by Howatt (1999).

TESTING YOUR KNOWLEDGE

ANSWERS

1. Social Interest   2. Motivated   3. Contributing   4. Reasons   5. Changed

---

TRUTH OR FICTION

QUIZ

1. True   2. True   3. False   4. True   5. False   6. True   7. False

REFERENCES

Aasved, M. (2002). *The psychodynamics and psychology of gambling: The gambler's mind (The gambling theory and research series)* (Vol. 1). Springfield, IL: Charles Thomas and Sons.

Aasved, M. (2003). *The sociology of gambling (The gambling theory and research series)* (Vol. 2). Springfield, IL: Charles Thomas and Sons.

Aasved, M. (2004). *The biology of gambling (The gambling theory and research series)* (Vol. 3). Springfield, IL: Charles Thomas and Sons.

Addiction Technology Transfer Centers National Curriculum Committee. (1998). *Addiction counseling competencies: The knowledge, skills, and attitudes of professional practice*. Treatment Assistance Publication @21. (DHHS Publication No. (SMA) 98-3171). Rockville, MD: Center for Substance Abuse Treatment.

American Psychiatric Association. (2000). *Diagnostic and statistical manual of mental disorders* (4th ed., text revision). Washington, DC: Author.

Anshel, M. H. (2006). *Applied exercise psychology: A practitioner's guide to improving client health and fitness*. New York: Springer Publishing.

Bauer, M. S. (2003). *Field guide to psychiatric assessment and treatment*. Philadelphia: Lippincott Williams & Wilkins.

Baumeister, R. F., & Exline, J. J. (1999). Virtue, personality and social relations: Self-control as the moral muscle. *Journal of Personality, 67,* 1165–1194.

Baumeister, R. F., & Vohs, K. D. (Eds.). (2004). *Handbook of self-regulation: Research, theory, and applications*. New York: Guilford Press.

Benhsain, K., Taillefer, A., & Ladouceur, R.. (2004). Awareness of independence of events and erroneous perceptions while gambling. *Addictive Behaviors, 29,* 399–404.

Berman, L., and Siegel, M. (1992). *Behind the 8-ball: A guide for families of gamblers*. New York: Fireside/Parkside.

Bien, T., & Bien, B. (2002). *Mindful recovery: A spiritual path to healing from addiction.* New York: John Wiley & Sons.

Blume, A. W. (2005). *Treating drug problems.* Hoboken, NJ: John Wiley & Sons.

Borkman, T. J. (1998). Is recovery planning any different from treatment planning? *Journal of Substance Abuse Treatment, 15,* 37–42.

Boutin, C., Dumont, M., Ladouceur, R., & Montecalvo, P. (2003). Excessive gambling and cognitive therapy: How to address ambivalence. *Clinical Case Studies, 2,* 259–269.

Breslin, F. C., Zack, M., & McMain, S. (2002). An information-processing analysis of mindfulness: Implications for relapse prevention in the treatment of substance abuse. *Clinical Psychology: Science and Practice, 9,* 275–299.

British Columbia Partnership for Responsible Gambling. (2004). Retrieved November 13, 2006, from http://www.bcresponsiblegambling.ca/.

Brown, M., & Lewis, H. G. (1999) Support vector machines for optimal classification and spectral unmixing. *Ecological Modeling, 120,* 167–179.

Burns, D. (1999). *The feeling good handbook* (Rev. ed.). New York: Plume.

Bütz, M. R., Chamberlain, L. L., & McCown, W. G. (1997). *Strange attractors: Chaos, complexity, and the art of family therapy.* New York: John Wiley & Sons.

Canada Safety Council. (2006). Retrieved November 13, 2006, from http://www.safety.council.org/info/community/gambling.html.

Ciarrocchi, J. W. (2002). *Counseling problem gamblers: A self-regulation manual for individual and family therapy.* San Diego, CA: Academic Press.

Coombs, R. H., & Howatt, W. A. (2005). *The addiction counselor's desk reference.* Hoboken, NJ: John Wiley & Sons.

Coombs, R. H. (Ed.). (2004). *Handbook on addictive disorders.* New York: John Wiley & Sons.

Coombs, R. H. (Ed.). (2005). *Addiction counseling review: Preparing for comprehensive, certification and licensing exams.* Mahwah, NJ: Erlbaum.

Coombs, R. H., Howatt, W. A., & Coombs, K. (Eds.). (2005). *Addiction recovery tools.* Mahwah, NJ: Erlbaum.

Corcoran, K., & Fischer, J. (2000). *Measures for clinical practice: A sourcebook, Vol. 2: Adults* (3rd ed.). New York: The Free Press.

Corey, G., Corey, M. S., & Callahan, P. (2006). *Issues and ethics in the helping professions.* Belmont, CA: Brooks/Cole.

Craig, R. J. (2005). *Clinical and diagnostic interviewing* (2nd ed.). Lanham, MD: Jason Aronson.

Cunningham, J. A. (2005). Little use of treatment among problem gamblers. *Psychiatric Services, 56,* 1024–1025.

Custer, R., & Milt, H. (1985). *When luck runs out: Help for compulsive gamblers and their families.* New York: Facts on File.

Dannon, P. N., Lowengrub, K., Musin, E., Gonopolski, Y., & Kotler, M. (2005). Sustained-release bupropion versus naltrexone in the treatment of pathological gambling: A preliminary blind-rater study. *Journal of Clinical Psychopharmacology, 25,* 593–596.

Deci, E. L., & Ryan, R. M. (2000). The "what" and "why" of goal pursuits: Human needs and the self-determination of behavior. *Psychological Inquiry, 11,* 227–268.

Dell'Osso, B., & Hollander, E. (2005). The impact of comorbidity on the management of pathological gambling. *CNS Spectrums, 10,* 619–621.

Dunstan, R. (1997). Gambling in California. California Research Bureau. Retrieved November 13, 2006, from http://www.library.ca.gov/CRB/97/03/Chapt2.html.

Federman, E. Drebing, C. E., & Krebs, C. (2000). *Don't leave it to chance: A guide for families of problem gamblers.* Oakland, CA: New Harbinger Publications.

Finley, J. R. (2004). *Integrating the 12-steps into addiction therapy: A resource collection and guide for promoting recovery.* Hoboken, NJ: John Wiley & Sons.

Finley, J. R., & Lenz, B. S. (2005). *The addiction counselor's documentation sourcebook: The complete paperwork resource for treating clients with addictions* (2nd ed.). Hoboken, NJ: John Wiley & Sons.

Fiorillo, C. D. (2004). The uncertain nature of dopamine. *Molecular Psychiatry, 9*(2), 122–123.

Fischer, J., & Corcoran, K. (1994). *Measures for clinical practice: A sourcebook* (2nd ed., 2 Vols.). New York: Free Press.

Fredrickson, B. L. (2003). The value of positive emotions: The emerging science of positive psychology is coming to understand why it's good to feel good. *American Scientist, 91,* 330–335.

Freeman, A., Felgoise, S. H., Nezu, A. M., Nezu, C. M., & Reinecke, M. A. (Eds.). (2005). *Encyclopedia of cognitive behavior therapy.* New York: Springer Science/ Business Media.

Gambler's Anonymous. (1957). Questions and answers. Retrieved November 13, 2006, from http://www.gamblersanonymous.org/recovery.html.

Ghodse, H. (2002). *Drugs and addictive behaviour: A guide to treatment* (3rd ed.). New York: Cambridge University Press.

Gilliland, B. F., & James, R. K. (2005). *Crisis intervention strategies* (5th ed.). Pacific Grove, CA: Brooks/Cole.

Glasser, W. (2000). *Choice theory.* New York: Harper Collins.

Glasser, W. (2004). *Warning: Psychiatry can be hazardous to your mental health.* New York: Harper.

Goleman, D. (1995). *Emotional intelligence.* New York: Bantam.

Grant, J. E., & Potenza, M. N. (2005). Tobacco use and pathological gambling. *Annals of Clinical Psychiatry: Official Journal of the American Academy of Clinical Psychiatrists, 17,* 237–241.

Grant, J. E., & Potenza, M. N. (Eds.). (2004). *Pathological gambling: A clinical guide to treatment.* Washington, DC: American Psychiatric Association.

Griffiths, M., Bellringer, P., Farrell-Roberts, K., & Freestone, F. (2001). Treating problem gamblers: A residential therapy approach. *Journal of Gambling Studies, 17,* 161–169.

Groover, J. (2005). States bet on online gambling revenues. *American City and County.* Prism Business Media, Inc.

Handelsman, M., Gottlieb, M. C., & Knapp, S. (2005). Training ethical psychologists: An acculturation model. *Professional Psychology: Research and Practice, 36,* 59–65.

Hersen, M., Rosqvist, J., Gross, A. M., Drabman, R. S., Sugai, G., & Horner, R. (Eds.). (2005). *Encyclopedia of behavior modification and cognitive behavior therapy, Vol. 1: Adult clinical applications.* Thousand Oaks, CA: Sage Publications.

Hodge, D. (2006, April). Responsible Gambling Conference sponsored by the Alberta Government. Alberta, Canada.

Hodgins, D. C. (2004). Addictive behavior. Retrieved November 13, 2006, from http://www.ncbi.nlm.nih.gov/entrez/query.fcgi?cmd=Retrieve&db=PubMed &list_uids=15451138&dopt=Abstract.

Hodgins, D. C. (2004). Workbooks for individuals with gambling problems: Promoting the natural recovery process through brief intervention. In L. L'Abate (Ed.), *Using workbooks in mental health: Resources in prevention, psychotherapy, and rehabilitation for clinicians and researchers* (pp. 159–172). New York: Haworth Press.

Hodgins, D. C., Wynne, H., & Makarchuk, K. (1999). Pathways to recovery from gambling problems: Follow-up from a general population survey. *Journal of Gambling Studies, 15*(2), 93–104.

Hollander, E., Sood, E., Pallanti, S., Baldini-Rossi, N., & Baker, B. (2005). Pharmacological treatments of pathological gambling. *Journal of Gambling Studies, 21,* 99–108.

Holy Bible, King James Version. (1999). New York: American Bible Society.

Howatt, W. (1999). *My personal success coach.* Kentville, Nova Scotia: A Way With Words.

Howatt, W. A. (2001). *Journal 45: A 45-day program to create a new beginning.* Kentville, Nova Scotia: A Way With Words.

Howatt, W. A. (2003). Six C's: Cognitive-behavioral recovery tools. *Counselor: The Magazine for Addictions Professionals, 5,* n1 62–67.

Howatt, W. A. (2006). Addiction screening tool vs. addiction clinical measures. *Counselor: The Magazine for Addiction Professionals, 7*(1), 48–53.

Hughes, J. R. (2005). The idiosyncratic aspects of the epilepsy of Fyodor Dostoevsky. *Epilepsy and Behavior, 7,* 531–538.

Humphrey, H. (2000). *This must be hell: A look at pathological gambling.* Lincoln, NE: Writers Club Press.

Isenhart, C. (2005). Motivational interviewing. In R. J. Craig (Ed.), *Clinical and diagnostic interviewing* (2nd ed.). Lanham, MD: Jason Aronson.

Johnson, E. E., Hamer, R. M. & Nora, R. M. (1988). The lie/bet questionnaire for screening pathological gamblers: A follow-up study. *Psychological Reports, 83*(3 Part 2), 1219–1224.

Jongsma, A. E., & Berghuis, D. J. (2005). *The addiction progress notes planner* (2nd ed.). Hoboken, NJ: John Wiley & Sons.

Jongsma, A. E., Peterson, M., & Bruce, T. (2006). *The complete adult psychotherapy treatment planner* (4th ed.). Hoboken, NJ: John Wiley & Sons.

Joukhador, J., Blaszczynski, A., & Maccallum, F. (2004). Superstitious beliefs in gambling among problem and social gamblers: Preliminary data. *Journal of Gambling Studies, 20*(2), 171–180.

Juniper, D. (2005). Leisure counseling, coping skills and therapeutic applications. *British Journal of Guidance and Counseling, 33,* 27–36.

Kausch, O. (2003). Patterns of substance abuse among treatment-seeking pathological gamblers. *Journal of Substance Abuse Treatment, 25,* 263–270.

Kawa, I., Carter, J. D., Joyce, P. R., Doughty, C. J., Frampton, C. M., Wells, J. E., et al. (2005). Gender differences in bipolar disorder: Age of onset, course, comorbidity, and symptom presentation. *Bipolar Disorders, 7,* 119–125.

Kearney, M. (2005). *The economic winners and losers of legalized gambling.* Washington, DC: The Brookings Institution.

Kelley, A. E., & Berridge, K. C. (2002). The neuroscience of natural rewards: Relevance to addictive drugs. *Journal of Neuroscience, 22,* 3306–3311.

Kessler, R. C., Adler, L., Ames, M., Demler, O., Faraone, S., Hiripi, E., et al. (2005). The World Health Organization Adult ADHD Self-Report Scale (ASRS): A short screening scale for use in the general population. *Psychological Medicine, 35,* 245–256.

Kessler, R. C., McGonagle, K. A., Zhao, S., et al. (1994). Lifetime and 12-month prevalence of *DSM-III-R* psychiatric disorders in the United States. *Archives of General Psychiatry, 51,* 8–19.

Knapp, S. J., & VandeCreek, L. D. (2006). Special topics in therapy. In S. J. Knapp & L. D. VandeCreek (Eds.), *Practical ethics for psychologists: A positive approach* (pp. 191–202). Washington, DC: American Psychological Association.

Korn, D., & Shaffer, J. (2002, November). *Poly-Drug Use: Multiple Problems, Multiple Challenge Poster Session* at the APHA Annual Conference. Philadelphia: CAS Harvard University.

Kottler, J. A. (2001). *Making changes last.* New York: Brunner-Routledge.

Kübler-Ross, E. (1969). *On death and dying.* New York: Macmillan.

L'Abate, L. (Ed.). (2004). *Using workbooks in mental health: Resources in prevention, psychotherapy, and rehabilitation for clinicians and researchers.* New York: Haworth Press.

L'Abate, L., & Kern, R. (2002). Workbooks: Tools for the expressive writing paradigm. In S. Lepore & J. Smyth (Eds.), *The writing cure: How expressive writing promotes health and emotional well being* (pp. 239–255). Washington, DC: American Psychological Association.

Ladouceur, R. (2005). *Journal of Gambling Studies, 21(1),* 49–57. Controlled gambling for pathological gamblers.

Ladouceur, R., & Shaffer, H. J. (2005). Treating problem gamblers: Working towards empirically supported treatment. *Journal of Gambling Studies, 21,* 1–4.

Ladouceur, R., Sylvain, C., Boutin, C., & Doucet, C. (2002). *Understanding and treating the pathological gambler.* New York: John Wiley & Sons.

Ladouceur, R., Sylvain, C., Boutin, C., Lachance, S., Doucet, C. L., Leblond, J., et al. (2001). Cognitive treatment of pathological gambling. *Journal of Nervous and Mental Disease, 189,* 774–780.

Ladouceur, R., Sylvain, C., Letarte, H., Giroux, I., & Jacques, C. (1998). Cognitive treatment of pathological gamblers. *Behavior Research Therapy, 36,* 1111–1120.

Laney, G., Rogers, G. E., & Phaison, R. (Eds.). (2002). Healing an addiction through a twelve step program ending in faith. In Jay C. Chung (Ed.), *The health behavioral change imperative: Theory, education, and practice in diverse populations* (pp. 153–169). New York: Kluwer Academic/Plenum Publishers

Larkin, M., & Griffiths, M. D. (2002). Experiences of addiction and recovery: The case for subjective accounts. *Addiction Research and Theory, 10,* 281–312.

Lee, B. (2000). *Born to lose: Memoirs of a compulsive gambler.* St. Paul, MN: Hazelden Publishing & Educational Services.

Leisure, H. R. & Blume, S. B. (1987). The South Oaks Gambling Screen (SOGS): A new instrument for the identification of pathological gamblers. *American Journal of Psychiatry, 144,* 1184–1188.

Lieblich, A., McAdams, D., & Josselson, R. (Eds.). (2004). *Healing plots: The narrative basis of psychotherapy* (The Narrative Study of Lives). Washington, DC: American Psychological Association.

Luepker, E. (2003). *Record keeping in psychotherapy and counseling: Protecting confidentiality and the professional relationship.* New York: Routledge.

Mack, J. E. (2002, February 2). Addictions: Individual and societal. Paper presented at the 25 Years of Addiction Treatment Conference. Boston, MA. Cited in Shaffer, H. J., & Albanese, M. J. (2005). Addiction's defining characteristics. In R. H. Coombs (Ed.), *Addiction counseling review.* Mahwah, NJ: Lahaska Press.

Marlatt, G. A. (2002). Buddhist philosophy and the treatment of addictive behavior. *Cognitive & Behavioral Practice, 9,* 44–49.

Marlatt, G. A., & Gordon, J. R. (Eds.). (1985). *Relapse prevention: Maintenance strategies in the treatment of addictive behaviors.* New York: Guilford Press.

Marlatt, G. A., & VandenBos, G. R. (Eds.). (1997). *Addictive behaviors: Readings on etiology, prevention, and treatment.* Washington, DC: American Psychological Association.

McClellan, A. T., Lewis, D., O'Brien, C., & Kleber, H. (2000). Drug dependence, a chronic medical illness: Implications for treatment, insurance and outcomes evaluation. *Journal of the American Medical Association, 284,* 1689–1695.

McCollum, E. E., & Trepper, T. S. (2001). *Family solutions for substance abuse: Clinical and counseling approaches.* Binghamton, NY: Haworth Clinical Practice Press.

McCown, W. G., & Chamberlain, L. L. (2000). *Best possible odds: Contemporary treatment strategies for gambling disorders.* New York: John Wiley & Sons.

McCown, W. G., & Johnson, J. L. (1993). *Therapy with treatment resistant families: A consultation-crisis intervention model.* New York: Haworth Press.

McKay, J. R., Lynch, K. G., Shepard, D. S., & Pettinati, H. M. (2005). The effectiveness of telephone-based continuing care for alcohol and cocaine dependence: 24-month outcomes. *Archives of General Psychiatry, 62,* 199–207.

Miller, W. R., & Rollnick, S. (1991). *Motivational interviewing: Preparing people to change addictive behavior.* New York: Guilford Press.

Miller, W. R., & Rollnick, S. (2002), *Motivational interviewing: Preparing people for change* (2nd ed.) 201–216. New York: Guilford Press.

Monahan, J., Steadman, H., Robbins, P., Appelbaum, P., Banks, S., Grisso, T., et al. (2005). An actuarial model of violence risk assessment for persons with mental disorders. *Psychiatric Services, 56,* 810–815.

Myers, P., & Salt, N. (2000). *Becoming an addictions counselor: A comprehensive text.* Sudbury, MA: Jones and Bartlett.

Nagy, T. F. (2005). *Ethics in plain English: An illustrative casebook for psychologists* (2nd ed.). Washington, DC: American Psychological Association.

National Research Council. (1999). *Pathological gambling: A critical review.* New York: National Academies Press.

Neff, J. A., Shorkey, C. T., & Windsor, L. C. (2006). Contrasting faith-based and traditional substance abuse treatment programs. *Journal of Substance Abuse Treatment, 30,* 49–61.

Ontario Problem Gambling Research Centre (OPGRC). Retrieved November 13, 2006, from http://www.gamblingresearch.org/contentdetail.sz?cid=2007.

Orford, J. (2001). *Excessive appetites: A psychological view of addictions* (2nd ed.). New York: John Wiley & Sons.

Pallesen, S., Mitsem, M., Kvale, G., Johnsen, B-H., & Molde, H. (2005). Outcome of psychological treatments of pathological gambling: A review and meta-analysis. *Addiction, 100*(10) 1412–1422.

Parker, J. D. A., Wood, L. M., Bond, B. J., & Shaughnessy, P. (2005). Alexithymia in young adulthood: A risk-factor for pathological gambling. *Psychotherapy and Psychosomatics, 74,* 51–55.

Petry, N. (2005a). Gamblers Anonymous and cognitive-behavioral therapies for pathological gamblers. *Journal of Gambling Studies, 21,* 27–33.

Petry, N. (2005b). *Pathological gambling: Etiology, comorbidity, and treatment.* Washington, DC: American Psychological Association.

Pope, K., & Vasquez, M. (2005a). Finding an attorney. In K. Pope & M. Vasquez (Eds.), *How to survive and thrive as a therapist: Information, ideas, and resources for psychologists in practice* (pp. 33–37). Washington, DC: American Psychological Association.

Pope, K., & Vasquez, M. (2005b). *How to survive and thrive as a therapist: Information, ideas, and resources for psychologists.* Washington, DC: American Psychological Association.

Potenza, M. N., Fiellin, D. A., Heninger, G. R., Rounsaville, B. J., & Mazure, C. M. (2002). Gambling: An addictive behavior with health and primary care implications. *Journal of General Internal Medicine, 17,* 721–732.

Potenza, M. N., Xian, H., Shah, K., Scherrer, J. F., & Eisen, S. A. (2005). Shared genetic contributions to pathological gambling and major depression in men. *Archives of General Psychiatry, 62,* 1015–1021.

Prochaska, J. O. (2004). Population treatment for addictions. *Current Directions in Psychological Science, 13,* 242–246.

Prochaska, J. O., & DiClemente, C. C. (1982). Transtheoretical therapy toward a more integrative model of change. *Psychotherapy: Theory, Research and Practice, 19,* 276–287.

Prochaska, J. O., DiClemente C. C., Norcross, J. C. (1992). In search of how people change: applications to addictive behaviors. *American Psychologist, 47(9),* 1102–1114. New York: William Morrow.

Reuter, J., Raedler, T., Rose, M., Hand, I., Giascher, J., & Bachel, C. (2005). Pathological gambling is linked to reduced activation of the mesolimbic reward system. *Nature Neuroscience, 8,* 147–148.

Robson, E., Edwards, J., Smith, G., & Colman, I. (2002). Gambling decisions: An early intervention program for problem gamblers. *Journal of Gambling Studies, 18,* 235–256.

Rogers, R. (2001). *Handbook of diagnostic and structured interviewing.* New York: Guilford Press.

Rosenthal, R. (2004). The role of medication in the treatment of pathological gambling: Bridging the gap between research and practice gambling. *Electronic Journal of Gambling Issues.* Retrieved December 4, 2005, from http://epe.lac-bac.gc.ca/100/202/300/egambling/html/2004/no10/issue10/ejgi_10_rosenthal.html.

Sajatovic, M., & Ramirez, L. F. (2001). *Rating scales in mental health.* Hudson, OH: Lexi-Comp, Inc.

Schouwenberg, H., Lay, C., Pynchl, L., & Ferrari, J. (2004). *Counseling the procrastinator in academic settings.* Washington, DC: American Psychological Association.

Shaffer, H. J., LaBrie, R., Sclanlan, K. M., & Cummins, T. N. (1994). Pathological gambling among adolescents: Massachusetts Gambling Screen (MAGS). *Journal of Gambling Studies, 10*(4), 339–362.

Shaffer, H., LaPlante, D., LaBrie, R., Kidman, R., Donato, A., & Stanton, M. (2004). Toward a syndrome model of addiction: Multiple expressions, common etiology. *Harvard Review of Psychiatry, 12(6),* 367–374.

Steel, Z., & Blaszczynski, A. (1996). The factorial structure of pathological gambling. *Journal of Gambling Studies, 12,* 3–20.

Sumitra, L. M., & Miller, S. C. (2005). Pathologic gambling disorder. *Postgraduate Medicine, 118,* 31–37.

Tavares, H., Zilberman, M. L., & el-Guebaly, N. (2003). Are there cognitive and behavioural approaches specific to the treatment of pathological gambling? *Canadian Journal of Psychiatry, 48,* 22–27.

Taylor, P., Funk, C., & Craighill, P. (2006). Gambling: As the take rises, so does public concern. Pew Research Center. Retrieved November 13, 2006, from http://64.233.161.104/search?q=cache:GlYZT_YkYGQJ:pewresearch.org/assets/social/pdf/Gambling.pdf.

Tims, F. M., Leukefeld, C. G., & Platt, J. J. (Eds.). (2001). *Relapse and recovery in addictions.* New Haven, CT: Yale University Press.

Toneatto, T., & Millar, G. (2004). Assessing and treating problem gambling: Empirical status and promising trends. *Canadian Journal of Psychiatry, 49,* 517–525.

Turner, N., & Horbay, R. (2004). How do slot machines and other electronic gambling machines actually work? CAMH. *Journal of Gambling Issues, 11,* 1–41.

Vallacher, R. R., & Wegner, D. M. (1985). *A theory of action identification.* Hillsdale, NJ: Erlbaum.

Wahab, S. P. (2005). Motivational interviewing and social work practice. *Journal of Social Work, 5,* 45–60.

Walker, M. B. (1992). *The psychology of gambling.* Elmsford, NY: Pergamon Press.

Weatherly, J. N., Sauter, J. M., & King, B. M. (2004). The "Big Win" and resistance to extinction when gambling. *Journal of Psychology: Interdisciplinary & Applied, 138,* 495–504.

Welte, J. W. , Barnes, G. M., Wieczorek, W. F., & Tidwell, M. (2004). Gambling participation and pathology in the United States: A sociodemographic analysis using classification trees. *Addictive Behaviors, 29,* 983–989.

Wiger, D. E. (2005). *The psychotherapy documentation primer* (2nd ed.). Hoboken, NJ: John Wiley & Sons.

Wildman, B. (2004). Ontario Problem Gambling Research Centre. Retrieved November 13, 2006, from http://www.gamblingresearch.org/ewildman.

Winters, K. C., & Kushner, M. G. (2003). Treatment issues pertaining to pathological gamblers with a comorbid disorder. *Journal of Gambling Studies, 19,* 261–277.

Winters, K. C., Specker, S. M., & Stinchfield, R. D. (2002), Measuring pathological gambling with the Diagnostic Interview for Gambling Severity

(DIGS). In J. J. Marotta, J. A. Cornelius, & W. R. Eadington (Eds.), *The down-side: Problem and pathological gambling* (pp. 143–148). Reno: Institute for the Study of Gambling and Commercial Gaming, University of Nevada.

Wulfert, E., Blanchard, E. B., & Martell, R. (2003). Conceptualizing and treating pathological gambling: A motivationally enhanced cognitive behavioral approach. *Cognitive & Behavioral Practice, 10,* 61–72.

Zuckerman, E. (2003). *The paper office: Forms, guidelines, and resources to make your practice work ethically, legally, and profitably* (3rd ed.). New York: Guilford Press.

INDEX